ASSESSMENT AND MODIFICATION OF EMOTIONAL BEHAVIOR

ADVANCES IN THE STUDY OF COMMUNICATION AND AFFECT

Volume 1 • NONVERBAL COMMUNICATION
Edited by Lester Krames, Patricia Pliner, and Thomas Alloway

Volume 2 • NONVERBAL COMMUNICATION OF AGGRESSION
Edited by Patricia Pliner, Lester Krames, and Thomas Alloway

Volume 3 • ATTACHMENT BEHAVIOR
Edited by Thomas Alloway, Patricia Pliner, and Lester Krames

Volume 4 • AGGRESSION, DOMINANCE, AND INDIVIDUAL SPACING
Edited by Lester Krames, Patricia Pliner, and Thomas Alloway

Volume 5 • PERCEPTION OF EMOTION IN SELF AND OTHERS
Edited by Patricia Pliner, Kirk R. Blankstein, and Irwin M. Spigel

Volume 6 • ASSESSMENT AND MODIFICATION OF EMOTIONAL BEHAVIOR
Edited by Kirk R. Blankstein, Patricia Pliner, and Janet Polivy

A Continuation Order Plan is available for this series. A continuation order will bring delivery of each new volume immediately upon publication. Volumes are billed only upon actual shipment. For further information please contact the publisher.

ADVANCES IN THE STUDY OF COMMUNICATION AND AFFECT

Volume 6

ASSESSMENT AND MODIFICATION OF EMOTIONAL BEHAVIOR

Edited by

Kirk R. Blankstein, Patricia Pliner, and Janet Polivy

Erindale College
University of Toronto
Mississauga, Ontario, Canada

PLENUM PRESS · NEW YORK AND LONDON

ISBN-13: 978-1-4684-3784-3 e-ISBN-13: 978-1-4684-3782-9
DOI: 10.1007/ 978-1-4684-3782-9

Proceedings of the Eighth Annual Symposium on Communications and Affect,
held at Erindale College, University of Toronto, Mississauga, Ontario, Canada, April 13–15, 1978.

Softcover reprint of the hardcover 1st edition 1980
A Division of Plenum Publishing Corporation
227 West 17th Street, New York, N.Y. 10011

Contributors

James R. Averill
Department of Psychology, University of Massachusetts, Amherst, Massachusetts

Thomas D. Borkovec
Department of Psychology, The Pennsylvania State University, University Park, Pennsylvania

Lynda Butler
Department of Psychology, University of Waterloo, Waterloo, Ontario, Canada

David C. Glass
Department of Psychology, Graduate School and University Center, City University of New York, New York, New York

J. B. Grayson
Department of Psychology, University of Iowa, Iowa City, Iowa

Irving L. Janis
Department of Psychology, Yale University, New Haven, Connecticut

Donald Meichenbaum
Department of Psychology, University of Waterloo, Waterloo, Ontario, Canada

ROBERT PLUTCHIK
Department of Psychiatry, Albert Einstein College of Medicine of Yeshiva University, Bronx Municipal Hospital Center, Bronx, New York

JANET POLIVY
Department of Psychology, Erindale College, University of Toronto, Mississauga, Ontario, Canada

LYNN P. REHM
Department of Psychology, University of Houston, Houston, Texas

MARVIN ZUCKERMAN
Department of Psychology, University of Delaware, Newark, Delaware

Contents

CHAPTER 1

Measuring and Modifying Moods

An Introduction

Janet Polivy

Department of Psychology
Erindale College, University of Toronto
Mississauga, Ontario, Canada

The attempt to understand the nature of emotion has occupied scientists since Hippocrates' theory of body fluids in the fourth century B.C. Modern scientists, from Charles Darwin and William James in the latter part of the nineteenth century, through the present day have sought to define, explain, and demonstrate the causes and meanings of the emotions. Various models of the purposes, sources, and interrelations of emotions have been proposed over the years. At the present time, however, there still is no consensus on the nature or even the number of emotions. This dissension among researchers may reflect the complexity of the phenomenon in question. As Plutchik points out in this volume (see also Averill's paper), emotion is a hypothetical construct inferred from behavior, facial expressions, body language, tone of voice, subjective report, and the reactions of others, to name just a few indicants. A large body of literature has been generated just on the issue of whether observers can identify what emotion a subject (or an actor) is feeling (or portraying). Although this literature does indicate that emotions can be recognized, the accuracy of this identification is far from perfect. Furthermore, research from our own laboratory at Erindale College (Polivy, Krames, & Bycio, 1979) indicates that, even when observers agree about which emotion a target subject is feeling, there is substantial disagreement about what that emotion means; that is, consensus about the emotion itself does not imply consensus about what the emoter wants, or is trying to communicate by expressing a particular feeling. Thus, emotions are neither especially obvious nor comprehensible in others.

Perhaps because of this inaccuracy, and because of the lack of specific physiological response patterns for different emotions,[1] emotion research has traditionally relied on subjects' self-reports of their emotional reactions. To this end, a large and occasionally bewildering variety of emotion assessment questionnaires has been devised and implemented over the years. Self-report adjective lists like Nowlis and Green's (1964) Mood Adjective Check List, Zuckerman and Lubin's (1965) Multiple Affect Adjective Check List (MAACL), Lubin's (1967) Depression Adjective Check Lists, and Spielberger, Gorsuch, and Luschene's (1969) State-Trait Anxiety Inventory, to name a few, proliferated and joined simple single question mood rating scales as the predominant dependent measures in laboratory mood-induction studies. (Laboratory studies tend to use "mood" and "emotion"—as well as words like "affect" or "feeling"—virtually synonymously, although it is generally recognized that there really is a difference in duration and/or intensity between a mood and an emotion. See Plutchik's chapter for a more extended discussion of this issue.) The typical laboratory emotion study, then, involves manipulating the subject's emotional state and then measuring it with a "mood scale." If a significant elevation appears in self reports of the target emotion (either measured pre- and post-manipulation or in an experimental and a control group), the manipulation is deemed a success, and the subject is assumed to be feeling that particular emotion. However, as Averill, Zuckerman, and Meichenbaum (among others) point out in this volume, there are several serious problems with this technique, and corresponding questions about the whole enterprise of assessing emotion through subjective reports.

One problem concerns the discriminant validity of these affective self-report scales. Averill and Zuckerman both question whether the scales measure separate emotions or simply general "good" versus "bad" feelings. In four studies using four different mood induction techniques and several affect assessment devices, we (Polivy, 1979) found disturbingly high intercorrelations among measures of hostility, anxiety, and depression. Regardless which of these three affects was supposed to be induced, all three tended to show significant elevations. Thus, if only the emotion presumably being induced is measured, everything seems fine, but if several emotions are measured, it appears that all have been induced. These data seem to support Averill's assertion that subjects will check off any negative adjective when

[1] A paper by Gary Schwartz in the next volume of this series presents new data along these lines. Schwartz has been finding specific patterns of micro-muscular facial responses for each of several different emotions. This technique may provide the accurate physical measure of emotional response for which researchers have been searching.

they are in an unpleasant situation, regardless of whether each adjective accurately refers to the specific negative affect they are experiencing. Also, the high intercorrelations among the three affects, often exceeding two alternative measures of the same emotion, replicate Zuckerman, Persky, Eckman, and Hopkins's (1967) similar unsettling results. One could conclude from these observations that the multiple adjective type of scale is to blame (rather than, say, the manipulations of mood state) and does simply lack discriminant validity. However, additional data from Polivy's (1979) studies suggest that the problem may not lie with the discriminant validity of the assessment devices, or even with the assessment procedure itself (i.e., demand effects), at least not solely. In addition to two different multiple affect adjective questionnaires, various of these studies included simple bipolar adjective scales (e.g., "How anxious do you feel?") with "one" indicating extremely anxious and "ten" being extremely calm and tranquil, and open-ended questions (e.g., "What exactly are you feeling right now?"). Even with these measures, manipulations intended to produce only anxiety, or anger, or depression produced two or more emotional responses. Responses on the unstructured questions, however, did tend to be simpler (i.e., fewer different emotions were acknowledged) than those on the structured single or multi-adjective scales. This suggests that the scales may be partially responsible for the subjects' reports of multiple emotions, either by suggesting moods the subject is really not feeling, by actually inducing other moods through this type of suggestion, or perhaps by reminding subjects of other affects they really are feeling but which were not sufficiently salient to be reported spontaneously. But the possible failings of the adjective scales only partially account for the emergence of multiple affects in emotion studies. Even with the unstructured self-report format, subjects were likely to report more than one emotion. Thus, some other factor must be contributing to the problem.

As Meichenbaum, Averill, and Plutchik all point out in this volume, self reports may not be the most accurate source of information about a subject's emotional state. Nisbett and Wilson (1977) reviewed evidence indicating that subjects are not even always accurate at telling why they have acted as they have, seeming to report what they think their cognitive processes ought to have been, rather than what they actually were. Self reports of emotion are notoriously suspect, not only because subjects may not have accurate access to their feelings, but because in many cases (e.g., guilt) subjects are psychologically motivated to "misdiagnose" their feelings.

The manipulations used to elicit emotion might certainly be another source of overlap. The so-called standard techniques used to induce emotion in the studies described above (Polivy, 1979) were shock threat (to induce anxiety), delay plus attack (to induce anger), and Velten's elation and depression statements (plus groups instructed to role play elation and depression). It is conceivable that at least the first three techniques might elicit more than simply the intended emotion (e.g., anger at being threatened with shock and depression because one has agreed to receive this pain, etc.). The role playing used to elicit elation and depression seems on the face of it less likely to elicit extraneous emotions since subjects were simply told to act elated or act depressed. Indeed, on the unstructured question, these subjects were more likely (than the Velten groups) to report single emotions. Yet, on the multiple adjective scales, these subjects reported large effects for all three measured emotions. Furthermore, a field study described in the same report (Polivy, 1979) indicates that, even when subjects were asked to indicate their naturally occurring emotions (over the course of several days), the intercorrelations were as high as in the laboratory. Schwartz and Weinberger (1978) also found reliable and complex patterns of emotional responses to questionnaire items designed to elicit specific emotions. The manipulations used in the laboratory may not be the problem, then.

If the problem is neither in the scales nor the manipulations, it could reside in the nature of the phenomenon itself. Izard (1972) asserted that emotions are simply not aroused singly, but that one emotion causes other related emotions to be experienced at the same time: "One emotion can almost instantaneously elicit another emotion that amplifies, attenuates, inhibits or interacts with the original emotional experience" (p. 77). Thus, once a specific mood is induced, either in the laboratory or the world, other feelings will arise from that emotion itself, so the original emotion does not exist in pure form for very long (perhaps not long enough to be measured). The finding of multiple affects when only one was supposed to be aroused may accurately reflect the actual experience of the subjects, then, who experience the target emotion plus other related emotions as a response to the target emotion. Schwartz and Weinberger's (1978) findings of patterned emotional responses to anxiety and depression stimuli lend further support to Izard. Izard's (1972) theory would thus maintain that neither the assessment devices nor the manipulations were imprecise, but that the failure to find discrete emotions reflects the intrinsic complexity of affective responses.

The source of the variability in self-reported affect may not yet be positively identified, but work continues on the issue. In Chapter 2, Averill begins with a general introduction to the concept of emotion. He shows that the connotations of defining a response as emotional account for the preponderance of negative over positive emotions, and discusses how this relates to assessment of emotional behavior. Chapter 3 (Plutchik) follows with an evolutionary framework for emotion, which has given rise to his new emotion–assessment technique, the Emotion Profile Index. He has applied this technique to personality, diagnosis and prediction of psychopathology, and assessment of emotion in animals, among other areas. Chapter 4, by Zuckerman, also introduces an innovative emotional assessment technique combining Zuckerman's earlier work on the MAACL and ZIPERS mood assessment scales with his research utilizing his sensation seeking scales. In addition to showing how these sets of scales in combination predict performance, Zuckerman examinies the implications of this technique for such applied problems as reducing negative affect and inducing positive feelings in psychotherapy patients.

Despite new assessment methods like those presented herein, however, the problems inherent in attempting to measure affect have not all been solved. But these shortcomings in the assessment area have not prevented people from working on techniques for modifying emotions. In Chapter 5 Rehm describes a specific program for modifying depressive feelings. and uses this to highlight continuing methodological and assessment problems in depression work. Clearly, changing emotional behavior introduces new problems in assessment. Borkovec (Chapter 6) follows with a well-organized account of techniques for modifying anxiety in patients with different personality profiles. His work illustrates the use of assessment in successfully modifying emotion.

An intriguing synthesis is also provided by Meichenbaum in Chapter 7 on cognitive ethology, the interaction of emotion, cognition, and behavior. After demonstrating the rapid fluctuation in feelings undergone in real life situations and pointing out the contribution to these overt feelings of covert cognitions and concerns, Meichenbaum explores the bidirectionality of the relation between cognitions and affect, and reviews the varied measurement techniques offered by cognitive ethology.

Finally, in the last two chapters, we move more fully into the applied aspects of modifying emotional behavior. Janis (Chapter 8) presents practical applications for affective and behavior change in the psychotherapeutic relationship, focussing on aspects of the therapist's behavior and client's personality which increase the likelihood of change. The last chapter, by Glass, presents an overview of his work over the last several years on identifying and modifying type A (heart attack prone) behavior.

The contributions herein thus provide a sampling of current theorizing and investigations into the intricacies, problems, and occasional successes in the quest for accurate measurement of emotion and the modification of dysfunctional or debilitating affects.

References

Izard, C. E. *Patterns of emotions*. New York: Academic, 1972.

Lubin, B. Adjective checklists for measurement of depression. *Archives of General Psychiatry*, 1965, *12*, 57–62.

Nisbett, R. E., & Wilson, T. D. Telling more than we can know: Verbal reports on mental processes. *Psychological Review*, 1977, *84*, 231–259.

Nowlis, V., & Green, R. F. Factor analytic studies of the Mood Adjective, Checklist. Technical report no. 11, NR 171–342, ONR Contract, 68(12), 1965.

Polivy, J., Krames, L., & Bycio, P. Communication value of emotional expressions to observers. Unpublished manuscript, University of Toronto, 1979.

Polivy, J. On the production of emotion in the laboratory—What are we producing? Unpublished manuscript, University of Toronto, 1979.

Schwartz, G. E., & Weinberger, D. A. Situational patterns of emotion: Self-reports of relationships among happiness, sadness, depression, anger, fear, and anxiety. Unpublished manuscript, Yale University, 1978.

Spielberger, C. D., Gorsuch, R. L., & Luschene, R. *The state-trait anxiety inventory* (*STAI*) *test manual* (*Form K*). Palo Alto: Consulting Psychologists Press, 1969.

Zuckerman, M., & Lubin, B. *Manual for the multiple affect adjective check list*. San Diego: Educational and Industrial Testing Service, 1965.

Zuckerman, M., Persky, H., Eckman, K. M., & Hopkins, T. R. A multitrait multimethod approach to the traits (or states) of anxiety, depression, and hostility. *Journal of Projective Techniques and Personality Assessment*, 1967, *31*, 39–48.

CHAPTER 2

On the Paucity of Positive Emotions

James R. Averill

Department of Psychology
University of Massachusetts
Amherst, Massachusetts

The positive emotions have proved to be a source of embarrassment to psychologists. Discussions of fear, anxiety, depression, anger, grief, etc., are plentiful in the psychological literature. But when it comes to emotions such as joy, mirth, love, mystical experiences, and the like, psychologists are often at a loss for words. Thus, in a content analysis of psychological textbooks, Carlson (1967) found that approximately twice as much space was devoted to negative as to positive emotions. Although Carlson's analysis is now somewhat out of date, I doubt that a survey of current textbooks would reveal a major change in emphasis (except perhaps for a recent upsurge of interest in issues related to sexual behavior, including romantic love).

A partial explanation for this one-sided emphasis may be that negative emotional states present personal and social problems that require the attention of psychologists. Professional interests are probably not the entire answer, however. I shall present evidence below that there also are fewer concepts in ordinary language that refer to positive as opposed to negative emotional states. Thus, in everyday discourse as well as in psychological disquisitions, there appears to be a relative neglect of positive emotions. Why should this be so? And what is the relationship between ordinary language and behavior (e.g., between emotional concepts and emotional reactions)? These are the main questions that I wish to address in this chapter.

The chapter is divided into five sections. The first section presents the empirical evidence concerning the relative frequency of positive and negative emotional concepts in ordinary language. The second section is devoted to a detailed analysis of the meaning of emotional concepts, in general, and of positive and negative emotional concepts, in particular. Since one of the most important of the criteria for classifying an emotion as positive or negative has to do with the consequences of the response, the third section deals with the attribution of emotion as a function of response outcomes. The relationship between emotional concepts and emotional behavior is the topic of the fourth section. Finally, in the fifth section, some of the implications of the present analysis for the assessment and modification of behavior are discussed.

The Relative Frequency of Positive and Negative Emotional Concepts

In ordinary language, how many words refer to positive emotional states, and how many to negative states? The answer to this question has long been the subject of debate. According to Wundt (1896/1897): "Obviously language has produced a much greater variety of names for unpleasurable emotions than for pleasurable. In fact, observation renders it probable that unpleasurable emotions exhibit a greater variety of typical forms of occurrence and that their different forms are really more numerous" (p. 180). Wundt provided no hard evidence for this assertion; he simply assumed that it was self-evident. It was not, however, self-evident to Titchener (1910), who argued:

> It has often been said that language is richer in words for unpleasant emotions; and Wundt has explained this difference on the grounds that "joyous emotions appear to be more uniform, less variously coloured, than the sorrowful." The author [Titchener] is disposed to doubt both statements. . . . Systematic study of a condensed dictionary, in any of the principal modern languages, reveals a wealth of terms for the pleasurable emotions; and the terms as they come, have their specific emotive feels upon them. (p. 492)

I would like to present some data relevant to this debate. These data were collected in connection with the construction of a Semantic Atlas of Emotional Concepts (Averill, (1975). The Atlas contains 558 terms, each rated on four dimensions of affective meaning—evaluation (e.g., good versus bad), activation (e.g., active versus inactive), depth of experience (e.g., deep versus shallow), and lack of personal control (e.g., involuntary versus intentional). Our main concern in the present discussion is with the relative distribution of terms on the evaluative dimension. However, since the validity of any conclusion regarding this distribution depends on the adequacy of the sample of emotional concepts, the construction of the Atlas must first be described briefly.

As an initial step, five judges went through the approximately 18,000 psychological terms compiled by Allport and Odbert (1936). If two or more judges believed that a term referred to a temporary emotional state, it was selected for further analysis. To help assure completeness, additional items were added to the list from other sources, including all the terms reviewed by Nowlis (1965) in connection with mood adjective checklists. Overlapping items were then eliminated, as well as most variants based on a single root (e.g., vengeful was retained, but revengeful was not). Also, for the sake of consistency, all terms were couched in either adjectival (e.g., angry), adverbial (e.g., lonely), or participial (e.g., grieving, thrilled) form. The result was a preliminary list of 717 concepts.

Each of the above concepts was then rated by 70 to 80 undergraduate students on a 7-point scale of emotionality. A concept was retained for inclusion in the Atlas if it (a) received a rating of 3 or more on the 7-point scale, and (b) was familiar to at least 75 percent of the subjects. A total of 535 emotional concepts met these criteria.

During or subsequent to the collection of the above data, several other studies appeared which involved analyses of emotional concepts (viz., Bush, 1972; Davitz, 1969; Izard, 1972). These publications were examined, and any item which did not appear in the original compilation of terms for the Semantic Atlas, but which on *a priori* grounds would seem to meet the above two criteria of emotionality and familiarity, were added to the list. A total of 23 words were thus added, bringing the final list to 558 terms.

The goal of the above procedure was to obtain a fairly complete sample of emotional concepts in the English language. It must be recognized, however, that concepts cannot be divided into two discrete categories, emotional and nonemotional. There are some terms which nearly everyone would agree refer to emotional states (e.g., "angry," "fearful," "grieving," "loving"), but such terms represent only one end of a continuum. At the other end are such terms as "logical," "deliberate," and "intelligent," which most people would agree do not refer to emotional states. Between these extremes, there are hundreds–perhaps thousands–of terms that have an emotional connotation but that do not necessarily refer to well-defined emotional syndromes. Any dividing line between emotional and nonemotional concepts is thus necessarily vague and somewhat arbitrary.

The list of the 558 emotional concepts that comprise the Semantic Atlas is arbitrary in another way. Many emotional terms have more than one variant based on the same root, often with subtle differences in meaning. Thus, "joyful," "joyous," and "enjoying" are a few of the variants of "joy." Only "joyful" was included in the Atlas. On the other hand, "grieving," "aggrieved," and "aggravated" also stem from the same root, but all were retained in the Atlas because they have distinct meanings. Decisions of this type were discretionary. A similar problem arose in the case of prefixes and suffixes. As a general rule, an attempt was made to include root words and to add prefixed or suffixed versions only if they were particularly common or had a marked difference in meaning (not just a shift from positive to negative). Thus, "delighted," "merciful," and "mirthful" were included, but "undelighted," "unmerciful," and "unmirthful" were not. On the other hand, both members of such pairs as "happy" and "unhappy," and "hopeful" and "hopeless," were included, since each member is very common.

With the above limitations in mind, I believe that the list of 558 terms included in the final version of the Semantic Atlas is a representative sample of emotional concepts in the English language. The list could undoubtedly have been enlarged, perhaps even doubled or tripled, if all the variants on a single root were included, and the criterion of emotionality was somewhat loosened. However, it is doubtful that any conclusions would be substantially altered if the sample had been thus expanded.

Following the selection of items in the above manner, each of the 558 terms was rated on 16 scales by 50 to 60 subjects. The mean ratings were then intercorrelated and the results were factor analyzed. Four factors were extracted. The first two factors referred to dimensions of evaluation (positive versus negative) and activation (arousal). The third factor referred to the depth of the emotional experience (e.g., whether the experience was regarded as profound, as in "grief," or rather superficial, as in "giddy"). The fourth factor referred to the degree of control a person has over the response and/or the situation (e.g., "berserk" and "astounded" versus "determined" and "cruel").

Our principal concern at this point is with the evaluative dimension, which is best represented by the mean rating on four scales: awful-nice, ugly-beautiful, bad-good, and sour-sweet. The distribution of these mean ratings depicted in Figure 1 is bimodal, with a majority of the terms (62%) being rated negatively.

A 62/38 ratio of negative to positive emotional concepts is statistically significant ($p < .001$), if one assumes as the null-hypothesis an equal (50/50) distribution in ordinary language. But what is the expected distribution of negative to positive terms in ordinary language? Is the preponderance of negative terms limited to emotional concepts, or is it a general feature of language? Although this question cannot be answered definitively, there is reason to believe that among nonemotional concepts, positive terms actually outnumber negative. For example, Osgood and his colleagues have compiled a Semantic Atlas of 500 common English words (Snider & Osgood, 1969), 84% of which have a positive connotation and only 16% a

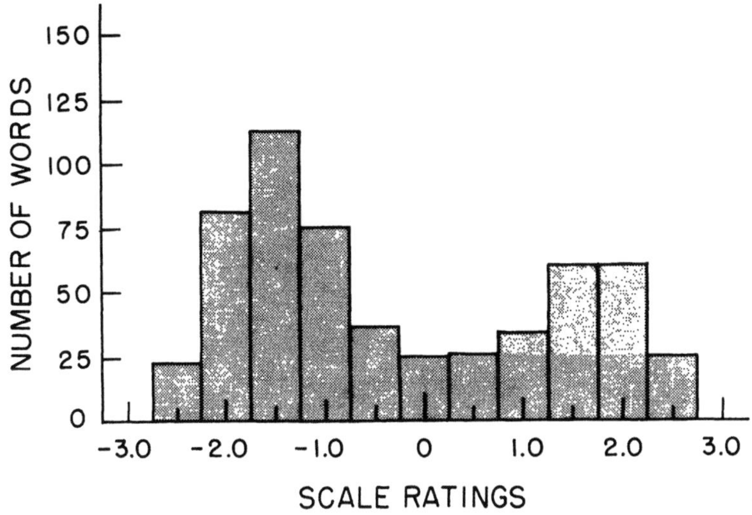

Fig. 1. Distribution of 558 emotional concepts on the evaluative dimension.

negative connotation. (In making this calculation, 36 words were eliminated from Osgood's list because they—or close variants—were also included in the Semantic Atlas of Emotional Concepts.)

The list compiled by Osgood *et al.* can be supplemented with another list by Brown and Ure (1969). These investigators had subjects rate 650 words on a variety of scales, including "good-bad" and "pleasant-unpleasant." The words were taken from previous lists used in research on word association. After eliminating the words that overlapped with Osgood's Semantic Atlas or the Semantic Atlas of Emotional Concepts, only 455 remained. Of these, 56% had scores above midpoint on *both* the bad-good and unpleasant-pleasant scales, whereas 44% had scores at or below the midpoint on either scale. This difference is statistically significant ($p < .05$), and again indicates a bias in the positive direction for nonemotional concepts.

The majority of the terms used by Osgood *et al.*, and by Brown and Ure are impersonal. It is possible that a list of terms restricted to personal characteristics might show a tendency in the negative direction, as do emotional concepts. To check this possibility, an examination was made of the likeableness ratings of common personality traits complied by Anderson (1968). Anderson's original list consisted of 555 trait names, of which 113 were also included in the Semantic Atlas of Emotional Concepts.[1] These

[1] Many terms that refer to relatively enduring personality traits can also refer to short-term emotional episodes (e.g., "anxious," "depressed," "shy," "sentimental," to name but a few). Hence, there was a considerable amount of overlap between the two lists.

overlapping items were eliminated. Nevertheless, many of the remaining 442 terms still had some emotional connotation. Therefore, three judges (graduate students) were asked to separate the terms into two categories: those that referred to emotional predispositions and those that referred to nonemotional predispositions.[2] Within each category, the percentage of terms that fell above the midpoint of Anderson's likableness scale was then calculated. The results are presented in Table 1.

The three judges used somewhat different criteria in deciding whether a term referred to a nonemotional or an emotional trait. Nevertheless, of the nonemotional traits, 57% (averaged over the three judges) had positive ratings on Anderson's likableness scale. By contrast, an average of only 26% of the emotional traits were positive.

The data presented thus far strongly suggest that a preponderance of negative terms is unique to emotional concepts and is not a characteristic of language in general. Some possible reasons for, and implications of, this finding will be discussed below. But first, one possible confounding factor should be considered. Zajonc (1968) has reported that positive words are used more frequently than are negative words. He found, for example, a correlation of .81 between the likableness ratings of Anderson's trait names and their frequency of usage as indicated by the Thorndike–Lorge (1944) word count. Moreover, Zajonc has presented considerable evidence that such a relationship is not limited to trait names but is a characteristic of words in general. Therefore, it is possible that, although fewer in number, positive emotional concepts are used more frequently than are negative emotional concepts.

Of the 558 terms contained in the Semantic Atlas of Emotional Concepts, 316 are also listed in exactly the *same form* in the Thorndike–Lorge wordcount. For another 207 terms, frequencies are available for some *close variant* (e.g., "annoy" instead of "annoyed"). For each of these sets of terms, correlations were calculated between the log transformation of the Thorndike–Lorge L count and the ratings on the evaluative dimension of the Semantic Atlas. For terms having exactly the same form in both lists, the correlation was an insignificant .10; for the close variants, the correlation was .29. Although this latter value is highly significant in a statistical sense ($p < .001$, $df = 205$), it indicates that less than 10% of the variance in the evaluative ratings can be accounted for by frequency of usage. It must be emphasized that even this value applies only to a minority of the terms examined (i.e., the close variants). Thus, in contrast to the findings of Zajonc (1968) for nonemotional terms, there appears to be little relationship

[2] Examples of emotional predispositions from Anderson's list are "ill-tempered" and "squeamish;" "intelligent" and "old-fashioned" are examples of nonemotional predispositions.

Table 1. Percentage of Nonemotional and Emotional Trait Names That Had Positive Ratings (>3.0) on Anderson's Likableness Scale

	Nonemotional traits		Emotional traits	
Judge[a]	Total number	Percentage positive	Total number	Percentage positive
A	237	62	205	28
B	317	56	125	22
C	329	52	113	28

[a] The results for the three judges are presented separately, since each judge used somewhat different criteria in deciding whether a trait name referred to a nonemotional or emotional predisposition.

between how positive (or negative) an emotional concept is considered to be and how frequently it is used in ordinary language.

The Meaning of Emotional Concepts

What accounts for the fact that there are fewer words in ordinary language that refer to positive as opposed to negative emotional states? To answer this question, we must first consider the meaning of emotional concepts, in general, and of positive and negative emotional concepts, in particular.

Of Emotion in General

Elsewhere (Averill, 1980) I have defined emotions as *transitory social roles (socially constituted syndromes) that are based on an individual's appraisal of the situation and that are interpreted as passions rather than as actions*. In this chapter, I will have something to say about each part of this definition. For the moment, however, I want to focus on the last aspect only, namely, the interpretation of emotions as passions.

When we look at the long history of psychology, as opposed to its short past, the use of the term "emotion" is relatively new. For most of Western history (from the time of the ancient Greeks to about the middle of the eighteenth century), the emotions were classified with the passions. The term "passion" is derived from the Latin *pati*, which means "to suffer" or "undergo change." The passions thus include those behaviors which seem to *happen* to a person, or over which a person has no control. This meaning of emotion is expressed colloquially by such phrases as "falling" in love, being "gripped" by anger, "seized" by fear, "torn" by jealousy, "transported" by joy, "subdued" by grief, etc.

The opposite of a passion is an action (i.e., a self-initiated response), or something a person does. In contrast to passions, actions are described by such terms as "deliberate," "rational," "premeditated," and the like.

The distinction between actions and passions is reflected in grammar as well as in words. Consider the difference between the active and passive voice. In the active voice (e.g., "I hit John"), the self is treated as the initiator of the response; in the passive voice (e.g., "I was hit by John"), the self is treated as the recipient of the response. A sentence in the passive voice can, of course, be turned around so that the subject becomes the object (e.g., "John hit me"). In a sense, then, the *I* (the subject of the active voice) demarcates the category of the actions, and the *Me* (the object of the active voice) demarcates the category of the passions. Stated more simply in phenomenological terms, the distinction between actions and passions corresponds to the *I* and the *Me*, the subject and object, of experience.

The distinction between actions and passions is illustrated in Figure 2. The upper left corner of the figure depicts what might be called the *total self-system*. This system represents those aspects of the individual, as a biosocial organism, that are concerned with the integration of behavior into a functional whole. Parts of the total self-system are concerned with monitoring and evaluating the individual's own behavior. When the monitoring subsystems involve conscious experience, we may speak of the *phenomenal self*. The phenomenal self may, in turn, be subdivided into two categories—*actions* and *passions*.

As depicted in Figure 2, actions and passions are broad categories that include a variety of different kinds of behavior. Some states, such as rational thought and *deliberately* motivated behavior, are actions by definition. Other states, such as unconditioned reflexes and fixed action patterns ("instincts"), are passions by definition. Most behaviors, however, can be classified as either actions or passions depending on the circumstances or the aspect of the response being emphasized. Consider perceptual responses, for instance. If I turn my head toward an object and keep my eyes open, I cannot help but see the object. In this sense, seeing is something that happens to me, something that I cannot deliberately control; it is a passion in the broadest sense. On the other hand, I can determine whether or not I look at an object, and hence looking is an action. The difference between

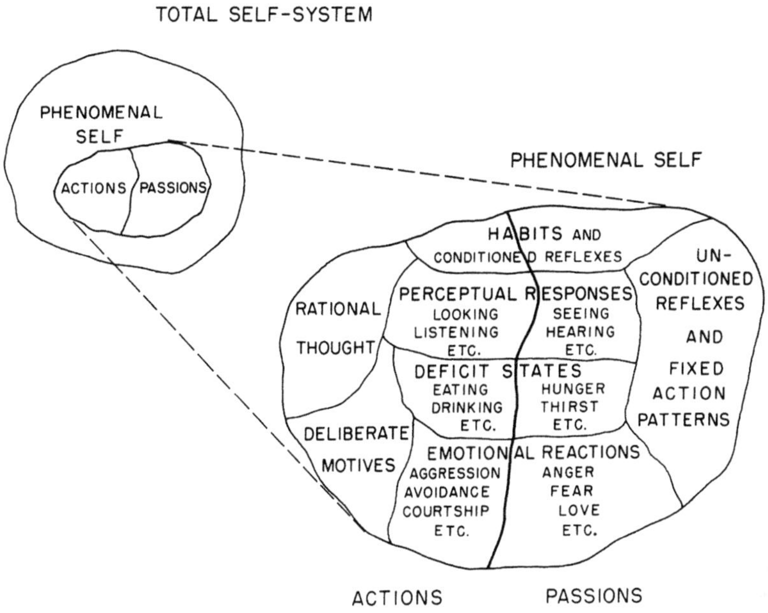

Fig. 2. A schematic representation of the self, illustrating the distinction between actions and passions.

looking and seeing is also evident in the adverbs that describe these responses. Thus, I may look carefully, but not see carefully; look attentively, but not see attentively; look disdainfully, but not see disdainfully, etc. It is important to note, however, that looking and seeing do not necessarily involve different responses (although on occasion they may). More often than not, looking and seeing are simply different ways of interpreting and categorizing the same response.

Similar considerations apply to deficit states. Eating, for example, is an action in the broadest sense, whereas hunger is a passion. Thus, a person may be urged to exercise self-control with regard to eating but not with regard to hunger, because in hunger the self is the object, not the initiator, of the response.

Turning to emotional reactions proper, we find an analogous distinction. When we speak of emotions as passions, we use such terms as anger, fear, love, etc. But when we want to emphasize the role of the self in initiating the response, we use a different set of terms and speak of instrumental aggression, avoidance, courtship, etc. Again, the principle is the same, namely, passions are something that happen to the individual, as opposed to something a person does.

What distinguishes the emotions proper from other kinds of passion (e.g., from perceptual responses and deficit states)? Without going into detail, it may be said that emotions are based on cognitive appraisals (i.e., an evaluation of the situation) as opposed to simple sensory experiences and/or organic changes. Moreover, the emotions tend to involve the entire organism. A glimpse, a twinge of hunger, a habit, or a reflex may occur while the person is preoccupied with something else; but the emotions monopolize. These distinctions are not absolute, of course, and hence it is not surprising that the emotions have often been characterized as perceptual phenomena (Leeper, 1970), as intervening drive variables (e.g., Brown & Farber, 1951), or as reflexes (Cannon, 1929).

There is another important feature about the emotions that helps to distinguish them from other passions. Most passions can be attributed (in a causal sense) to events in the external or internal environment. Thus, simple perceptual experiences and reflexes are "due" to the stimulating object; hunger is "due" to internal bodily changes, etc. By contrast, the emotions seem to be a product of the self—they are "passions of the soul" and not just of the body. But how can a response be a product of the self and yet happen to the self? Historically, the most common solution offered to this paradox is that the emotions are primitive, "instinctive" responses. We cannot help responding the way we do in the case of emotion because that is part of our nature. Although this line of thought is generally couched in evolutionary terms (cf. Izard, 1977; Plutchik, 1962), it can be traced back to the ancient Greeks and to concerns that are as much symbolic (e.g., ethical or aesthetic) as biological (Averill, 1974).

In contrast to theories which view the emotions as primitive response patterns, I have defined the emotions as socially constituted responses (Averill, 1976, 1980). This is not the place to discuss the reasons for defining the emotions in social rather than in biological terms or to explore all the ramifications of such a definition. There is one point that does require emphasis, however. If emotions are socially constituted responses, then the dividing line between actions and passions is, in part, a matter of social custom. Figure 2 may be used to illustrate this point. The diagram of the phenomenal self depicted in Figure 2 is like a map. It is not, however, like a geological map that demarcates the natural or "innate" contours of the land; rather, it is like a geopolitical map that demarcates socially constituted entities (e.g., nations, states). The socially constituted entities, may, of course, follow natural contours, as when the border of a country coincides with a river or a mountain range; it does not follow from this fact, however, that a nation, say, is an inevitable or natural product of the land. Analogously, certain passions may coincide largely with biologically based patterns of behavior. This does not mean, however, that the emotions can be identified with, or are a natural product of, innate response tendencies.

In short, the location of the boundary between actions and passions as depicted in Figure 2 is dependent on a variety of biosocial ("geopolitical") considerations, and hence it is somewhat arbitrary. I shall illustrate this point in a subsequent section on the attribution of emotion as a function of response outcomes. But before that, I want to consider briefly six of the more specific connotations of emotional concepts that will further explicate the bases for classifying a response as a passion rather than as an action.

1. Emotional concepts imply that the behavior in question is *uncharacteristic* of the individual. For example, a mild verbal rebuke may be quite unusual for Bill, and hence may be taken as a sign of anger, whereas the same words spoken by Joe might be typical, and hence might be interpreted as nonemotional. To say that a response is uncharacteristic divorces it from the self-as-agent, and thus places it within the category of the passions. ("I don't know what came over me; it is not at all like myself to behave that way.") Animal as well as human behavior can also be described as "uncharacteristic," and this is one basis for attributing emotions to animals (albeit somewhat metaphorically). Thus, as Hebb (1946) has shown, emotional attributions to chimpanzees cannot be made simply on the basis of the animal's immediate response, even with knowledge of the eliciting conditions. Rather, an emotional attribution requires a familiarity with the animal's typical behavior; the "emotion" is a response that is somehow "out of character" for the animal.

2. Emotional concepts also carry the connotation of *irrationality*. For example, the hope of a mother that her severely ill child will recover may be considered emotional to the extent that it is not supported by empirical evidence or logical argument that recovery is possible. Rationality, it might also be noted, has long been considered a hallmark of humankind; hence, behavior that seems to be irrational is likely to be disclaimed or separated from the self, and one way of doing this to classify the response as a passion rather than as an action.

3. Of course, not all emotional responses are regarded as irrational. Thus, if I meet a bear in the woods, no one would accuse me of being irrational if I flee. My behavior would, however, be nondeliberate or *intuitive*. I "see" the danger immediately and do not have to think about it. In this respect, the emotions are like perceptual phenomena. (As described earlier, responses such as seeing, hearing, etc., have also been traditionally classified among the passions in the broadest sense.)

4. An emotional attribution also implies that the response in question is *impulsive* or intrinsically motivated. If a response is made for extrinsic

reasons, such as monetary reward or external coercion, then it may not be interpreted as emotional. The fearful person wants to flee, the angry person seeks revenge, etc. This is why homicides committed during emotion (crimes of passion) are classified as voluntary manslaughter, rather than as murder (which implies malice aforethought) or as involuntary manslaughter (due to accident or negligence). In ordinary discourse, however, the emotions are typically regarded as *involuntary*, since they are supposedly beyond personal control. The term "impulsive" captures this connotation of involuntariness while also recognizing that the emotions are intrinsically motivated.

5. Many emotional concepts also imply that the response is *intense*. Thus, the person who runs from a bear is typically regarded as more fearful than the person who walks away quickly; and the person who attacks an antagonist with vehemence is likely to be judged more angry than a person who retaliates in a calm and collected fashion. Intense responses are, of course, also accompanied by physiological arousal, which is one reason why physiological changes have often been considered an integral part of emotional syndromes.

6. Closely related to intensity is the notion of *persistence*. In general, the more persistent a response, the more likely it is to be identified as emotional. Thus, if a person seeks revenge over a long period and can think about or do nothing else in the meantime, his behavior may be described as emotional. He has, it might be said, a passion for revenge.

There are still other connotations of emotional concepts that could be mentioned, but the underlying themes quickly become redundant. For example, behavior which is very intense and/or persistent is also likely to be regarded as uncharacteristic, irrational, intuitive, and/or impulsive (involuntary). There is, therefore, a great deal of overlap among the various connotations of emotional concepts, and it is this overlap that allows us to speak of the emotions as passions. However, none of the features mentioned above represents a necessary or sufficient condition for the attribution of emotion. The concept of emotion is like a net woven from many different strands (connotations), none of which is essential to the integrity of the whole. Moreover, the concept of emotion is a very broad net which, when cast upon the psychological waters, captures many diverse phenomena.

It will also be noted that most of the connotations described above have a slightly negative quality. Other things being equal, behavior that is considered to be uncharacteristic, irrational, intuitive, impulsive, intense, and persistent will be less highly regarded than behavior that is characteristic, rational, deliberate, voluntary, calm, and flexible. This fact suggests one reason why there are fewer terms in ordinary language for positive as opposed to negative emotions; namely, the concept of emotion (passion) has connotations that make it less applicable to positive, as opposed to negative, states. But before we can pursue this suggestion further, we must examine more fully the meaning of positive and negative emotional concepts.

Of Positive and Negative Emotions

At first, the distinction between positive and negative emotions might seem rather simple and intuitively obvious. It is not, as a little history will indicate. When psychology was founded as an independent discipline, its ostensible aim was to analyze the contents of consciousness. Wundt, who is generally regarded as the "father" of the new discipline, originally recognized only one kind of mental element—sensation. Sensations, he believed, have three attributes: quality, intensity, and feeling tone. The first two attributes refer to the objective nature of the sensation, whereas the third (feeling tone) reflects the relation of the sensation to the experiencing subject. Like most theorists before him, Wundt believed that feeling tone, which forms the basis for emotional experience, was completely characterized by a single dimension ranging from the unpleasant (negative emotions) to the pleasant (positive emotions).

In 1896, Wundt radically revised this original system with the introduction of his famous tridimensional theory of feeling. According to this new theory, feeling is not just another attribute of sensation. Rather, feelings are separate elements of consciousness. Moreover, Wundt postulated, feelings can vary along three independent dimensions; pleasantness–unpleasantness (*Lust–Unlust*), excitation–inhibition (*Erregung–Hemmung*), and strain–relaxation (*Spannung–Lösung*). This tridimensional theory of feeling had a dramatic impact on psychology at the time, for it called into question two hoary and commonly accepted notions. The first notion was the empiricist assumption that all experience is ultimately based on sensation; and the second was the assumption that emotional experiences could be ordered along a single dimension of pleasantness–unpleasantness. A great flurry of research naturally followed.

The first aspect of Wundt's theory to come under attack was the hypothesis that feelings could vary along three independent dimensions. Experiments conducted in Tichener's laboratory at Cornell University seemed to show that feelings of excitation–inhibition and of strain–relaxation could be reduced to one or a combination of three factors: (a) organic sensations, (b) past associations, and/or (c) feelings of pleasantness–unpleasantness. Tichener (1908) therefore concluded that feelings are unidimensional (pleasantness–unpleasantness) after all, and that the other characteristics attributed to them by Wundt could be accounted for in terms of sensory and associative mechanisms. This conclusion set the stage for a study by Nafe (1924), which is a model of analytic introspection.

Nafe presented trained observers with a wide variety of pleasant and unpleasant stimuli. A careful analysis of the introspective reports of these observers led Nafe to conclude that pleasantness and unpleasantness also could be reduced to sensory phenomena (e.g., pleasantness to bright pressurelike experiences and unpleasantness to heavy, dull pressurelike experiences). Nafe (1925) believed this was a major discovery that would "help materially to stabilize affective doctrine, and so to settle one of the major uncertainties of experimental psychology" (p. 542.). Unfortunately, by the time Nafe published his findings, Wundtian psychology was already being eclipsed. Nafe's "discovery" came too late to receive much attention.

I mention the Nafe episode because history seems to be repeating itself. Based on multivariate analyses of, among other things, facial expressions (e.g., Schlosberg, 1954) and the connotative meaning of words (Osgood, Suci, & Tannenbaum, 1957), a number of contemporary psychologists have developed tridimensional theories of emotion. For ease of discussion, I will limit the present remarks to theories based on semantic analyses. Osgood (1969) has postulated three dimensions of affective or connotative meaning (evaluation, activation, and potency) which he relates directly to the pleasantness–unpleasantness, excitation–inhibition, and strain–relaxation dimensions postulated by Wundt. Noting that these three dimensions can be identified in different linguistic groups. Osgood (1969) suggests that they reflect "the innateness of the emotional reaction system of the human animal." In a similar vein, Russell and Mehrabian (1977) have presented what they call a "three-factor theory of emotions" based largely on semantic analyses. According to this theory, the three dimensions of pleasure–displeasure, arousal–nonarousal, and dominance–submissiveness "are both necessary and sufficient to adequately define emotional states" (p. 273).

The same questions must be asked of these modern tridimensional theories as were asked of Wundt's original theory: Are the postulated dimensions truly necessary and sufficient to define emotional states? And are the dimensions unitary? That is, does each represent some fundamental process–perhaps of biological origin–as Osgood (1969) and others (e.g., Blumenthal, 1977) have suggested, or are they explicable in terms of other processes? Our major concern here, of course, is with the meaning of the evaluative (good–bad, pleasant–unpleasant) dimension. But before getting to that, a few words need to be said with regard to other possible dimensions.

In our previous discussion of the Semantic Atlas of Emotional Concepts (Averill, 1975) we indicated that four factors were necessary, but not necessarily sufficient, to describe the domain of emotion. These factors were evaluation, activation, control, and depth of experience, the last two representing a breakdown of Osgood's potency dimension. Additional research by Russell (1978) confirms the existence of the control and depth of experience dimensions, but suggests that they are limited to certain subsets of emotional concepts and/or that they can be even further broken down into more specific factors (e.g., control over external events, control over one's own behavior). The only dimensions that seem to be representative of the whole range of emotional phenomena are evaluation and activation. But there is also reason to believe that the latter dimension is not unitary or fundamental. For example, in a factor-analytic study of words signifying high or low arousal, Thayer (1967) found four different and independent dimensions, each of which is related to "activation" in one sense or another. In a cluster analysis of the way people describe emotional experiences, Davitz (1969) also found that activation could be divided into four different varieties. Moreover, multiple patterns of activation are not limited to verbal reports but can also be observed in physiological and behavioral responses as well (Lacey, 1967).

Thus, we come back once again to the most widely recognized and accepted dimension of emotion, namely, the evaluative (positive–negative) dimension. What is the meaning of this dimension? Is it unitary? Or can it, too, be broken down into components?

Criteria for Identifying an Emotion as Positive or Negative. It requires only a moment's reflection to realize that an emotion may be regarded as positive or negative for any of four reasons: (1) the emotion is accompanied by a feeling state that is either pleasant or unpleasant; (2) the object of the emotion is appraised as either good or bad; (3) the behavior displayed during the emotion is regarded favorably or unfavorably; and (4) the consequences of the emotion are either beneficial or harmful. These four criteria are not independent, but it will be helpful to analyze them separately.

1. Some emotions (such as sexual arousal) are accompanied by pleasurable feelings, whereas others (such as grief) are marked by pain and anguish. However, in discussing Wundt's tridimensional theory of emotion, and especially the experiment of Nafe, we saw how difficult it is to specify what constitutes a feeling of pleasure or pain. Certainly, there does not appear to be any one thing which is common to all pleasant experiences and which separates these from the unpleasant. Rather, "pleasant" is a term which applies to a diverse class of experiences that share, at best, a certain "family resemblance" (to borrow a phrase from Wittgenstein, 1953).

Consider the pleasure of a cool drink and remove from it all the specific stimuli related to the taste of the drink and to the relief of specific bodily discomforts, for example, a parched throat. What remains? And does *it*–the "raw feeling" of pleasure–have anything in common with what we experience on a pleasant afternoon in the company of friends, or during the excitement of a football game, or upon the completion of a job well done? Conversely, does the unpleasantness of grief share elements in common with the malaise that accompanies a severe flu, the pain of a broken leg, or the noxious smell of rotten eggs?

If the "raw feels" of pleasantness and unpleasantness share anything in common, no one has been able to identify it, and not for the lack of trying. The distinction between positive and negative emotions cannot, therefore, rest solely on this criterion. Among other things, the individual's appraisal or judgment of the situation must be taken into account.

2. Consider the following statements:

I am delighted to see you.
I am sorry to learn of your father's death.
I have nothing but contempt for him.
I am disgusted by the whole affair.

In these statements, the emotional concepts (delight, sorrow, contempt, disgust) refer not so much to feelings as to judgments. And although this judgmental feature is more evident in some uses of emotional concepts than in others, all emotions are based on an individual's appraisal of the situation, and hence all emotions are judgmental to at least some degree. Moreover, if the object of the emotion is judged positively, then the emotion as a whole may be regarded as positive, even if it is accompanied by unpleasant feelings. Unrequited love is a case in point. Conversely, if the emotion entails a negative judgment, then the entire emotion may be considered negative, even if it is accompanied by pleasurable feelings. Anger, for example, typically involves the appraisal of some wrongdoing, and it also is regarded as a negative emotion. However, anger may be experienced as pleasant: "Anger, sweeter far than trickling honey, waxeth like smoke in the breasts of men" (Homer, *Iliad*).

The confounding of subjective feelings with an evaluation of the stimulus object is to commit what Titchener (1910) called the "stimulus error." But as Henle (1971) has pointed out, not even so erudite a systematist as Titchener could avoid the stimulus error, and with good reason. Although one can speak in the abstract of raw feelings and sensations, uncontaminated by cognitive appraisals, such abstractions are divorced from reality and have proved to be theoretically sterile.

3. Many of the same considerations that apply to the appraisal of stimulus objects also apply to the evaluation of one's own behavior during emotion. To take a rather extreme example, the person who regards sex as "dirty" is likely to consider sexual arousal as a negative emotion, even though the stimulus object (a loved one) may be highly regarded and the subjective experience pleasurable. Of course, most people do not consider sexual behavior as wrong under appropriate conditions. But consider such common emotional terms as "smug," "coy," "peevish," and "giddy." These terms imply an evaluation of behavior, just as "delighted," "contempt," etc., imply an evaluation of some stimulus object. Moreover, the connotation of a term such as "smug" is slightly negative, even though the person who is smug feels good and is evaluating a situation favorably. (This is why smugness is something we typically attribute to others, not ourselves.)

4. A response may be regarded as good or bad because of its intrinsic characteristics, as indicated above, or because of the consequences to which it leads. Consider an emotion such as courage. By definition, courage must be elicited by a situation that is evaluated negatively (e.g., dangerous) and/or there must be pain and anguish involved. Moreover, the courageous act itself may be regarded as foolish (e.g., rushing into a burning house), particularly if it does not succeed. Yet, courage is considered a positive emotion because it often does lead to beneficial outcomes, and hence is encouraged. A similar point, but from the negative side, is illustrated by vengeance. Vengeful acts are regarded negatively, in large part because they often lead to harmful consequences.

It must again be emphasized that the above four criteria for classifying an emotion as positive or negative (i.e., subjective feelings, stimulus appraisal, response evaluation, and outcomes) are not independent. There are no "raw feels," or uninterpreted sensations of pleasantness or unpleasantness. Rather, all experience is conditioned by an evaulation of the eliciting conditions, the accompanying behavior (including ideation), and the actual or potential consequences. Similarly, any evaluation of behavior, say, is conditioned by an appraisal of the instigation, feeling states, and consequences. Of course, during the course of an emotion, one or another of these factors may assume greater importance, only to become muted at a later time; and the overall relative weight of each factor may differ from one emotion to another (e.g., in joy, eliciting conditions may be more important than response consequences).

In short, the experience of emotion represents a dynamic whole. This does not, however, negate the fact that the classification–and the experience–of an emotion as positive or negative represents a complex judgment involving a number of different criteria.

The Attribution of Emotion as a Function of Response Outcomes

In the preceding section, we reviewed some of the connotations of emotional concepts in general, and also the criteria for identifying a response as either positive or negative. We may now return to the question: Why are there fewer concepts in ordinary language for positive as opposed to negative emotions? To answer this question completely, we would have to consider how the various connotations of emotional concepts (e.g., the implication that emotional responses are uncharacteristic, irrational, etc.) apply to each of the criteria for classifying a response as positive or negative. That, however, would be beyond the scope of this chapter. Therefore, I will limit the discussion to one of the four criteria for classifying behavior as positive or negative, namely, the outcome of the response. In any case, this is the most important of the criteria. In the long run, the real or fancied consequences of a response determine how eliciting stimuli are appraised and also how the response itself will be evaluated; and even simple sensory experiences of pleasure and pain can be influenced by subsequent rewards and punishments.[3]

To simplify matters even further, I will not consider separately each of the various connotations of emotional concepts. Rather, I will focus on a common theme that emerges when these connotations are considered together. Specifically a behavior that is regarded as uncharacteristic of the individual, that is irrational, intuitive, impulsive, etc., tends to be classified as a passion rather than as an action. This means, among other things, that a person may not be held fully responsible for the outcome of an emotional response.

As a kind of thought experiment, consider a person who kills another in a fit of rage—the typical "crime of passion." If the plea of passion is accepted, the charge will be reduced from murder (premediated homicide) to manslaughter. Now contrast this event with the action of a person who uncharacteristically and impulsively donates a large sum of money to a worthy cause. The donor is unlikely to classify his response as a passion, implying that he could not help himself, that he was overcome by charity. Unlike crimes of passion, which are legion, good deeds of passion are rare, not necessarily because evil is more prevalent than goodness. Rather, it is because responses with positive outcomes are not typically described as emo-

[3] Pavlov (1927) found, for example, that when burns and electric shocks were followed by food, dogs would respond with calm anticipation; however, unconditioned animals would show strong defensive reactions to the same stimuli.

tional, for that would imply a diminished responsibility on the part of the individual for his behavior.

It is not necessary to rely on a thought experiment to illustrate the importance of positive and negative outcomes for the attribution of emotion. In a recent series of experiments by Averill, DeWitt, and Zimmer (1978), students were asked to work on problems that ostensibly were part of a culture-free test of academic ability. The problems were presented together with potentially arousing stimuli (e.g., photographs of nudes from *Playboy* and similar magazines, and photographs of mutilated corpses from homicide files). The prediction was that the photographs would be rated as more arousing (e.g., the nudes as more beautiful and the corpses as more horrible) if they were accompanied by failure rather than by success, for this would provide subjects with an ego-syntonic rationale for their poor performance. This prediction was confirmed in three separate studies. Moreover, emotional attributions were most likely to occur (a) when subjects were highly ego-involved in the problem-solving task; (b) when they were confronted by the experimenter with the pattern of their success and failure; and (c) when the cues in the situation were potentially arousing, as in the case of the nudes and corpses, as opposed to affectively neutral.

A study conducted by Semin and Manstead (1977) also illustrates the importance of response outcomes for the attribution of emotion. These investigators presented subjects with a series of short vignettes describing the inadvertant breaking of some social rule (e.g., noticing that the zipper of one's trousers is open), or some accidental event involving physical danger but no social violation (e.g., tripping on some stairs). The vignettes were presented under four different orientations—as happening in public or in private, and as happening to the subject or to someone else. The subjects then rated the person to whom the event occured on a variety of scales, some of which represented personality characteristics (e.g., intelligent–unintelligent, competent–incompetent), and some of which represented immediate emotional reactions to the situation (e.g., anxious–calm, embarrassed–unembarrassed).

Not surprisingly, if the event involved the breaking of some social rule, the attribution of emotion was much greater when the setting was public rather than private; if, on the other hand, the event involved some physical danger, emotional reactivity was about the same in both settings (although slightly higher in public). Of greater interest is the way subjects rated the personality characteristics of the actor. Such ratings were made from two orientations—that of the actor and that of a bystander observing the event. Subjects who took the bystander's perspective did not rate the actor any more harshly (e.g., as more incompetent) than did subjects who took the actor's perspective. However, subjects who took the actor's perspective *believed* that bystanders would rate them more harshly than they would rate themselves.

In other words, a person who commits a minor social faux pas tends to assume (unrealistically) that others will attribute the transgression to a defect in character. Semin and Manstead postulate that an emotional reaction on the part of the actor in such a situation serves to stem the flow of (presumed) negative criticism. By showing embarrassment, nervous tension, or other signs of upset, the actor is in effect saying: "This was an unusual thing that happened to me. Please don't infer that I am always so clumsy or ignorant."

Semin and Manstead speculate that disruptions of social rules that have positive consequences may give rise to positive emotions, but they present no data. Indeed, they caution against assuming that the process would be simply the reverse of the negative case. They note, for example, that an unexpected positive performance can often lead to embarrassment—a negative emotion.

According to the present analysis, events with positive outcomes would elicit fewer self-attributions of emotion than would events with negative outcomes, unless in the former case the actor had some reason not to assume full responsibility. Thus, we do sometimes become embarrassed at positive deeds, especially if we believe others may evaluate us too highly, or more than we deserve. But more often, we are only too glad to accept credit for positive outcomes, and too much emotion, even too much glee, may imply that it was not altogether deserved. (Compare, for example, the person who "jumps for joy" after winning a lottery, and the same response by a person who has just passed an important examination. In the latter case, we might wonder: Was passing the exam so unexpected? Was it so chancy? And if so, did the person really deserve it?)

To summarize briefly, the research by Averill *et al.* (1978) and by Semin and Manstead (1977) illustrates different ways in which the attribution of emotion and/or the display of emotional upset may help to protect the individual from the negative consequences of his behavior. I do not wish to insinuate, however, that a deflection of responsibility for negative outcomes is the primary reason for becoming emotional. Obviously, positive outcomes can also be associated with emotional states, and we must also account for this fact.

As discussed earlier, emotional concepts have a variety of connotations, any of which may contribute to a response being classified as a passion rather than as an action. For example, a response that is regarded as uncharacteristic, irrational, intuitive, impulsive, etc., may also be interpreted as emotional, for attributes such as these imply a certain lack of personal control. This is true even when the outcome of the response is positive.

Consider an emotion such as courage. Although a person may be described as courageous in a dispositional or trait sense, most courageous acts are performed by ordinary people behaving in extraordinary or uncharacteristic ways. Moreover, since a courageous act is often inimical to the immediate well-being of the individual, it may also be considered irrational. Why, for example, should a person risk his own life to save that of another, especially if the other person is a stranger and there is no immediate reward or coercion involved? Courageous acts also tend to occur in emergency situations in which there is little time to think or deliberate. Hence they may be characterized as intuitive and impulsive. And, of course, a courageous act often requires a great deal of energy (intensity) and persistence in order to overcome the danger.

In short, the typical act of courage has many of the characteristics of a passion. There is a problem, however. Not only does courage often lead to favorable outcomes; the individual who responds courageously is also the subject of much praise. But how can a person accept credit, and be honored, for an emotional response, which is ostensibly beyond personal control? This question highlights a certain ambiguity in the concept of courage. According to one set of criteria, courage qualifies as a passion; but according to other criteria (involving the attribution of responsibility), it is treated more like an action.

In view of the above considerations, it is not surprising that some people deny that courage is even an emotion.[4] There may, of course, be a variety of reasons for such a denial; but one of them is, I suspect, the reluctance to describe as emotional a response that leads to a positive outcome.

Indeed, courage is, only one of many positive emotions recognized in ordinary language. If this were an essay on the positive emotions *per se*, analyses would have to be made of states such as love, mirth, joy, empathy, awe, ecstasy, and hope, to name but a few. Such analyses are beyond the scope of this chapter; to avoid misunderstanding, however, one thing should be emphasized. I am not contending that emotional concepts are inapplica-

[4] For example, in the discussion following the presentation of this material at the Erindale Symposium, several members of the audience questioned whether courage is a true emotion. No definitive answer can be given to such a question. However, in ordinary language, terms such as "courageous," "daring," and "brave" are judged to have a strong emotional connotation (Averill, 1975); moreover, in many classical discussions of the topic, courage is treated as a basic or fundamental emotion (cf. Aquinas, *Summa Theologica*, 1a2ae. 45, 1).

ble to positive states, only that their range of applicability is more limited in the case of positive as opposed to negative responses. And the attribution of emotion as a function of positive and negative outcomes simply illustrates one of the limiting conditions.

Perhaps it would be helpful at this point to take stock of where we have been, and to preview briefly where we are going in the remainder of this chapter. Thus far, we have (a) established that there are fewer concepts in ordinary language for positive as opposed to negative emotions; (b) examined the meaning of emotional concepts, in general, and the criteria for identifying positive and negative emotions, in particular; and (c) illustrated how the meaning of emotional concepts makes them less applicable to positive states, using outcome as the criterion for classifying a response as positive or negative. I shall argue next that the limited applicability of emotional concepts to positive states is not just a linguistic curiosity. Rather, there is a close relationship between language and behavior, such that there is paucity of positive emotions in deed as well as in word. More generally, I shall argue that emotional behavior is fashioned according to many of the same rules that help determine the use (meaning) of emotional concepts.

The Relationship between Emotional Concepts and Emotional Behavior

I have devoted so much space to demonstrating the greater applicability of emotional concepts to negative than to positive states, not because I believe this is a problem of great importance in its own right, but rather because it forces us to consider some issues of fundamental importance for theories of emotion. The present section is devoted to an examination of those issues. At the outset, therefore, let me make a brief digression to place the discussion within a broader context.

Among current theories of emotion, perhaps the most influential is that adumbrated by Stanley Schachter (1964, 1971). Central to Schachter's formulation is the following proposition:

> Given a state of physiological arousal for which an individual has no immediate explanation, he will "label" this state and describe his feelings in terms of the cognitions available to him. . . . Precisely the same state of physiological arousal could be labeled "joy," or "fury," or any of a great variety of emotional labels, depending upon the cognitive structure of the situation. (1971, p. 4)

There are two things to note about this proposition. The first is the assumed lack of identity between emotional states and *specific* physiological reactions. This assumption does not rule out any physiological differences among emotional states. (Sexual arousal obviously involves some physiological responses—tumescence, for example–that are not typically found in fear, say, or grief.) The assumption does, however, highlight the fact that a variety of different physiological reactions are at least compatible with any given emotion. This means, among other things, that emotions cannot be reduced to built-in (genetically determined) patterns of responses. But more of that shortly.

The second thing to note about the above proposition is the emphasis on the "labeling" of emotion. Actually, it is not really the emotional state that is being labeled, according to Schachter; it is, rather, some state of physiological arousal. In fact, exactly the same state of arousal can be labeled differently depending on the "cognitive structure of the situation." This implies that the experience of emotion results from the same processes that lead a physiological response to be labeled as emotional. And what are those processes? Reference to the "cognitive structure of the situation" is not sufficient explanation, for the appraisal of situational cues supposedly does not occasion the experience of emotion in the absence of physiological arousal. Yet, there is nothing in Schachter's formulation to suggest why physiological arousal *per se* should add an emotional quality to experience.

In short, Schachter's theory highlights the three-way interaction between verbal responses, physiological arousal, and the experience of emotion, but it leaves vague the nature of the relationships involved. Since each aspect of the interaction is important for understanding the others, I will begin with a discussion of how physiological arousal contributes to the experience of emotion.[5] We will then be in a better position to examine how the "labeling" of a response can influence, and even transform, an emotional experience.

The Contribution of Physiological Arousal

Because of the limited space, it will be helpful to approach this issue historically, using the observations of others as stepping stones. Our im-

[5] Some theorists (e.g., Solomon, 1976) maintain that the emotions are a form of judgment or cognition, and hence that physiological arousal is not an essential part of an emotional syndrome. I agree that physiological arousal, in the strict sense of visceral change, is not necessary for the experience of emotion. I would contend, however, that some form of response, actual or intended, is necessary. In the following discussion, therefore, I will be using "physiological arousal" as a catchword for all kinds of responses. The nature of the argument (that the experience of emotion depends ultimately on the *meaning* of the response) does not depend on whether the response is conceived of in terms of visceral changes, expressive reactions, overt behavior, central neural activity, or whatever.

mediate goal is to answer the question: How does physiological arousal plus the appraisal of situational cues contribute to the experience of emotion? Few questions in psychology are without precedent, and this one is no exception. William James (1890), like Schachter, believed that feedback from visceral changes and other postural adjustments adds the glow of emotion to otherwise neutral perceptions. We are fearful, according to James, because we run; sad because we cry; mirthful because we laugh; and so forth. However, James did not attribute to interoception (e.g., visceral feedback) any special properties not explicable in terms of ordinary perceptual processes. This led Irons (1894) to wonder: "How then can one perceptive process of itself suffuse with emotional warmth the cold intellectuality of another?" (p. 85).

The challenge posed by Irons was taken up, not by James, but by Dewey (1894, 1895); and, in the discussion that follows, I will draw heavily on Dewey's analysis.

In a previous section of this chapter, I noted that the distinction between positive and negative emotions could be made on the basis of feelings, appraisals, responses, and/or outcomes. Dewey made a similar, but somewhat simpler, distinction among three phases of an emotion: (1) the feel or "affective *quale*," which he attributed to feedback from visceral and other bodily changes; (2) the response or what he called a "teleological coordination"; and (3) the appraised object of the emotion.

Using this threefold distinction as a starting point, Dewey addressed the question of how bodily feedback (interoception) can add an emotional quality to other (exteroceptive) perceptual processes. The answer is to be found, according to Dewey, in the response phase of the emotion. The other two phases, the feeling and the appraised object, are coproducts of the response, as will be described below.

With regard to the feeling of emotion, Dewey agreed with James that this must follow rather than precede the response. Diagrammatically, these two phases can be related as follows:

$$\text{RESPONSE} \rightarrow \text{FEELING}$$

But the response, for Dewey, is not simply a physiological reaction. It is a *teleological coordination*. The meaning of this phrase can best be conveyed through an example, such as laughter. If one took the James–Lange theory literally, all laughter should result in feelings of mirth. That obviously is not the case. Anticipating this criticism, James suggested that bodily changes that do not result in emotional feelings are somehow incomplete. But in what way are they incomplete? What would have to be added to transform laughter into mirth? Would the contraction of a few more muscles suffice, or the addition of glandular secretions? According to Dewey (1894):

> The change from mere cachination to mirthful emotion is a distinct change in psychical quality, and this change of quality does not seem to be adequately *accounted* for by the mere addition of more discharges—though, I repeat, simply adding on more discharges will undoubtedly *make* this difference. If these supplementary factors report the meaning or value of past co-ordinations, this change of quality is reasonable and inevitable; if not, if they are simply some more accidental discharges, the peculiar qualitative "feel" is miraculous—it admits of no explanation. (p. 562)

In other words, the qualitative change from simple sensory feedback to emotional experience occurs when the total response forms a meaningful pattern or "co-ordination." But this simply raises another question: What makes a pattern meaningful? In addressing this issue, Dewey relied primarily on Darwin's (1872/1965) analysis of emotion. Emotional responses are meaningful because they at one time had a use (e.g., in the struggle for survival). In the case of laughter, Dewey speculated that

> all expectancy, waiting, suspended effort, etc., is accompanied for obvious teleological reasons, with taking in and holding a full breath, and the maintenance of the whole muscular system in a state of considerable tension. . . . The sudden relaxation of this strain, so far as occurring through the medium of the breathing and vocal apparatus, is laughter. (p. 559)

Whether this is a correct explanation of laughter is not of concern here. The important point is that, according to Dewey, laughter will not result in feelings of mirth unless the laughter occurs in a manner related to some such meaningful function. For Dewey, then, emotional behavior is the recurrence, in modified form, of a teleological (functional) act, and the feeling of emotion is a "reflexion" (reflection) of that act. Reflection, in Dewey's sense, involves feedback from motor and visceral discharges, as James had postulated. However, since the bodily changes represent *meaningful* patterns, the feeling of emotion also involves the "realization of ideas" (1895, p. 15).

Turning now to the object phase of the emotion, this is what the response is *about*. The object of mirth, for example, might be a cartoon; and the object of fear, a bear in the woods. The object of an emotion, Dewey emphasized, cannot precede the response without violating James's principle that the experience of emotion is a function of response feedback because a person does not laugh at any cartoon, only a *funny* one; similarly, a person does not run from any bear, only a *frightening* one. But *ex hypothesi*, funniness and fear are a realization of the meaning of the response and not inherent properties of the exciting event. Or, stated somewhat differently,

> it is not the idea of the bear, or the bear as object, but a certain *act of seeing*, which by habit, whether inherited or acquired, sets up other acts. It is the kind of *coordination of acts* which, brought to sensational consciousness, constitutes the bear a fearful, or a laughable, or an indifferent object. (Dewey, 1895, p. 19)

Taking into account the fact that the object as well as the feeling is a coordinate product of the response, we may expand the earlier diagram of an emotional syndrome as follows:

$$\text{OBJECT} \leftarrow \text{RESPONSE} \rightarrow \text{FEELING}$$

But if the object is a coordinate product of the response, what initiates the emotion? According to Dewey (1895):

> We have certain organic activities initiated, say in the eye, stimulating through organized paths of association in the brain, certain activities of hands, legs, etc., and (through the coordination of these motor activities with the vegetative functions necessary to maintain them) of lungs, heart, vaso-motor system, digestive organs, etc. The "bear" is psychologically, just as much a discrimination of certain values, within the total pulse of coordination of action, as is the feeling of "fear." The "bear" is constituted by the excitations of eye and coordinated touch centers, just as the "terror" is by the disturbances of muscular and glandular systems. (p. 20)

These cryptic references to sensory activities and hypothetical neural centers do not, of course, explain how an emotion is aroused. However, Dewey's point is as much logical as psychological. That is, the object is part of an emotional syndrome and not a causal antecedent. For example, a man may fall in love because he is lonely, in a strange locale, and meets a girl who reminds him of more pleasant times in the past. These circumstances are the *causes* of his love, not the object. That is, the man is not in love with his loneliness, the strange locale, or past pleasures; in fact, there is a sense in which the object of his love is not even the girl he meets. Love is blind, as the saying goes, and when the man recovers he may well wonder what he ever "saw" in his former sweetheart. Similar remarks could be made with regard to the objects of fear, disgust, anger, or any other emotion. The basic point is, simply, that the object of an emotion is a construction, a part of the entire syndrome, and not an objectively existing reality.

With the above considerations in mind, the entire emotional syndrome may now be diagrammed:

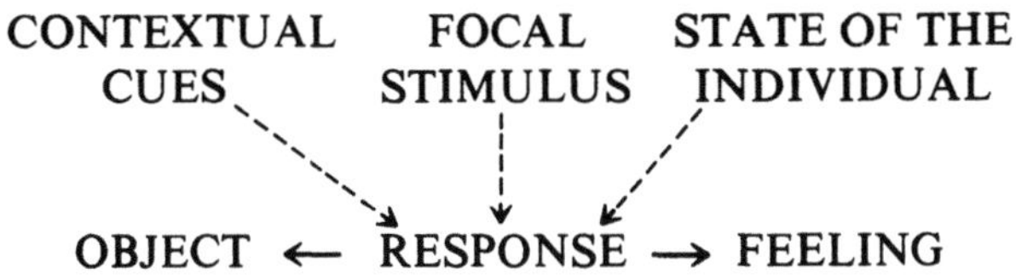

And how do these considerations bear upon the relationship between emotional concepts and behavior? We began this discussion with an analysis of Schachter's proposition that the same state of physiological arousal may be "labeled" as joy, fury, etc., depending on the cognitive structure of the situation. This proposition highlights the close relationship between language and emotion. However, it also raises more questions than it answers. In particular, it implies that both the labeling and the experience of emotion are the result of similar processes, but it does not indicate the nature of those processes. Nevertheless, the implication is clear: If we understand the *labeling* of emotion, we will also understand to a large extent the experience of emotion, and vice versa.

Because the nature of emotional experience has long been debated, I have chosen to start with this side of the equation, even though subjective experience presents a more difficult problem than the language of emotion. Schachter, who considers his theory to be "neo-Jamesean", contends that the feeling of emotion is a joint production of physiological arousal and the cognitive structure of the situation. But, as we have seen, this contention is subject to the same criticism that Irons (1894) raised in connection with the James–Lange theory of emotion (namely, there is nothing about physiological arousal *per se* that will add emotional warmth to the cold perception of an environmental event); and we have considered the reply that Dewey (1894, 1895) made to Irons. In a word, the experience of emotion depends on the *meaning* of the response.

If we accept Dewey's reply, then the basic question becomes: How do emotional responses accrue meaning? Basically, I agree with Schachter (1971) that emotional responses, in the sense of physiological arousal and other bodily adjustments, are not inherently meaningful, and that precisely the same response can be labeled (and experienced) as joy, fury, or fear, depending on the cognitive structure of the situation. On the other hand, I also agree with Dewey that situations are not inherently joyful, infuriating, or fearful, but that these are meanings imposed on events as part of the emotional response.

If the meaning of the response is dependent on the cognitive structure of the situation (Schachter), and the cognitive structure of the situation is dependent on the response (Dewey), we would seem to be caught in a vicious circle. The way out, of course, is to postulate a common source of meaning for both the response and the cognitive structure of the situation. This is basically the move that Dewey made when he argued that emotional responses accrue meaning primarily because of their role in biological evolution. Such a move, however, does not really resolve the issue; it merely fails to recognize the possibility that emotional responses lack inherent meaning. In Dewey's day, such a failure was perhaps reasonable. However, I believe that the data presented by Schachter and others are quite convincing. The emotions cannot be reduced in any simple or direct fashion to genetically determined "instincts" (by whatever name). But another possibility exists, namely, that the meaning of emotional responses is primarily social in origin.

There is not space here to examine in any detail the social determinants of emotional behavior (see Averill, 1976; 1980). However, some fundamental aspects of the problem can be clarified by considering further the meaning of emotional concepts (which few would deny is social in origin, and which, for reasons already described, stands in a close functional relationship to the experience of emotion).

A Further Note on the Meaning of Emotional Concepts

In an earlier section, I examined various connotations of emotional concepts as they relate to the distinction between actions and passions. For present purposes, we must broaden our concern to the nature of meaning itself. That is, how do emotional concepts (or any other kind of concept, for that matter) accrue meaning, regardless of specific connotations?

The nature of meaning has long plagued philosophers and linguists, and there is still little agreement on the subject. However, two general trends or lines of thought can be distinguished. The first is associated with the philosophical tradition that William James (1907) labeled "tough minded" (empiricist/positivistic) and the other with what he termed "tender minded" (rationalistic). More specifically, the first may be called the *referential* theory of meaning, and the second (following Taylor, 1975) the *expressivist* theory.[6]

The referential theory of meaning takes proper names as a paradigm case. The word "John," for example, has meaning because it refers to a specific person. As a name, however, "John" has no special relationship to

[6] A more accurate, but much more cumbersome, term for the second point of view might be the "meaning-as-use" theory. Emotional terms do not express feelings in the same way that the yelp of a dog, say, expresses the animal's pain. Through the use of language, a new, and uniquely human, dimension of meaning is added to experience. But more of that shortly.

the intrinsic characteristics of the person (who could just as readily have been named "Bill" or "Joe"). The relationship between a name and the object named is arbitrary, subject only to mutual agreement. Stated somewhat differently, the referential theory assumes that the object named has meaning independent of any labels attached to it, and in this sense, the theory *objectifies* events.

Because of its simplicity, intuitive plausibility, and, above all, its "tough mindedness," the referential theory of meaning has had considerable influence on theories of emotion. Debate has raged, for example, about the referent of such terms as "anger," "fear," "grief," etc. Do these terms name feelings, physiological responses, drive states, or what? Some theorists (e.g., Duffy, 1962), finding nothing unique to which emotional terms might refer, have even concluded that the concept of emotion is meaningless from a scientific point of view. Underlying these debates is the assumption that emotional terms must refer to some independently existing object or event, or else they must be meaningless, like signs that point nowhere.

Historically, the referential theory of meaning can be traced to the Enlightenment period, which was characterized by an optimistic faith in the advancement of science (conceived largely along mechanistic lines). Not surprisingly, therefore, the reaction to the Enlightenment gave rise to a different theory of meaning—the expressivist. Herder's *On the Origin of Language* (1772/1966) was seminal in this regard. Taylor (1975) has eloquently described the implications of Herder's work:

> For [Herder's] Enlightenment predecessors representative consciousness, the understanding that something stands for or refers to something else, was taken for granted. . . . But for Herder the existence of this representational or linguistic consciousness is the central question. What is it which makes it possible for us to have this distinct, focussed awareness of things, where animals remain caught in the dream-like, melodic flow of experience? It is language that makes this possible. Hence language must be probed from an entirely different point of view. It is not just a set of signs which have meaning in virtue of referring to something, it is the necessary vehicle of a certain form of consciousness, which is characteristically human, the distinct grasp of things which Herder calls "reflection" (*Besonnenheit*). In other terms, *words do not just refer, they are also precipitates of an activity in which the human form of consciousness comes to be.* (p. 19, italics added)

Herder believed that each cultural group develops its own spirit and laws, its own unique way of realizing the human potential. Moreover, the realization of man is made possible by, and is manifested through, language. Herder's work thus gave strong impetus to the study of philology and ethnopsychology (*Völkerpsychologie*), two characteristic endeavors of nineteenth-century German scholars.

Among recent theorists, the later Wittgenstein has been the most influential advocate of an expressivist view of language.[7] "A child has hurt himself and he cries; and then adults talk to him and teach him exclamations and, later, sentences. They teach the child new pain-behavior" (Wittgenstein, 1953, p. 244). In other words, the term "pain" in an expression such as "I have a pain" accrues meaning as part of an ongoing stream of behavior.

From a broader perspective, it may be said that the meaning of a term derives from the use to which it is put, not just the feeling it expresses. Wittgenstein (1953) illustrates this point with the example of a building assistant who picks up a flat stone upon hearing the command, "Slab!" The assistant's response is based on an agreement with the builder that the word "slab" will have a certain use (meaning) in connection with the work they are doing. In this example, the construction project represents what Wittgenstein calls a "language game." The notion of a language game focuses attention on the fact that words have meaning only as part of a larger activity in which a person is engaged. Of course, language "games" are not games in the ordinary sense of that term. In a manner reminiscent of Herder, Wittgenstein (1958, p. 98) speaks of them as part of the "natural history" of the group.

On a more psychological level, Bates (1976) has presented an analysis of meaning which combines some aspects of the expressivist theory as represented by Wittgenstein with the genetic epistemology of Piaget (e.g., 1970). According to Piaget's point of view, objects and events are not knowable in themselves. Rather, all knowledge results from the imposition on events of cognitive schematas built up through interaction with the environment. According to Bates (1976),

> Within this framework, a symbol or representation is the internal reenactment (re-presentation) of the activities originally carried out with objects or events. Just as the child originally KNEW a triangle by imitating its contours with movements of the eye, touch, etc., he later SYMBOLIZES a triangle by recalling or imitating the scheme (or part of the scheme) of movements that were originally used to know that pattern. (p. 11)

Or, stated somewhat differently, "meaning is a coordinated set of internalized action patterns which can be associated with a set of symbols in systematic ways, for the purpose of communication" (p. 12).

[7] By juxtaposing Herder and Wittgenstein in this fashion, I do not wish to imply a greater commonality between the two than actually exists. Herder is generally considered the father of German Romanticism; Wittgenstein belongs to another age, in spirit and style, as well as in time. But their contrasting approaches to other issues simply adds weight to their common insights regarding the meaning and use of language.

In short, the expressivist theory can be stated in two versions. One version is sociocultural, that is, the meaning of a concept depends on the *natural history* of the behavior (language game) of which it is a part. The other version is psychological, that is, the meaning of a concept is based on *internalized action patterns* or cognitive structures that symbolically represent aspects of the appropriate language game.

Emotions as Transitory Social Roles

We have now considered separately the two sides of the relationship between language and emotion, namely, the nature of emotional syndromes and the meaning (as use) of emotional concepts. It remains to combine these two considerations into a single formulation.

Earlier in this chapter, I defined emotions as "transitory social roles." The theoretical and empirical rationale for such a definition has been presented in detail elsewhere (Averill, 1976, 1980), and I do not wish to repeat those arguments here. I will therefore confine my remarks to a few observations on the relevance of this definition to the relationship between emotional concepts and emotional behavior. And, corresponding to the two versions of the expressivist theory of meaning outlined above, two aspects of this relationship need to be considered.

The Natural History of Emotion. At first, the definition of an emotion as a transitory social role might seem somewhat strange (and, indeed, it is a metaphorical way of speaking). However, consider again the example of a language game offered by Wittgenstein (1953). The command "Slab!" is given meaning in the context of a set pattern of interaction between the construction boss and the assistant. Should the assistant quit the project, another might be hired in his stead, and likewise for the boss. These are, in short, social roles, of which the command "Slab!" is one manifestation. The social roles of construction boss and assistant are, in turn, only one aspect of a larger social structure that helps determine the division of labor, the kinds of material used in construction, etc.

Now consider the person who exclaims, "I am angry!" He too expects some kind of response on the part of another (an apology, perhaps, or at least a change in behavior). And similarly, the person who hears that exclamation can expect certain further behavior on the part of the person who is angry. The angry person and his target have, in a sense, entered into transitory social roles vis-à-vis one another.

But let us return for the moment to the construction boss and his assistant. A critic might admit that the command, "Slab!" epitomizes the social roles of the participants in this example. Yet the slab itself—as a piece of stone or building material—does not change. It has its own characteristics regardless of how the construction boss and his assistant interact. Similarly, this critic might maintain, anger has its own (innate) characteristics that do not change in any fundamental way as a function of how it is expressed in social interaction.

The above objection would have some merit if human behavior were as rigid and unyielding as a piece of building material. But that is not the case. Human behavior is remarkably malleable and variable; and emotional responses are no exception. Take anger, for example. A person may become angry for many different reasons, some constructive and others malevolent, and anger may be expressed in innumerable different ways (Averill, 1979a). The belief that there is some specific thing or event to which the term "anger" must refer (e.g., a feeling, neurological circuit, or whatever) is based on an implicit acceptance of the referential theory of meaning described earlier. If, on the other hand, one adopts the expressivist theory, then the meaning of a term such as anger is determined not by what it refers to, but by the way it is used. Going further, it may be said that the meaning of emotional concepts is determined by many of the same rules that determine the meaning of emotional behavior, and those rules are primarily social in origin.

The Experience of Emotion. The overt expression of emotion, whether verbal or behavioral, is governed by social norms and rules. That, no one would deny. But how can one account for the experience of emotion in terms of social roles? Surely, the person who is infuriated by an insult is not simply acting.

To say that emotional syndromes are transitory social roles is not to imply that the experience of emotion is counterfeit or disingenuous. Social roles are not theatrical performances. They are part of reality. With this in mind, two aspects of emotional role-enactment may be distinguished. The first aspect has to do with understanding the meaning or use of the role within a broader social context. Such understanding is acquired during socialization as the child (and sometimes, adult) learns how to respond, and to *conceptualize events*, in terms of anger, fear, etc. From a psychological point of view, the resulting concepts represent cognitive schemata or "internalized action patterns" in the sense of Bates (1976).

The second aspect of role-enactment that must be considered is the monitoring of behavior. Monitoring may occur on two levels (cf. Harré & Secord, 1972). First-order monitoring involves the correction or control of behavior through afferent feedback loops. It is this order of monitoring that, according to a simplistic interpretation of the James–Lange theory, should account for the experience of emotion. But for reasons already discussed, afferent feedback from visceral and other bodily changes is not sufficient to infuse with emotional warmth the cold perception of an exciting event. For that, a second order of monitoring is required.

In the case of second-order monitoring, afferent feedback is assimilated into, or given meaning by, the cognitive schemata that represent the individual's understanding of the emotional role. And, as described above, such understanding is intimately related to the meaning (use) of emotional concepts. The experience of emotion is thus "reflective" in the sense of Herder (1772/1966) and later phenomenological psychologists. Also, the notion of second-order monitoring gives new meaning to Dewey's (1895) insight that "emotional excitation is the felt process of realization of ideas" (p. 15).

Implications for the Assessment and Modification of Emotional Behavior

In concluding this chapter, I would like to say a few words about the relevance of the present analysis for the assessment and modification of emotional behavior, the explicit topic of this symposium.

Implications for Assessment

Although much maligned because of their presumed lack of veracity (cf. Nisbett & Wilson, 1977), verbal reports are still the most commonly used means of assessing emotional reactions. Therefore, it is of considerable importance to understand the relationship between emotional concepts and emotional behavior. According to the present formulation, verbal reports are not just labels for internal states or feelings; rather, they are *part of* the entire emotional syndrome. However, each kind of response that enters into, or forms part of, an emotional syndrome is under multiple control. Take a simple response, such as a change in heart rate, as an example. Heart rate cannot change in just any fashion when a person is emotional, for it is regulated by a variety of homeostatic feedback mechanisms that operate quite independently of the emotion. Similarly, overt behavior is subject to a variety of controls (e.g., rules of etiquette and probity) that apply to both emotional and nonemotional responses. And the same can be said with regard to self-reports. Verbal behavior is subject to a great many rules and constraints (linguistic, social, etc.) that help determine what a person will say in any given situation.

In most instances (i.e., during the course of everyday affairs), the verbal expression of emotion is unambiguous and straightforward. However, if the subject is placed in an unusual situation, such as a psychology experiment or a clinical session, then the meaning of a self-report may be questionable. This is not because persons tend to dissimulate–consciously or unconsciously–in such situations (although that sometimes may be the case). Rather, it is because the rules governing verbal behavior are often unclear when taken out of their ordinary context, and self-reports become correspondingly ambiguous.

In my own experimental research on stress (e.g., Averill, O'Brien, & DeWitt, 1977), the subject is typically asked to indicate his or her emotional state by means of an adjective check list (usually patterned after that by Nowlis, 1965). The most common finding is that under conditions of threat (e.g., waiting for an electric shock) subjects will check any adjective that has a negative connotation, regardless of why the connotation is negative. Thus, the subject may report being anxious, angry, depressed, fatigued, etc. This does not necessarily mean that the individual is actually angry or depressed in the situation. It means simply that the situation is negative and unusual. (How often does a person find himself sitting in an easy chair, attached to a polygraph, awaiting a noxious stimulus, in order to test some hypothesis that he knows nothing about?) Moreover, the means of obtaining the self-reports is also unusual. (How often does a person express his emotions by running through a list of adjectives, checking those which supposedly describe his state at the moment?) No one should be surprised if, under such conditions, the different dimensions of emotion defined by the adjectives do not have a great deal of "discriminative validity." Perhaps the best we can–or should–hope for is that the subject will be able to make some gross distinctions along such dimensions as positive versus negative, and perhaps levels of activation.

I want to emphasize, however, that the above considerations do *not* mean that self-reports are generally ambiguous, unreliable, etc., especially in everyday affairs. It simply means that a self-report, like any other kind of response, must be interpreted within a context. Language is, to repeat Wittgenstein's metaphor, like a game; and to correctly interpret self-report data, we must understand the rules of the particular game we are playing.

In addition to the above general considerations, the fact that there are fewer terms in ordinary language for positive than negative emotions also has implications for assessment. Specifically, it implies that the categories used for positive emotions may be more inclusive and less differentiated than those for negative emotions. And, since more inclusive categories encompass a greater variety of behavior, it is not surprising that the assessment of positive emotional states tends to be more reliable across cultures

(Ekman, Friesen, & Ellsworth, 1972) and more stable across time within our own culture (Epstein, 1979). One must be cautious, however, about overinterpreting findings such as these. Comparisons between positive and negative emotions can be misleading unless the differential applicability of emotional concepts to such states is taken into account.

Implications for the Modification of Behavior

A verbal response can be used not only to assess but also to modify emotional behavior. Indeed, of all the responses that constitute an emotional syndrome, the verbal may be the most instrumental for inducing change. This is because verbal responses are primarily symbolic. The muscular contractions involved in a statement such as "I am angry" are trivial compared with the visceral and other behavioral reactions that may accompany anger. Yet the verbal report symbolizes the entire syndrome in a way that few other responses can.

Like a magnet that draws iron filings to it, the self-report may draw together and help organize disparate response elements. For this reason, if a subject is led to label his behavior as "anger," then he may begin to see the situation as provocative and to respond aggressively (cf. Berkowitz & Turner, 1974). Conversely, if a person who is angry can be induced to describe this condition in nonemotional terms, then his behavior may be modified accordingly. This is illustrated well by Meichenbaum's (1977) use of "internal dialogues" to reduce anger and other negative emotions.

Of course, verbal responses are not everything. We are all familiar with the person who shouts: "I'm not angry, dammit; and if you keep insisting that I am, I'll punch you in the nose!" On a more serious level, the clinical literature is replete with descriptions of persons who are caught in an emotional episode (e.g., of anger, fear, jealousy, etc.), but who, for one reason or another, cannot admit the emotion either to themselves or to others.

Emotional syndromes are complex. For example, in the earlier discussion of Dewey's theory, three phases of an emotion were distinguished: the response, the feeling, and the object. If any of these phases (or significant components thereof) are modified, so, too, will be the entire episode. Thus, any procedure (e.g., relaxation) which disrupts or interferes with the response may alter the appraised object and the feeling state as well. Similarly, altering a person's appraisal of the object may modify the response and feeling. One may even alter the way a person interprets his feelings (e.g., by providing information about the nature and causes of an emotional reaction), and this in turn may influence the appraisal of, and response to, a threatening event (Averill, 1979b; Leventhal, 1979).

From the above considerations, it would be expected that the most effective way to modify emotional reactions would be a procedure that involves all aspects of a person's cognitive–behavioral repertoire (i.e., verbal responses, overt behavior, physiological change, and subjective experience). This perhaps accounts for the success of role-playing and related techniques (e.g., Bandura's, 1976, "participant modeling") in promoting change.

These last observations bring us back to our earlier definition of emotions as transitory social roles and to the paucity of positive emotions. The negative emotions may outnumber the positive, for reasons already discussed. On the whole, however, people generally report being more satisfied than dissatisfied. That is true today in our own society (Campbell, Converse, & Rogers, 1976; Flanagan, 1978), and it probably has been true at most periods in all societies. Nevertheless, as Samuel Johnson observed: "A peasant and a philosopher may be equally *satisfied*, but not equally *happy*. Happiness consists in the multiplicity of agreeable consciousness. A peasant has not capacity of having equal happiness with a philosopher" (Boswell, 1791/1934, p. 9).

I doubt that the fine conceptual distinctions that philosophers are prone to make would contribute more to the multiplicity of positive than negative states of consciousness. Nevertheless, Johnson's point should be well-taken; "happiness," as a generic term for all the positive emotions, does require some cognitive and behavioral preparation for its realization.

References

Allport, G. W., & Odbert, H. S. Trait-names: A psycho-lexical study. *Psychological Monographs*, 1936, *47*, (1, Whole No. 211).

Anderson, N. H. Likableness ratings of 555 personality-trait words. *Journal of Personality and Social Psychology*, 1968, *9*, 272–279.

Averill, J. R. An analysis of psychophysiological symbolism and its influence on theories of emotion. *Journal for the Theory of Social Behavior*, 1974, *4*, 147–190.

Averill, J. R. A semantic atlas of emotional concepts. JSAS *Catalogue of Selected Documents in Psychology*, 1975, *5*, 330. (Ms. No. 421)

Averill, J. R. Emotion and anxiety: Socio-cultural, biological, and psychological determinants. In M. Zuckerman & C. D. Spielberger (Eds.), *Emotion and anxiety: New concepts, methods and applications*. New York: LEA-Wiley, 1976.

Averill, J. R. Anger. In H. Howe & R. Dienstbier (Eds.), *Nebraska Symposium on Motivation*: 1978. Lincoln: University of Nebraska Press, 1979. (a)

Averill, J. R. A selective review of cognitive and behavioral factors involved in the regulation of stress. In R. A. Depue (Ed.), *The psychobiology of the depressive disorders: Implications for the effects of stress*. New York: Academic, 1979. (b)

Averill, J. R. A constructivist view of emotion. In R. Plutchik & H. Kellerman (Eds.), *Theories of emotion*. New York: Academic, 1980.

Averill, J. R., DeWitt, G. W., & Zimmer, M. The self-attribution of emotion as a function of success and failure. *Journal of Personality*, 1978, *46*, 323–347.

Averill, J. R., O'Brien, L., & DeWitt, G. W. The influence of response effectiveness on the preference for warning and on psychophysiological stress reactions. *Journal of Personality*, 1977, *45*, 395–418.

Bandura, A. Social learning perspective on behavior change. In A. Burton (Ed.), *What makes behavior change possible?* New York: Brunner/Mazel, 1976.

Bates, E. *Language and context: The acquisition of pragmatics*. New York: Academic, 1976.

Berkowitz, L., & Turner, C. Perceived anger level, instigating agent, and aggression. In H. London & R. E. Nisbett (Eds.), *Thought and feeling: Cognitive alteration of feeling states*. Chicago: Aldine, 1974.

Blumenthal, A. L. *The process of cognition*. Englewood Cliffs, N. J.: Prentice-Hall, 1977.

Boswell, J. *The life of Johnson*. Vol. II. (L. F. Powell, Ed.). Oxford: Clarendon Press, 1934. (Originally published, 1791.)

Brown, J. S., & Farber, I. E. Emotions conceptualized as intervening variables–with suggestions toward a theory of frustration. *Psychological Bulletin*, 1951, *48*, 465–495.

Brown, W. P., & Ure, D. M. J. Five rated characteristics of 650 word association stimuli. *British Journal of Psychology*, 1969, *60*, 233–249.

Bush, L. E., II. Successive intervals scaling of adjectives denoting feelings. JSAS *Catalogue of Selected Documents in Psychology*, 1972, *2*, 140.

Campbell, A., Converse, P. E., & Rogers, W. L. *The quality of American life*. New York: Russell Sage Foundation, 1976.

Cannon, W. B. *Bodily changes in pain, hunger, fear, and rage* (2nd ed.). New York: Appleton, 1929.

Carlson, E. R. The affective tone of psychology. *Journal of General Psychology*, 1966, *75*, 65–78.

Darwin, C. *The expression of emotion in man and animals*. Chicago: University of Chicago Press, 1965. (Originally published, 1872).

Davitz, J. R. *The language of emotion*. New York: Academic, 1969.

Dewey, J. The theory of emotion. I: Emotional attitudes. *Psychological Review*, 1894, *1*, 553–569.

Dewey, J. The theory of emotion. II: The significance of emotions. *Psychological Review*, 1895, *2*, 13–32.

Duffy, Elizabeth. *Activation and behavior*. New York: Wiley, 1962.

Ekman, P., Friesen, W. V., & Ellsworth, P. *Emotion in the human face: Guidelines for research and a review of findings*. New York: Pergamon, 1972.

Epstein, S. The ecological study of emotions in humans. In P. Pliner, K. R. Blankstein, & I. M. Spigel (Eds.), *Advances in the study of communication and affect*. Vol. 5: *Perception of emotions in self and others*. New York: Plenum, 1979.

Flanagan, J. C. A research approach to improving our quality of life. *American Psychologist*, 1978, *33*, 138–147.

Harré, R., & Secord, P. S. *The explanation of social behavior*. London: Basil Blackwell, 1972.

Hebb, D. O. Emotion in man and animal: An analysis of the intuitive processes of recognition. *Psychological Review*, 1946, *53*, 88–106.

Henle, M. Did Titchener commit the stimulus error? The problem of meaning in structural psychology. *Journal of the History of the Behavioral Sciences*, 1971, *7*, 279–283.

Herder, J. G. [*On the origin of language*] (J. H. Moran & A. Gode, Eds. and Trans.). New York: Frederick Ungar, 1966. (Originally published, 1772.)

Irons, D. Professor James' theory of emotion. *Mind*, 1894, 3 (N.S.), 77–97.
Izard, C. E. *Patterns of emotions*. New York: Academic, 1972.
Izard, C. E. *Human Emotions*. New York: Plenum, 1977.
James, W. *Principles of psychology* (Vol. 2). New York: Henry Holt, 1890.
James, W. *Pragmatism*. New York: Longman, 1907.
Lacey, J. I. Somatic response patterning and stress: Some revisions of activation theory. In M. H. Appley & R. Trumbull (Eds.), *Psychological stress: Issues in research*. New York: Appleton-Century-Crofts, 1967.
Leeper, R. W. The motivational and perceptual properties of emotions as indicating their fundamental character and role. In M. B. Arnold (Ed.), *Feelings and emotions: The Loyola symposium*. New York: Academic, 1970.
Leventhal, H. A perceptual–motor processing model of emotion. Applications to the study of pain and humor. In P. Pliner, K. R. Blankstein, & I. M. Spigel (Eds.), *Advances in the study of communication and affect*. Vol. 5: *Perception of emotions in self and others*. New York: Plenum, 1979.
Meichenbaum, D. *Cognitive–behavior modification: An integrative approach*. New York: Plenum, 1977.
Nafe, J. An experimental study of the affective qualities. *American Journal of Psychology*, 1924, *35*, 507–544.
Nisbett, R. E., & Wilson, T. D. Telling more than we know: Verbal reports on mental processes. *Psychological Review*, 1977, *84*, 231–259.
Nowlis, V. Research with the Mood Adjective Check List. In S. S. Tomkins & C. E. Izard (Eds.), *Affect, cognition, and personality*. New York: Springer, 1965.
Osgood, C. E. On the whys and wherefores of E, P, and A. *Journal of Personality and Social Psychology*, 1969, *12*, 194–199.
Osgood, C. E., Suci, G. J., & Tannenbaum, P. H. *The measurement of meaning*. Urbana: University of Illinois Press, 1957.
Pavlov, I. P. *Conditioned reflexes*. Oxford: Oxford University Press, 1927.
Piaget, J. *Genetic epistemology*. New York: Norton, 1970.
Plutchik, R. *The emotions*. New York: Random House, 1962.
Russell, J. A. *Evidence of convergent validity on the dimensions of affect*. Unpublished manuscript, University of British Columbia, 1978.
Russell, J. A., & Mehrabian, A. Evidence for a three-factor theory of emotions. *Journal of Research in Personality*, 1977, *11*, 273–294.
Schachter, S. The interaction of cognitive and physiological determinants of emotional state. In L. Berkowitz (Ed.), *Advances in experimental social psychology*. Vol. 1. New York: Academic Press, 1964.
Schachter, S. *Emotion, obesity, and crime*. New York: Academic, 1971.
Schlosberg, H. Three dimensions of emotion. *Psychological Review*, 1954, *61*, 81–88.
Semin, G. R., & Manstead, A. S. R. *The beholder beheld: A preliminary investigation of social emotions*. Unpublished manuscript, University of Sussex, 1977.
Snider, J. G., & Osgood, C. E. (Eds.). *Semantic differential technique*. Chicago: Aldine, 1969.
Solomon, R. C. *The passions*. Garden City, N.Y.: Doubleday Anchor, 1976.
Taylor, C. *Hegel*. Cambridge: Cambridge University Press, 1975.
Thayer, R. E. Measurement of activation through self-report. *Psychological Reports*, 1967, *20*, 663–678.
Thorndike, E. L., & Lorge, I. *The teacher's wordbook of 30,000 words*. New York: Teachers College, Columbia University, 1944.
Titchener, E. B. The tridimensional theory of feeling. *American Journal of Psychology*, 1908, *19*, 213–231.

Titchener, E. B. *A textbook of psychology* (Rev. ed.). New York: Macmillan, 1910.
Wittgenstein, L. *Philosophical investigations*. Oxford: Basil Blackwell & Mott, 1953.
Wittgenstein, L. *The blue and brown books*. Oxford: Basil Blackwell & Mott, 1958.
Wundt, W. *Outlines of psychology*. Leipzig: Engelmann, 1897. (Originally published, 1896.)
Zajonc, R. B. Attitudinal effects of mere exposure. *Journal of Personality and Social Psychology Monograph*, 1968, 9 (2, Pt. 2).

CHAPTER 3

Measurement Implications of a Psychoevolutionary Theory of Emotions

Robert Plutchik

Department of Psychiatry
Albert Einstein College of Medicine
Yeshiva University
Bronx Municipal Hospital Center
Bronx, New York

Most people usually think of emotion as a subjective feeling of a certain kind, the kind for which labels like happy, sad, and frightened are appropriate. However, there is much evidence to suggest that this is too narrow a way to define emotion, that the facts available to us and the current uses of the term imply the need for a different and broader conceptualization.

In contrast, it may be proposed that an emotion is not a subjective experience *per se*, but is rather a construct or inference based on various classes of evidence. The evidence is of several different types, and includes verbal reports, expressive behaviors, goal-directed activities, and peer group reactions, among others.

Emotions as Inferences

The concept of emotions as inferences is widely accepted by psychologists and psychiatrists of quite diverse backgrounds. Psychoanalysts rely on dreams, free associations, slips of the tongue, postures, facial expressions, and voice quailty to make judgments about a person's emotions. Ethologists working within the Darwinian tradition rely on expressive behavior as well as goal-directed actions as a basis for judging emotions in animals. Skinner has pointed out that we identify states of anger and fear, not by noticing how fast someone's heart beats, and not even by what someone says, but rather by noticing how an individual's behavior affects the environment (Holland & Skinner, 1961). Similarly, Cannon, who has contributed so much to our understanding of visceral physiology has concluded that visceral changes tell us little about emotions; rather, such changes are homeostatic adjustments that help the body prepare for action (Cannon, 1929). Young (1961) has likewise pointed out that we judge the presence of emotions in another person on the basis of various kinds of evidence, such as (1) a knowledge of the situation; (2) a knowledge of how a person typically reacts to various situations; and (3) the physical signs of disturbance.

Charles Brenner, a leading contemporary psychoanalyst, points out that conscious, subjective reports of emotions (or affects as the psychoanalysts prefer to call them) are often unreliable simply because most affect states are characterized by mixtures of both pleasant and unpleasant feelings, as well as expectations or memories of both "good" and "bad" events. Such ambivalences are the rule rather than the exception. In addition, part of or all these affects may be repressed or modified, so that a conscious report is seldom what it seems (Brenner, 1974).

Lest it be thought that this issue is of concern only to psychoanalysts, the work of Hebb may be cited (1946). After several years of extensive observations of chimpanzee behavior at the Yerkes Laboratory in Florida, he came to the conclusion that emotion should not be defined as a conscious process, nor as a pattern of motor or glandular activity. In order to recognize or infer emotions in chimpanzees or in humans, Hebb reported that a great deal needs to be known about the individual, since the choice of a correct term depends on a knowledge of the stimulus, of the response, of the subject's past behavior in similar situations, and the behavioral characteristics of the species. Reports of a lack of consistent recognition of emotions occur only in situations dealing with momentary response patterns as in typical studies of the judgment of facial expressions. When long-term observations are made of other individuals, recognition of emotional states and prediction of behavior are much more accurate.

Hebb denies that subjective naming of emotional feelings is always more accurate than the naming of a state by outside observers. For example, an outside impartial observer is more likely to describe correctly the pattern of jealousy than the person "experiencing" it, since to him, it may appear as indignation or annoyance. Hebb writes: "When observers agree among themselves and the subject disagrees it is often accepted that the observers' report is more trustworthy (and a better guide to future behavior), even when the subject is not lying" (1946).

Experimental psychologists have recognized sources of bias in research for a long time. These include such things as dissembling, failure to understand instructions, refusal to believe the experimenter's avowed reasons for the experiment, and fear of exposure of personal inadequacies. All these factors act to raise questions about the veracity and validity of the verbal responses of subjects.

An interesting illustration of one of these factors is seen in the study by Schachter and Singer (1962). In this study, the investigators exposed groups of college students to conditions designed to arouse feelings of euphoria or anger. To assess the extent to which these emotions were produced, the subjects rated their feelings of "happiness" and "anger" on a scale. The results showed that the subjects reported themselves as more "happy" than "angry" in the euphoria condition, as was predicted. However, in the anger condition, subjects still reported themselves as more "happy" than "angry." This puzzle was resolved after the experiment was over. It was then learned that the subjects in the anger condition actually felt angry, but were afraid to say this publicly since the experimenter had promised them two extra points on their final exam for participating; they were afraid that telling the truth might jeopardize their grades. This again emphasizes the point that verbal responses describing emotional states cannot always be taken at face value, particularly when the situation allows various secondary gains (e.g., money, grades, goodwill, etc.).

The Language of Emotion

There is no doubt that the language of emotion is confusing. The confusions relate not only to the meanings of particular emotion words but also to the distinctions that have been made between *emotions* and other closely related states. What, for instance, is the difference between an emotion, an affect, a motivation, a feeling, a mood and a temperament? These terms have not only been used interchangeably by psychologists, but our everyday language usage does not make clear distinctions between them. Some writers consider a mood to be a long-persisting emotion, whereas others consider an emotion to be an intense mood. Some writers use the term *feeling* as a general way of describing any reportable internal state, whereas the word *temperament* is interpreted by some authors as indicating a disposition to show certain emotions with high frequency. Psychoanalysts use the word *affect* sometimes to refer to a subjective state, and sometimes to refer to a hypothetical inferred unconscious state. Some motivations, such as greed, are labeled by the same word that others would call an emotion.

The work of Davitz (1970) illustrates some of the confusions inherent in the introspective language of emotions. In his research he asked students to write brief reports about emotional experiences they had had. From these reports he selected the words and phrases used to describe emotions and ended up with a list of 556 descriptive terms.

To illustrate the complexity of these terms, consider some that were used to describe depression:

> I feel empty, sluggish, tired, sleepy.
> I feel sorry for myself; I feel vulnerable; I feel insignificant.
> I want to withdraw, disappear, draw back, be alone.
> I have no appetite; I can't smile or laugh. (Davitz, 1970)

It is obvious, in looking at these descriptions of depression, that they present a picture of a complex internal state having many elements. There are physical symptoms ("tired," "sleepy"), self-attitudes ("feel vulnerable"), impulses to action ("want to withdraw"), and physiological changes ("no appetite"). It is important to note that any one class of descriptions is only a partial image of the total state called an emotion.

Nonverbal Communication of Affect

The language of emotion is more than words. People also convey information about their feelings by nonverbal signs or cues, and these two sources of information are not always consistent. This inconsistency was illustrated in a study conducted by Mehrabian and Weiner (1967). In this investigation, actors said certain things about a hypothetical third person at the same time that they expressed a positive or negative attitude by tone of voice or by facial expression. The judges usually rated an actor's attitude as expressed by his tone of voice rather than by the meaning of his spoken words. For example, if the actor used a negative tone of voice with the words "dear," or "thanks," the judges rated the actor as having a negative feeling toward the third person. Similarly, if the actor said the words "don't" or "terrible" with a positive tone, the judges rated the actor as feeling positive.

These observations raise further doubts about the extent to which verbal reports of feeling states can be taken at face value. It is evident that every communication between two people involves a *context* as well as a *content*. The listener (or observer) has to consider nonverbal cues, such as tone of voice, facial expression, body posture, and mannerisms, in interpreting (or decoding) the message which has been sent. The conclusion reached by the listener about the emotions that may be present is a complex inference based on multiple cues, only some of which are verbal. After reviewing a number of studies of this sort, Speer (1972) concluded that there are no one-to-one relations between verbal labels, nonverbal cues, and subjective feelings.

The inherent ambiguity of the affect language is further documented in an extensive cross-cultural review of studies of depression by Marsella (1976). He cites reports indicating that in some languages there are no terms for depression as such, and that different investigators have reported widely varying prevalence rates for depression depending on their theoretical expectations as well as the specific measures they used. It appears that some cultures do not label inner mood states. The more westernized a culture, the more likely are psychological components to be included in a description of depression. The fact that a society does not have a word for it, however, does not mean that a particular emotion does not exist.

For these and other reasons, we must conclude that a verbal report of an inner emotional state is only a rough approximation to whatever that state is. We conclude that an emotion is not to be considered as synonymous with a presumed inner feeling state. Instead we conclude that the word *emotion* refers to a complex theoretical term whose characteristics can only be inferred on the basis of a congruence of various classes of evidence. One of these classes of evidence consists of verbal reports of supposed inner states, but such evidence has no greater logical priority than do the other classes of evidence. This approach is exactly analogous to that taken in other parts of psychology or the physical sciences. Such terms as memory, perceptions, traits, atoms, genes, and DNA molecules are hypothetical constructs whose properties are inferred on the basis of various kinds of evidence. If these basic conclusions are accepted, then some interesting implications follow.

Emotions in Animals

Since the concept of emotion applies to adult patients with repressions, to the mentally defective, to young children with limited verbal repertoires, and to infants with none, there is no reason why the concept cannot be applied to animals. Folklore is filled with animal images that are connected with certain personality traits or emotions. Lions are courageous, foxes are sly, tortoises are persistent, bears are moody, poodles are playful. In folklore and mythology, animals behave as humans, loving and hating, seducing and submitting.

Experimental and comparative psychologists also are willing to infer the existence of emotions in lower animals. For example, Hebb has written: "The dog is definitely capable of jealousy and occasionally, in some dogs, there are signs of sulking. In the chimpanzee, however, we have the full picture of human anger in its three main forms: anger, sulking and the temper tantrum" (1972).

Hebb also points out that not only are such basic emotions as anger, fear, and curiosity seen quite clearly in chimpanzees, but so too is altruistic behavior; that is, behavior which functions to help another person or animal even at the risk of danger or death.

Given the fact that an inference is made of an emotional state in an animal, is there any way of verifying the judgment? Hebb states that the validity of the label is seen in its practical ability to predict the animal's behavior. In other words, if an animal is called "shy," caretakers know what to expect of it in the future. If an animal is called "angry," or "hostile" the caretakers will know enough to be cautious in its presence.

Peer Group Behavior

Another important way to identify emotional reactions in an animal (as well as in a human) is by observing the behavior of other animals toward the identified one. Delgado gives several illustrations of this same idea. He points out that the behavior of one monkey in a colony will produce emotional reactions from other animals. If submissiveness or retaliation is provoked from the other monkeys, it indicates that threat has occurred. Which of these two reactions occurs depends on the relative positions of the animals within the dominance hierarchy; higher dominance animals will retaliate, whereas lower dominance animals will usually become submissive. We can thus identify the nature of the initial emotional stimulus by carefully observing the ensuing behavior of the other animals in the troop (Delgado, 1966).

Another example of this point is given by Delgado in relation to the effects of electrical stimulation of the brain in monkeys and cats. An electrode was placed in the rhinal fissure at the tip of the temporal lobe in a rhesus monkey. Electrical stimulation of this point produced opening of the mouth, rotation of the head, and scratching of the face, a pattern which, to a human observer, looked like aggression. However, this evoked behavior had no effect on the social behavior of the other members of the monkey colony. In contrast, electrical stimulation of the central gray area of the brain produced behavior that caused the other animals to withdraw, grimace, and show submissive behaviors (Delgado, 1964). We can thus reasonably infer that stimulation of the central gray area produced aggressive behavior whereas stimulation of the rhinal fissure did not, even though there were some superficial similarities in the two patterns of behavior.

Conclusion

The foregoing material has been presented to support the idea that emotion is a hypothetical construct based on inferences. In order to make these inferences, a variety of types of evidence is used. There is no reason to suppose that verbal reports have a more valid or special relation to the inferred emotions than do the other kinds of evidence. It thus appears scientifically valid to infer the existence of emotions in lower animals. However, the important issue is not so much whether or not animals have emotions, but rather, the function or significance of emotion in the lives of both humans and animals. The examination of this issue requires an evolutionary framework.

Emotions and Evolution

The ideas that have been presented imply the need for a general conception of emotions that has relevance to both humans and animals. Such a model has been presented in my book *The Emotions: Facts, Theories and a New Model* (1962), and in a number of subsequent papers (Plutchik, 1970; Plutchik, Kellerman, & Conte, 1978). My new book presents the model and its empirical supports in greater detail (Plutchik, 1980). The remainder of this chapter will deal with one aspect of the theory; that is, its implications for the measurement of emotional states and their derivatives.

The theory is based on the assumption that there are certain classes of adaptive responses, involving the whole organism, which are the prototype patterns of emotions in animals and humans. The theory assumes that the environment of all organisms creates certain common problems; for example, identifying prey and predator, food, or mate. Emotions are total body reactions, involving both physiological and behavioral changes, to these kinds of basic survival problems created by the environment. Emotions are attempts by the organism to achieve control over certain events that relate to survival. Emotions are the "ultra-conservative" evolutionary behavioral adaptations, the "innate reactions," that have been found to be successful (like amino acids, DNA, and genes) in increasing the chances of survival of organisms. Therefore, they have been maintained, in functionally equivalent form, through all phylogenetic levels.

Among the basic postulates of the theory is one which states that there is a small number of basic, primary, or prototypical emotions. All other emotions are mixed or derivative states. In addition, the primary emotions can be conceptualized in terms of pairs of polar opposites.

Our experience with emotions indicates that emotions can vary in at least three important characteristics: intensity, similarity, and polarity. We distinguish between fear and panic, or sadness and grief. We consider joy and optimism more similar than joy and disgust. We also recognize certain polarities: joy and sadness, love and hate. This set of characteristics of intensity, similarity, and bipolarity is the logical basis for the well-known three-dimensional color solid. The same characteristics justify conceiving of a three-dimensional emotion solid.

The previous discussion has also implied that emotions can be described in a number of different ways, that we may use several different kinds of "languages" to describe them. Three of these languages are shown in Table 1.

The *subjective* or introspective language refers to words used by humans to describe inner feeling states, and although most of us feel comfortable with this terminology, it is fairly narrow since it can be used only by human adults with certain kinds of linguistic experiences. The *behavioral* language refers to species-specific behaviors that are sometimes associated with the introspective states, which include such behaviors as running away, biting an enemy, crying for help, etc. The *functional* language is most general and describes the goals or functions of each type of behavior. Thus, the goal of running is protection; the goal of sadness is succorance; etc.

There is also an implied set of relations among the three languages which goes something like this: a survival-related stimulus occurs in the environment of an organism (e.g., appearance of a predator). A cognitive process evaluates the stimulus as a threat to survival, leading to a subjective feeling of fear (or its homologue in lower animals). The fear strongly increases the probability of certain classes of escape behaviors. These behaviors may or may not occur depending on the conditions of the environment (e.g., presence of a fence), and the condition of the animal (e.g., fatigue). If the behavior occurs and it enables the organism to escape, the goals of protection and individual survival are served. The concept of emotion refers to this total process.

However, it should be evident that partial reactions are possible. The predator may appear, and the prey may not adequately or correctly evaluate

Table 1. Three Languages Used To Describe Emotional States

Subjective language	Behavioral language	Functional language
Fear, terror	Running or flying away	Protection
Anger, rage	Biting, hitting	Destruction
Joy, ecstasy	Courting, mating	Reproduction
Sadness, grief	Distress cries	Reintegration
Acceptance, trust	Sharing, grooming	Incorporation
Disgust, loathing	Vomiting, pushing away	Rejection
Expectancy, watchfulness	Examining, planning	Exploration
Surprise, astonishment	Stopping, alerting	Orientation

the extent of the danger. Even if it does, it is possible for the internal, subjective state to occur at various levels of arousal, but for no behavioral action to follow. Finally, it is possible for the animal to attempt to escape but to be unsuccessful, so that the protective function is not served and the animal fails to survive.

One of the implications of the theory is that primary emotions can be mixed to produce compounds, or blends, of emotions. However, what is especially interesting about the naming of emotion mixtures is the fact that many of the terms are words normally used to describe personality traits. Thus, words such as "aggressive," "cruel," "friendly," "pessimistic," and "anxious" can be used just as well to describe personality traits or to describe emotions. In fact, further studies have shown that all personality traits, when defined in terms of interpersonal relations, can be conceptualized as resulting from the mixing of emotions.

In one study, judges were given a long list of personality and emotion words and asked to rate which words were used primarily as a description of emotional states, which were used primarily as a description of personality traits, and which were used to describe *both*. It was found that some words such as *terrified* were considered to apply to emotions only. Some words such as *anxious* were considered to apply to both emotions and traits. Most interesting of all was the fact that no term was believed to describe personality traits but not emotions. This result is consistent with the idea that personality traits are derived from more fundamental emotions.

Given the conclusion that no sharp distinctions could be made between mixed emotions and personality traits, the implication follows that personality traits should have the same type of similarity structure as emotions, and that concepts of similarity and bipolarity could be used to describe the relations among personality traits.

The idea of a circular organization of personality traits is actually an old one, and various writers have independently suggested a similar schema. For example, there is the Leary Interpersonal Circle (Freedman, Leary, Ossorio, & Coffey, 1951); the Stern Activities Index Circle (1958); the Schaefer Circumplex for Parent–Child Behavior Interactions (1959); the Becker and Krug Child Behavior Circumplex (1964); the Lorr and McNair Interpersonal Behavior Circle (1965); and the Schaefer–Plutchik Personality–Emotion Circumplex (1966), among others.

The most extensive empirical circumplex analysis of personality traits was developed by Conte (1975). She began by identifying a universe of personality trait terms based on the lists of Allport and Odbert (1936), Norman (1967), Anderson (1968), and others. A large number of words were then excluded on such grounds as ambiguity, slanginess, metaphor, etc., or because the term did not appear on a majority of the lists. These exclusions produced a final pool of 223 trait terms.

Using a modified paired comparison method, a group of judges rated the relative similarity of the trait terms to each other. Positive ratings indicated relative similarity of terms, while negative ratings indicated relative dissimilarity. The mean ratings were converted to angular placement on a circle.

To check the validity of the angular placements, a totally independent method, utilizing the semantic differential, was used. A subsample of 40 trait words were rated for connotative meaning on each of 30 semantic differential scales. The average ratings for a group of judges produced a semantic profile for each trait. These profiles were then correlated in a 40×40 matrix. The correlations produce measures of profile shape similarity of the different traits in accordance with the descriptions given by Nunnally (1967) and by Stone and Coles (1970).

The matrix of correlations was then factor analyzed and the first two factors were found to account for 91% of the variance, which clearly implied that a two-dimensional surface would be adequate to describe the relations among the traits. The empirical locations of each of the 40 traits were plotted on the basis of their factor loadings and were then transformed into angular placements. The placements using the second method correlated +.99 with the placements using the first method, thus giving strong support to a circumplex organization of personality traits. These placements are shown in Figure 1. This circumplex implies that all personality traits, defined by the exclusion rules listed above, can be located on a circle in terms of their relative similarity. It implies that every trait has a similar neighboring trait, as well as an opposite trait. It also implies that factors of personality are probably artifacts of poor sampling or selection of terms.

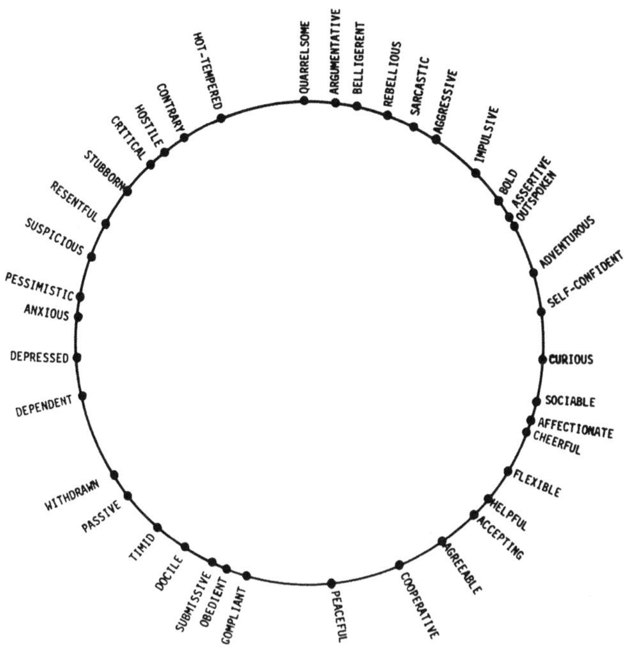

Fig. 1. A circumplex organization of a sample of personality traits, based on direct similiarity scaling and confirmed by a factor analysis of semantic differential ratings (from Conte, 1975).

Further, it suggests that personality tests of known structure can be developed within this theoretical framework.

Tests of Emotion–Personality

To illustrate how the concept of a circular structure of emotions and personality traits has practical implications for measurement, I should like to describe the *Emotions Profile Index* developed by Kellerman and myself and recently published by Western Psychological Services (Kellerman, 1964; Kellerman & Plutchik, 1968; Plutchik & Kellerman, 1974).

With the exception of several personality tests based upon Murray's Need System, most personality tests in current use have little or no theoretical rationale. In contrast, the Emotions Profile Index (EPI) was developed directly on the basis of Plutchik's psychoevolutionary theory of emotion.

The EPI provides measures of the eight basic emotions postulated by Plutchik (1955, 1958, 1960, 1965, 1970). It is based on the idea that all interpersonal personality traits can be conceptualized as resulting from the mixture of two or more primary emotions; which means that a person who describes himself as "shy" or "gloomy" is implicitly telling us something about the primary emotions that go to make up these traits. Shyness, for example, implies frequent feelings of fear; gloominess, however, implies frequent feelings of sadness.

The EPI was developed initially by having 10 clinical psychologists rate the primary emotion components of a large number of traits. Twelve trait terms were finally selected on the grounds of high interjudge consistency on the components and a wide sampling of the trait universe described by Schaefer's (1959; 1961) factor-analytic studies. These twelve terms were then paired in all possible combinations, yielding 66 pairs. Four of the pairs were found to have identical scoring categories and were dropped, leaving 62 pairs of trait terms for the final form of the test (Kellerman, 1964).

The EPI is a forced-choice test. The respondents are simply asked to indicate which of two paired words is more self-descriptive; for example, are they more "quarrelsome" or "shy"? The choices are scored in terms of the primary emotions implied by the trait word. Each time the respondents make a choice between two trait words they add to their scores on one or more of the eight basic emotion dimensions. Thus, rather than measure only anxiety, the test also simultaneously measures anger, sadness, joy, etc. Because the implications of the choices are not always clear to the respondents, they cannot easily fake their answers. Finally, due to the forced-choice format of the EPI, the test tends to reduce response bias (i.e., the tendency to choose socially desirable traits) because many of the choices must be made between two equally undersirable or two equally desirable traits. In addition, a *bias* score is built into the test as a measure of the responsents' tendency to choose socially desirable (or undersirable) traits in those cases where the items are not matched.

The twelve terms used in the EPI are the following: *adventurous*, *affectionate*, *brooding*, *cautious*, *gloomy*, *impulsive*, *obedient*, *quarrelsome*, *resentful*, *self-conscious*, *shy*, and *sociable*. A brief definition is provided in the test for each term. The total score for each of the eight primary emotion dimensions is converted into a percentile score based on data obtained from 1000 normal men and women. The percentile scores are then plotted on a circular diagram where the center of the circle represents zero percentile and the outer circumference, 100 percentile. The larger the dark wedge-shaped area, the stronger the emotional disposition that is revealed.

When the EPI was first developed, we used the functional names for the emotions to describe each category, such an *incorporation*, *protection*, and *exploration*. Later, when the test was prepared for publication (Plutchik & Kellerman, 1974), we decided to use a trait language to describe the primary dimensions on the grounds that it would be more familiar to people who wished to use the EPI as a clinical or diagnostic tool.

Let me illustrate the usefulness of the EPI by referring to several studies that we did dealing with suicide. On a research ward for the study of manic-depressive patients, one patient began to act increasingly belligerent and depressed. After several weeks on the ward, this 49-year-old woman tried to commit suicide by slashing her wrists. Fortunately, the attempt was unsuccessful, but a large amount of data had been collected on this woman including weekly self-report EPIs. Figure 2 shows the EPI profile obtained just one day prior to her suicide attempt. It reveals a high depression and aggression score, but also a low fear or anxiety score. After the suicide attempt, the EPI profile rapidly changed to a more "normal" pattern and the patient was discharged in two weeks.

What was especially interesting about this multidimensional analysis of affective changes associated with a suicide attempt was the fact that, contrary to popular impressions, anxiety was *low* rather than high at the time of the attempt. We concluded that anxiety acts as an inhibitor of action, and that when the anxiety diminshes while the anger and depression remain high, the risk of suicide is greatest (Platman, Plutchik, & Weinstein, 1971). This observation has since been confirmed by two other studies. The

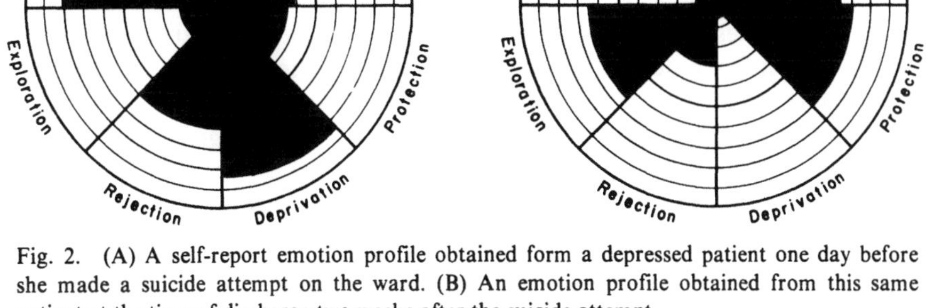

Fig. 2. (A) A self-report emotion profile obtained form a depressed patient one day before she made a suicide attempt on the ward. (B) An emotion profile obtained from this same patient at the time of discharge two weeks after the suicide attempt.

EPI has also been used in studies of patient groups, sex differences, stereotyping, diagnostic labeling, and violence. The EPI reveals not only the simultaneous operation of many basic affect states, but also major areas of affective conflict, making it particularly useful as a clinical tool.

However, obviously there are certain types of populations for whom self-reports of emotional states are not possible: severely ill mental patients; mentally retarded patients; infants; and animals. For such populations rating scales have been used, but here too, such scales frequently suffer from a lack of theoretical relevance.

Therefore, the EPI has been adapted for use with animals (Buirski, Kellerman, Plutchik, Weininger & Buirski, 1973), although this version could be used with humans of limited verbal capacities. Ten terms descriptive of emotional behavior were selected and defined. The terms were: *belligerent*, *fearful*, *inquisitive*, *irritable*, *defiant*, *depressed*, *dominant*, *playful*, *sociable*, and *submissive*. The emotion components of each of these states was determined by consensus of a group of judges. The terms were then paired in all possible combinations, and the resulting form was used in a study of baboons at the Nairobi National Park in Kenya, Africa.

Three observers watched a small troop of seven baboons for 35 hours over a three-week period. Every incident of grooming was noted in terms of who groomed who, and the length of time of the act. At the end of the 35 hours of observation the baboons in the troop were independently ranked on dominance, and the baboon version of the EPI was independently completed for each animal by each observer. The rater simply picked one word from each pair which best described the behavior of the baboon under observation. Interjudge reliability for each of the eight EPI scales was fairly high with most intraclass correlations being over +.75.

Among the many interesting findings of this investigation is the fact that the animals rated lowest on the fearfulness dimension of the EPI, and highest on the aggressiveness dimension were groomed the most by the other baboons.

The rating schema enabled us to plot the emotion profiles for each member of the troop. An illustration is shown in Figure 3. It compares the emotion profiles of "Big Harry" the dominant male in the troop with that of "Norman," the next oldest male (who was ranked fifth on dominance). The figure illustrates a general tendency noticed in that troop; the more dominant animals showed less sociability and more aggression than the subordinate animals.

This modified technique was adapted for two other species (by Kellerman [1966] for use with dolphins, and by Buirski, Plutchik, & Kellerman [1978] for use with chimpanzees). The latter study will be described in more detail.

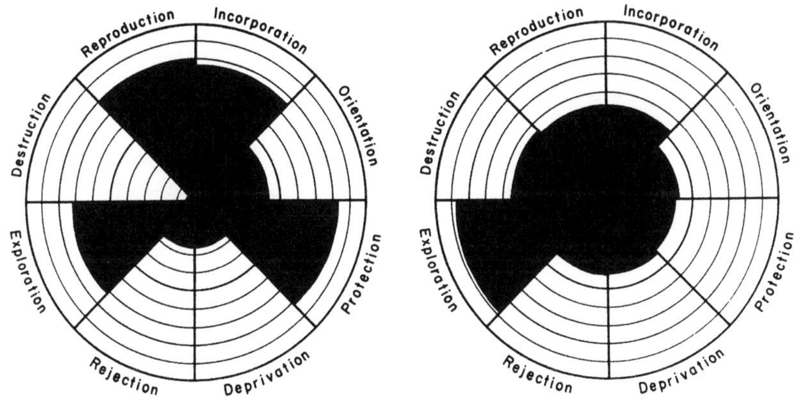

"NORMAN" "BIG HARRY"

Fig. 3. Emotion profiles of two members of a baboon group resulting from the average ratings of three independent observers. The profile for "Norman" is on the left; the right profile belongs to "Big Harry."

Observations were made at the Gombe Stream Research Centre in Tanzania, East Africa on 23 free-living chimpanzees, 13 males and 10 females. This center had been established by Jane Goodall. Ratings were made by seven graduate students living at the camp, who were quite familiar with the day-to-day behavior of most of the chimps. Raters were asked to rate, in terms of the EPI scales, those chimpanzees with whose behavior they were most familiar. The students picked one word from each of the 45 pairs that best described the behavior of the chimp under observation. Most of the interjudge reliabilities were over +.70.

Figure 4 shows the average EPI profiles for the male and for the female chimps. Significant sex differences were found for five of the eight emotions. (These diagrams use the language of personality traits to describe the animals, but a functional language, as shown in Figure 2, is equally appropriate.) For example, the female chimps were rated as more timid, more depressed and more trustful than the males, while the males were judged as more gregarious and more distrustful. If we were interpreting the profiles in human terms we would add that the females have more conflict in the area of social contacts (i.e., the gain or loss of social relations) while the males have more conflict in the area of passivity and aggression.

The dominance rank of each male was independently estimated from brief biographies of the animals. The rank position was then correlated with each of the eight EPI affect dimensions. The set of correlations suggested a profile: dominant animals tend to be aggressive and distrustful, while nondominant animals tend to be timid, dyscontrolled (impulsive), and trustful.

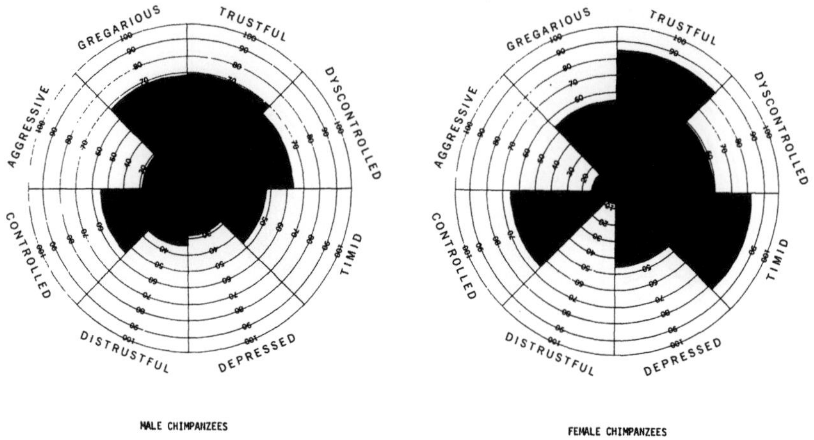

Fig. 4. Average emotion profiles for a group of 13 male and a group of 10 female chimpanzees observed at the Gombe Stream Research Centre in Tanzania, East Africa.

Other Theory-Based Measures

There are at least five different methods by which emotions have been measured. One method involves the use of self-reports of subjective feelings; a second involves descriptions of one's own behavior. These procedures are useful mainly with human adults. A third method for judging emotions is through ratings made of the behavior of some other individual. Such ratings can be used with adults, children, mentally retarded persons, and with lower animals. A fourth way to evaluate emotions is through a rating of the product of someone's behavior; for example, handwriting or figure drawings. Finally, information about emotions may be obtained through the use of physiological recordings of bodily changes. In this concluding section, I should like to describe two more theory-based measures to illustrate some of these ideas.

Parent–Child Interactions

Previous research dealing with mother–child interactions has been concerned primarily with a mother's general attitudes about child-rearing. Such studies have tended to demonstrate low correlations between general maternal attitudes and levels of adjustment in children. Therefore, it seemed worthwhile to approach the problem in a different way. Instead of focusing on attitudes, it seemed more useful to develop a mother–child interaction scale that would reflect actual practices rather than general attitudes. In addition, since basic emotions can be expressed through particular interpersonal styles, it seemed evident that styles of parent–child interaction could be described in terms of the eight basic dimensions of emotion.

With this framework in mind, a group of psychiatrists and psychologists working with me developed a series of items designed to described parental behavior that reflects each of the eight basic emotion dimensions. The labels for the dimensions in this context are given in Table 2, and each is illustrated with two items. For example, a Rejection item would be: "Do you punish your child by not talking to him (her)?" An Aggression item is: "Do you hit your child if he (she) doesn't obey you?" Preliminary work has demonstrated that the scales have high internal reliability, and can easily be completed as a self-report scale by mothers of very limited educational backgrounds. The ability of the scales to discriminate different levels of maternal as well as child psychopathology is now under investigation.

Ego Defenses

The most recently developed scale based upon my theory of emotion is concerned with the measurement of ego defenses. The concept of ego

Table 2. Examples of Items Representing Eight Basic Patterns of Parent–Child Interactions

Acceptance	
Example:	"If your child gets into an argument with another child, do you let them handle it themselves?"
Rejection	
Example:	"Do you punish your child by not talking to him (her)
Sociability (contact)	
Example:	"Do you spend as much time as you can playing with your child?"
Depression (isolation)	
Example:	"After punishing your child, do you make up for it by giving him (her) something?"
Anxiety	
Example:	"Do you give your child his (her) own way when he (she) sulks or pouts?"
Aggression	
Example:	"Do you hit your child if he (she) doesn't obey you?"
Control	
Example:	"Do you insist on your child's having good manners?"
Dyscontrol	
Example:	"Are you inconsistent in the way you act with your child?"

defenses is among the most important contributions of psychoanalysis to personality theory and clinical practice. It is an idea that has received wide acceptance among psychologists and is described in most elementary textbooks.

From a psychoanalytic point of view, ego mechanisms of defense are hypothetical mental processes that attempt to resolve conflicts between emotions and external reality when an individual is threatened by anxiety. Psychoanalysts have written about defenses in relation to both children and infants, and ethologists have demonstrated the operation of certain defense mechanisms such as displacement and regression, in lower animals (Goodall, 1967; Lorenz, 1966). These observations suggest that the concept of defenses can be placed within a broad evolutionary perspective.

When we examine the literature, it appears that there is little agreement among clinicians on just how many defenses there are, or even on how they should be labeled. Various similarities among defenses have been noted (for example, *denial* and *repression*), and it has been said that there are no distinct boundaries separating one defense from another (English & Finch, 1964). Some defenses are bipolar; for example, *introjection* and *projection.*

These characteristics of defenses; namely, similarity and bipolarity suggest again the relevance of a circular model for describing their relations. Such a model has been proposed by Plutchik *et al.* (1978). The model is based on certain relations that exist among emotions, defenses, and diagnostic labels. For example, the relation of *displacement* to anger or aggression is seen in the literature on scapegoating. *Projection* and paranoid personality are also related. Persons who are paranoid tend to be highly critical and rejecting. The use of projection becomes an attempt to see the world as a threatening environment in order to justify one's own rejecting feelings. Still another example of a relation between defense and diagnosis is the connection between denial and the hysterical personality style. These connections are shown in Table 3 in a systematic way.

This table shows the proposed relations among six different languages. For example, the feeling of *fear* is probably associated with the behavior of *escape* which *protects* the individual. When this sequence is frequently observed, we may describe the individual as *timid* and likely to use the ego defense of *repression.* When this pattern is more extreme, we would diagnose the individual as a *passive* type. To take another example, the feeling of *expectation* leads a person to learn more about his environment, or in other words, to try and *map* it. The function of mapping is *exploration* which has high adaptive value for survival. A person who has a strong tendency to explore his environment might be described by the trait of

Table 3. *Emotions and Their Derivatives*

Subjective language	Behavioral language	Functional language	Trait language	Diagnostic language	Ego-defense language
Fear	Escape	Protection	Timid	Passive type	Repression
Anger	Attack	Destruction	Aggressive	Aggressive type	Displacement
Joy	Mate	Reproduction	Sociable	Manic state	Reaction-formation
Sadness	Cry	Reintegration	Gloomy	Depression	Compensation
Acceptance	Groom	Incorporation	Agreeable	Hysteric	Denial
Disgust	Vomit	Rejection	Contemptuous	Paranoid state	Projection
Expectation	Map	Exploration	Curious	Obsessive-compulsive	Intellectualization
Surprise	Alert	Orientation	Impulsive	Psychopathic	Regression

curiosity. Under conditions of stress, such an individual might try to cope by *intellectualizing*; if his problems were difficult to solve he might develop *obsessive–compulsive* traits, which in extreme form constitutes a diagnostic label.

The model implied by these observations is based on the assumption that ego defenses act to protect the individual from the painful or frightening feelings associated with an emotion that has been generated. The purpose of each defense is to manage, or deal with, a particular emotion when the direct expression of that emotion is, in some sense, dangerous. Thus, when the direct expression of *anger* is dangerous, it may be *displaced* to an object or person perceived as less dangerous. When feelings of *sadness* result from the experience of loss, this is sometimes managed by sublimating in order to obtain a substitute gain. This in turn makes one's own critical feelings more acceptable. Finally, when even the expression of fear is dangerous, the defense of *repression* totally inhibits it.

This conceptualization of ego defenses has led to the development of scales for the measurement of defenses. Kellerman, Conte, and I have developed a series of self-report items which we believe reflect the operation of eight basic ego defenses. We established content validity through the judgments of experienced clinicians and reduced an initial pool of 224 items to 92 by means of a series of item analyses and factor analyses. The internal reliabilities of the eight ego defense scales are quite high. The test, which we call the *Life Style Index*, has been found to discriminate between a normal group and a group of schizophrenics on seven of the eight scales. For all scales except one, the schizophrenics had higher scores on the use of ego defenses than did a normal sample of college students. Further evidence of construct validity was found by correlating self-esteem and Taylor Manifest Anxiety scores with the ego defense scores. Results showed that the greater the self-esteem of a person, the less are his scores on most of the ego defenses. Conversely, the higher the anxiety scores, the greater the tendency to use regression, projection, displacement, etc. The *Life Style Index* thus appears to be a useful theoretically-based clinical and research tool for an important domain. Table 4 lists sample items for each of the eight ego defenses.

One other derivative set of concepts is worth noting. In Table 3 the last column refers to coping styles, the conscious procedures that individuals use to deal with problems. For example, some people are optimists and they tend to minimize the magnitude of life problems. *Minimization* may thus be considered to be the conscious derivative of the unconscious process of *denial*. Similarly, some people handle conflicts by attributing blame to other people. In the unconscious process, this is called *projection*, but when this is done in a more deliberate, conscious way, it might simply be called *fault-*

Table 4. Examples of Items Representing Eight Basic Ego Defenses

Denial
Example: "I am not prejudiced against anyone."

Repression
Example: "I have trouble remembering people's names."

Regression
Example: "I get irritable when I don't get attention."

Compensation
Example: "In my daydreams, I am always the center of attention."

Projection
Example: "If I'm not careful, people will take advantage of me."

Displacement
Example: "When I drive a car, I sometimes get an urge to hit another car."

Intellectualization
Example: "I always take work with me when I go on vacation."

Reaction Formation
Example: "I feel outraged at dirty movies."

finding. Still another example is the use of jokes or humor to deal with difficult situations. This might be called *reversal* and can be conceptualized as the conscious coping style that corresponds to the unconscious process of *reaction formation.* A new set of self-report scales have been developed on the basis of this conceptualization, and validating studies are now in progress.

Summing Up

In summing up I should like to recapitulate my basic themes. First, an emotion is not a subjective experience *per se*, but is rather a hypothetical state whose existence is inferred on the basis of a number of lines of evidence. No single index of emotions is free of some bias, and therefore, different types of measurement approaches should be used. Secondly, this view of emotion is shown to apply to lower animals as well as humans, so that emotions are seen in a broad evolutionary context. Thirdly, the concept of basic or primary emotions leads to a structural model which has many implications. For example, it implies the need to measure different basic emotions simultaneiously because of their different properties and their complex interactions. It leads to the view that personality traits are, in fact, mixtures of emotions. Not only are personality traits derivatives of emotions, but so too, are diagnostic labels and ego defenses. This concept of primary emotions and their derivatives provides guidelines and a framework for developing a series of tests and scales for the measurement of these basic dimensions. Theory determines what dimensions to measure, and theory helps establish a connection between observable indices and the hypothetical states called emotions. The various measurement procedures described here provide a beginning step toward the integration of a number of diverse content areas. They also help us document the essential continuity of emotional processes in all living creatures.

References

Allport, G. W. & Odbert, H. S. Trait names: A psychological study. *Psychological Monographs*, 1936, *47* (Whole No. 211).

Anderson, N. H. Likeableness ratings of 555 personality trait words. *Journal of Personality and Social Psychology*, 1968, *9*, 272–279.

Becker, W. C. & Krug, R. S. A circumplex model for social behavior in children. *Child Development*, 1964, *35*, 371–396.

Brenner, C. On the nature and development of affects. A unified theory. *The Psychoanalytic Quarterly*. 1974, *43*, 532–556.

Buirski, P., Plutchik, R., & Kellerman, H. Sex differences, dominance and personality in the chimpanzee. *Animal Behavior*, 1978, *26*, 123–129.

Buirski, P., Kellerman, H., Plutchik, R., Weininger, R., & Buirski, N. A field study of emotions, dominance, and social behavior in a group of baboons (Papio anubis). *Primates*, 1973, *14*, 67–78.

Cannon, W. B. *Bodily changes in pain, hunger, fear and rage*. New York: Appleton, 1929.

Conte, H. R. A circumplex model for personality traits. (Doctoral dissertation, New York University, 1975.) *Dissertation Abstracts International*, 1975. (University Microfilms No. 2601731)

Davitz, J. R. A dictionary and grammar of emotion. In M. Arnold (Ed.), *Feelings and emotions. The Loyola Symposium*. New York: Academic, 1970.

Delgado, J. M. R. Free behavior and brain stimulation. In C. C. Pfeiffer and J. R. Smythies (Eds.), *International Review of Neurobiology*, Vol. VI. New York: Academic, 1964.

Delgado, J. M. R. *Emotions*. Dubuque, Iowa: Wm. C. Brown, 1966.

English, O. S., & Finch, S. M. *Introduction to psychiatry*. New York: Norton, 1964.

Freedman, M. B., Leary, T. F., Ossorio, A. G., & Coffey, H. S. The interpersonal dimension of personality. *Journal of Personality*, 1951, *20*, 143–161.

Goodall, J. Mother–offspring relationships in the free ranging chimpanzees. In D. Morris (Ed.), *Primate ethology*. Chicago: Aldine, 1967.

Hebb, D. O. Emotion in man and animal. An analysis of the intuitive process of recognition. *Psychological Review*, 1946, *53*, 88–106.

Hebb, D. O. *Textbook of psychology*. Philadelphia. Saunders, 1972.

Holland, J. G., & Skinner, B. F. *The analysis of behavior*. New York: McGraw-Hill, 1961.

Kellerman, H. *The development of a forced-choice personality index and its relation to degree of maladjustment*. Unpublished Ph.D. Dissertation, Yeshiva University, 1964.

Kellerman, H. The emotional behavior of dolphins (Tursiops Truncatus): Implications for psychoanalysis. *International Mental Health Research Newsletter*, 1966, *8*, 1–7.

Kellerman, H., & Plutchik, R. Emotion-trait interrelations and the measurement of personality. *Psychological Reports*, 1968, *23*, 1107–1114.

Lorenz, K. *On aggression*. New York. Harcourt-Brace, 1966.

Lorr, M., & McNair, D. M. Expansion of the interpersonal behavior circle. *Journal of Personality and Social Psychology*, 1965, *2*, 823–830.

Marsella, A. J. Cross-cultural studies of depression: A review of the literature. Paper presented at the *Symposium on Cross-Cultural Aspects of Depression*. International Association of Cross-Cultural Psychology, Tilburg, Netherlands, 1976.

Mehrabian, A. & Weiner, M. Decoding of inconsistent communications. *Journal of Personality and Social Psychology*, 1967, *1*, 109–114.

Norman, W. T. 2800 personality trait descriptors: Normative operating characteristics for a university population. Ann Arbor, Michigan: Office of Research Administration, 1967.

Nunnally, J. *Psychometric theory*, New York: McGraw-Hill, 1967.

Platman, S. R., Plutchik, R., and Weinstein, B. Psychiatric, physiological, behavioral and self-report measures in relation to a suicide attempt. *Journal of Psychiatric Research*, 1971, *8*, 127–137.

Plutchik, R. Some problems for a theory of emotion. *Psychosomatic Medicine*, 1955, *17*, 306–310.

Plutchik, R. Outlines of a new theory of emotion. *Transactions of the New York Academy of Sciences*, 1958, *20*, 394–403.

Plutchik, R. The multifactor analytic theory of emotion. *Journal of Psychology*, 1960, *50*, 153–171.

Plutchik, R. *The emotions: Facts, theories and a new model*. New York. Random House, 1962.

Plutchik, R. What is an emotion? *Journal of Psychology*, 1965, *61*, 295–303.

Plutchik, R. Emotions, evolution and adaptive processes. In M. Arnold (Ed.), *Feelings and emotions: The Loyola Symposium*, New York: Academic, 1970.

Plutchik, R., & Kellerman, H. *Manual for the Emotions Profile Index*. Los Angeles: Western Psychological Services, 1974.

Plutchik, R., Kellerman, H., and Conte, H. R. A structural theory of ego defenses. In C. E. Izard (Ed.), Emotions, personality, and psychopathology. New York: Plenum, 1978.

Plutchik, R. *Emotions in humans and animals: A psychoevolutionary synthesis*. New York: Harper and Row, 1980.

Schachter, S., & Singer, J. E. Cognitive, social and physiological determinants of emotional state. *Psychological Bulletin*, 1962, *69*, 379–399.

Schaefer, E. S. A circumplex model for maternal behavior. *Journal of Abnormal and Social Psychology*, 1959, *59*, 226–235.

Schaefer, E. S. Converging conceptual models for maternal behavior and for child behavior. In *Parental attitudes and child behavior*. John Glidewell (Ed.), Springfield, Ill: C. C. Thomas, 1961.

Schaefer, E. S. & Plutchik, R. Interrelationships of emotions, traits, and diagnostic constructs. *Psychological Reports*, 1966, *18*, 399–410.

Speer, D. C. Nonverbal communication of affective information. *Comparative Group Studies*, 1972, *3*, 409–423.

Stern, G. G. *Activities index*. Syracuse: Syracuse University Psychological Research Center, 1958.

Stone, L. A., & Coles, G. J. Correlational similarity: The basis for a new revised method of similarity analysis. *Studia Psychologica*, 1970, *12*, 258–265.

Young, P. T. *Motivation and emotion*. New York: Wiley, 1961.

CHAPTER 4

To Risk or Not to Risk

Predicting Behavior from Negative and Positive Emotional States

Marvin Zuckerman

Department of Psychology
University of Delaware
Newark, Delaware

Certainly there must be some peculiar Calvinistic streak in modern psychology that accounts for our preoccupation with negative emotions, particularly the unholy trinity of *fear*, *anger*, and *depression*. This most persistent FAD (i.e. fear, anger, and depression) may represent the influence of clinical psychology and psychiatry. With the exception of the hypomanic, clinical subjects are not noted for their joyfulness or high spirits. But, is FAD, or its absence, all there is to emotions? The heavily-tranquilized patient may not be anxious, but he is not usually euphoric either. How many trait and state tests of FAD do we have compared to tests of positive affects such as surgency, elation, affection, or interest? How many studies are entitled "The Effect of Anxiety upon . . ."? I do not recall ever seeing a study entitled "The Effects of Interest . . ." or "The Effects of Elation . . ." on anything.

Many theories seem to regard positive emotions as the mere absence of negative emotions. Harry Stack Sullivan (1953) provides a very good example:

> Absolute euphoria can be defined as a state of utter well-being. The nearest ap-

> proach to anything like it . . . might occur when a very young infant is in a state of deep sleep. . . . Now it is a peculiarity of life that the level of euphoria and the level of tension are in reciprocal relation; that is, the level of euphoria varies inversely with the level of tension. (pp. 34–35)

In a similar fashion, Freud defined pleasure as the absence of or reduction of sensation, thereby disallowing the possibility of intrinsically pleasurable types of sensation. In *Beyond the Pleasure Principle* (Freud, 1920/1961) pain is defined as an increase, and pleasure as a decrease, of stimulation. Ten years later, in *Civilization and its Discontents* (Freud, 1930/1961), he states:

> What we call happiness in the strictest sense comes from the (preferably sudden) satisfaction of needs which have been damed up to a high degree, and it is from its nature only possible as an episodic phenomena. . . . In the last analysis all suffering is nothing else than sensation. . . . (p. 23)

Freud's limited vision of pleasure is perhaps attributable to the fact that he suffered daily intense pain from his mouth cancer in these later years, and heroically refused the pleasures of morphine in order to continue thinking and writing with a clear mind.

According to the logic of this tension-reduction concept of hedonism, the building of sexual tensions must be aversive and the only joy in sex must come at the moment of orgasm. Foreplay is foul play, or frustrating play at best, according to Freud.

In order to account for the fact that humans often voluntarily engage in behavior which seems to increase rather than decrease tension, analysts have invoked dubious constructs like the *need for mastery*, *counter-phobic*, or *repetition-compulsion*.

The Multiple Affect Adjective Check List (MAACL)

I confess that I have also suffered from this narrow clinical view of emotions. When I constructed the Multiple Affect Adjective Check List (Zuckerman & Lubin, 1965), the "multiple" included only three affects: anxiety, depression, and hostility, the old FAD trinity. There were plenty of positive affect words in the test, so you may ask "what happened to the positive affects?" The answer is in the way the test was constructed. We used the empirical method for item selection. Items comprising the anxiety scale, for instance, consisted of words checked as self-descriptive by patients rated as anxious with greater or lesser frequency than normals. A second criterion was that the frequency of checking words had to change in normals going from a normal hypnotized state to a suggested state of anxiety. The clinical type of criterion was used to develop the depression scale, and hypnotically induced anger was used to select words for the hostility scale. Since the scales were developed sequentially rather than simultaneously, the only attempt to keep them pure was the elimination of items from the previous scales in the latter scales.

We were not surprised when the positive affect words ended up as "minus" words on the anxiety, depression, and hostility scales, since we were thinking in terms of bipolar emotion factors. *Cheerfulness* and *content* are the opposite of *fearfulness* and *worrying*. *Enthusiasm* and *gladness* are the opposite of *gloominess* and *sadness*. *Agreeableness* and *cooperativeness* are the opposite of *angry* and *cruel*. But, are they really?

Damn the factor analyses and full speed ahead with the empirical studies! The success of these studies in such diverse areas as examination stress, ego-threat, stress reduction, drugs, etc. (Zuckerman & Schwartz, 1977) made us complacent. The scales showed, and continue to show, extreme sensitivity to all kinds of natural and experimental treatments. The first doubts arose from the extremely high correlations between the three negative affect scales. Things called by different names such as anxiety, depression, and hostility should not correlate as highly as these scales did with one another. Many times, I cursed myself for not leaving well enough alone, and sticking with the solitary anxiety scale in the earlier Affect Adjective Check List (AACL) (Zuckerman, 1960). Further failure of discriminant validity was found in the study by Zuckerman, Persky, Eckman, and Hopkins (1967) where we found that while anxiety and depression scores correlated with observers ratings for these affects, anxiety correlated as highly with the ratings for depression as those for anxiety. To make matters worse, hostility scores correlated more with the ratings for anxiety than those for hostility.

In our initial studies, using psychiatric patients the negative affect groups of items did correlate with positive affect items within the anxiety and depression scales (but not in the hostility scale) (Zuckerman & Lubin, 1965). Later studies showed less correlation between positive and negative affect items. Like Banquo's ghost, the positive affects were returning to spoil our triumph. They refused to be defined as the mere opposite of negative affects. While the MAACL had excellent convergent and experimental validity, as far as discriminant validity went, the MAACL was a mackeral. The fact that patients checked more of the negative affect words and fewer of the positive affect words was due to the fact that they differed from normal on two factors, negative *and* positive affect, not just one bipolar factor.

Dimensions of Affect

Basic dimensions of affect have been postulated on rational and empirical (particularly studies of facial expressions) bases in several theories. Two outstanding theories are those of Plutchik (1962) and Izard (1971, 1977). In addition to the negative affects, such as anger, fear, sorrow (guilt-remorse), and disgust, both theorists define positive affects of joy and curiosity, or interest-excitement. Plutchik also describes "acceptance" as a primary emotion related to the prototype activity of ingestion of food and water. In his system, "expectation or curiosity" is related to the activity of exploration in animals.

Nowlis (1965) described the primary dimensions of affect appearing in factor analyses of subjects' responses on self-rating affect tests. Nowlis also expected to find bipolar factors, but instead found that "bipolarity was almost nonexistent in the obtained axes."

Apart from the usual negative affect factors of anger, anxiety, and sadness, Nowlis found some interesting positive affect factors:

Surgency describes a factor based on the following adjectives: "carefree," "playful," "witty," "lively," and "talkative."

Elation is composed of: "elated," "overjoyed," "pleased," and "refreshed."

Concentration may be described as: "attentive," "earnest," "serious," "contemplative," "concentrating," and "engaged in thought."

Social affection is defined by: "affectionate," "forgiving," "kindly," and "warmhearted."

Vigor is an activation dimension described by three adjectives: "active," "energetic," and "vigorous."

Nowlis examined other factor-analytic studies of self-reported mood and found some evidence for the replicability of most of these factors, although some did not appear simply because no provision was made for them by including the relevant words beforehand. You cannot get anything out of a factor analysis that is not included in the variables going into the correlation matrix. Another problem is that the tests are often given under relatively neutral conditions when arousal of particular affects is unlikely.

This point will be touched on again in a discussion of the attentive-coping factor in the Zuckerman Inventory of Personal Reactions.

After discovering that the MAACL scores did not describe the actual factors in the test, I had hoped to remedy this shortcoming by finding what factors actually existed in the test.

This hope was dashed by a cluster analysis done by Datel and Guerjoy (personal communication). The subjects for this study were 305 soldiers tested with the MAACL during their third week of basic training. The results on the standard MAACL scales were described in publications by Datel and his co-workers.

A large negative affect cluster was found which included 56 negative affect words—practically all the ones contained in the three scales, anxiety, depression, and hostility. Even cluster analysis could not break down this gargantuan factor. Only two small hostility subclusters could be teased out: one which included the following: *contrary*, *incensed*, *indignant*; and another which contained: *cruel* and *mean*. Perhaps this lack of affect discrimination is unique to soldiers in the middle of basic training who just feel generally "lousy." But the results are in accord with the high correlations obtained between the three MAACL scales in other studies. What is notable is that none of the positive affect words correlated negatively with the cluster.

Positive affect words formed more discriminative clusters. One cluster which might be described as the elation factor found in prior analyses included: *cheerful*, *friendly*, *gay*, *gentle*, *glad*, *good-natured*, *happy*, *joyful*, *kindly*, *lucky*, *merry*, *peaceful*, *pleasant*, *pleased*, *satisfied*, and *steady*.

Another factor was a more active, potent kind of positive affect, akin to the surgency and vigor factors discovered by Nowlis. It included the words: *energetic*, *enthusiastic*, *fine*, *fit*, *good*, *healthy*, *inspired*, *powerful*, *rough*, and *strong*.

Other narrow positive affect clusters were found including: *mild*, *tame*, *tender*, *timid* (docility?); *agreeable*, *cooperative*, *understanding* (conformity?); *affectionate*, *loving* (social affection); and *safe*, *secure*.

Overall, the results were not encouraging for the prospects of developing factor scales from the MAACL. One basic problem is the check-list format of the MAACL. While simple to take, this kind of test requires a considerable number of adjectives to make up a scale which will give any kind of score distribution. The small clusters of a few items each could not be used to construct scales.

It was at this point that I decided to construct a new trait-state test for affects; one capable of measuring positive as well as negative affects. There was another reason to develop a new test. I had just read Mischel's (1968) book on personality assessment and had begun to ponder the problems of broad trait measurement. The general form of the MAACL is an affect-trait test in which subjects describe how they "generally" feel. I decided to construct a different kind of trait test based on the idea that situation-specific traits would predict self-report behavioral, and physiological emotional responses more effectively than general trait tests. I am not going to talk about the trait version here or the studies to test the idea of situation-specific traits, but will only discuss the state measure of the Zuckerman (1976a, 1977) Inventory of Personal Reactions (ZIPERS).

ZIPERS State Test

Words were selected on the basis of the Nowlis (1965) analyses to represent each of the major, replicated dimensions of affect. In addition, subjective reports of physiological change (e.g., heart, breathing changes) and four rating scales for implicit response tendencies were included to give further definition to the affect (e.g., "I want to avoid or get out of the situation."). The first form of the ZIPERS state test included 16 scales on which the subjects rated from 1 to 5 to describe how they felt "now at this time." The state test was given to 153 undergraduates on two occasions: once during a normal class day, and three weeks later, just prior to taking an examination. Previous research with the AACL and MAACL (Zuckerman, 1960, Zuckerman, Lubin, Vogel, & Valerius, 1964) has shown that anxiety is typically increased in a group waiting to take an examination. I wanted to see if the state factors would be changed in a situation which increases negative affect.

Details of the factor-analytic results can be found in my chapter (Zuckerman, 1976a) in the book *Emotions and Anxiety*. Factor analyses of the classes's responses in both the neutral and arousal situations revealed: (a) a *fear arousal* (FA) factor consisting of the self-report "I feel fearful" plus reports of increased physiological arousal; (b) a *positive affect* (PA) factor containing all of the positive affect words; and (c) an *angry-aggression-avoidance* (AAA) factor which included the ratings for these affects and response tendencies as well as the affect response "I feel sad." Analysis of responses in the neutral class session indicated another aggression factor which included physiological arousal. The analysis in the examination situation revealed an *attentive-coping* (AC) factor consisting of the feeling of attentiveness and the desire to get further into the situation or through with it. It is interesting that the AC factor appeared in the examination situation and not in the more neutral situation. This confirmed my suspicion that the appearance of some state factors might be dependent on situations which elicit arousal of the relevant state.

The final factors that I decided on were based on the factor analyses of both trait and state versions and included:

1. Fear arousal (FA): heart beats faster, breathe faster, feel fearful.
2. Positive affect (PA): feel carefree; affectionate, elated and act friendly or affectionately.
3. Anger-aggression-avoidance (AAA): feel angry and act aggressively and/or avoidantly.
4. Attentive-coping: feel attentive and feel like getting further into situation or through with it.
5. Sad: feel sad.

Sad was taken out of the AAA factor where it actually loaded because, as an independent factor, it helped define specific patterns of response to particular situations in the trait version.

The convergent and discriminant validity of the fear arousal factor score of the ZIPERS was tested in a study by Mellstrom, Cicala, and Zuckerman (1976) and also discussed in Zuckerman (1977). The FA score showed high correlations with other state test and behavioral measures of fear in three phobic situations, and these convergent validity coefficients were generally higher than the correlations of the FA scale with itself or other measures in other situations. This kind of discriminant validity is unique to state tests which are reliable internally but have low retest reliability. They provide an exception to the dictum that validity cannot exceed reliability, if reliability is of the retest type.

Further validity studies of the ZIPERS state test have recently come out of studies by Roger Ulrich (1978a,b), a geographer at the University of Delaware. Ulrich examined the effects of viewing urban and nature scenes on the affects measured by the ZIPERS in students who had just completed a classroom examination. The group viewing urban scenes of buildings showed significant increases on sadness and decreases on attentiveness. The group who saw nature scenes showed significant decreases on fear arousal and increases on positive affect scores.

A second study conducted in Sweden with a translated form of the ZIPERS used subjects who were exposed to the slides without any preceeding stress experience. Again the urban scenes increased the sadness factor, and resulted in decreased scores on attentiveness relative to nature-water scenes. Levels of fear arousal only increased slightly in response to urban scenes, but decreased markedly in response to nature-water scenes.

These studies by Ulrich show the sensitivity of the ZIPERS factor scales to the relatively mild influence of slide-viewing, and confirm the tranquilizing effects of nature as opposed to urban scenery. Another type of validity concerns the predictive value of state measures for subsequent responses. Before discussing these studies I would like to describe the development of one more affect measure.

Development of a Sensation Seeking State Scale

As you probably know, I have spent many years developing a trait measure of something I call "Sensation Seeking" and have used this scale to explore the construct and its ramifications in behavior (Zuckerman 1971, 1974, 1978, 1979a). It is my conviction that every trait, not only emotion traits such as anxiety, has an affective arousal component which can be measured by a state test. Patrick, Zuckerman, and Masterson (1974) showed how the traits measured by the Gough–Heilbrun (1965) Adjective Check Test could be measured as states, and Patrick and Zuckerman (1977) have shown a validity application for one of these motive-state measures: need for achievement.

My own persuasive arguments on the trait-state problem necessitated the development of a state scale for the sensation-seeking motive, for self-consistency if for no other reason. Actually, we needed a state scale to develop an experimental approach to sensation seeking. Much of the validity of the trait SSS depended on subjects' reports of their life experiences. We wanted to see how well we could actually predict their behavior in contrived laboratory situations.

Past experiences with prediction of behavior in actual situations showed that prediction was better accomplished with a state test, taken just before the experimental treatment, than a general trait test of the same construct. Zuckerman, Persky, and Link (1967), for instance, showed that MAACL state scales of depression and hostility, taken before a standard test of hypnotic susceptibility, could predict subsequent hypnotizability, whereas trait measures of these affects could not. Actually, the positive affect words in these scales accounted for prediction as much as negative affect words. Gouax, Lamberth, and Friedrich (1972) showed that the MAACL state scales could predict "interpersonal attraction" to a stranger, whereas trait scales could not. Neary and Zuckerman (1976) found that the MAACL state measure of anxiety was related to the magnitude of the *electrodermal orienting reflex* (OR), whereas the Manifest Anxiety Scale trait measure was not. It stands to reason that the immediate motive or affect arousal at the time behavior is observed is more likely to be predictive of that behavior than any general trait measure based on a report of how one "usually" feels.

Neary (1975) developed the Sensation Seeking and Anxiety States Test (SSAST), and the development is described in Zuckerman (1976b, 1978). An initial pool of adjectives was derived from the Gough–Heilbrun (1965) ACL, the Zuckerman (1960) AACL, and the ZIPERS (Zuckerman, 1976a, 1977). As with the MAACL, we started with an empirical method of item selection. Subjects who scored in the high or low ranges of the trait SSS were given four hypothetical risky situations, asked to visualize the scenes, and rate how they would feel using the 156 items on the preliminary form I of the SSAST. Item analyses were done by comparing the responses of persons high and low on the trait SSS. Adjectives which were checked significantly more often by one group than the other group in response to at least 2 of the situations were selected for further study.

The items checked more by the high sensation seekers than by the lows included: interested, elated, adventurous, pleased, lucky, daring, enthusiastic, amused, imaginative, confident, zany, curious, cooperative, joyful, and playful. They seem to represent a mixture of "surgency" and "elation" as these factors were defined by Nowlis (1965).

The items checked more by the lows included: desperate, frightened, panicky, terrified, upset, and worrying. All were items from the AACL anxiety scale! Here we were facing the implication of a bipolar factor. But, this time, I knew better than to assume the existence of the factor from the results of empirical item selection. Furthermore, studies of the relationship between the trait SSS and the usual kinds of general anxiety trait measures showed no correlation (Zuckerman 1974, 1978), so why should anxiety, or its absence, be part of the sensation-seeking state?

The items discriminating the criterion groups were given to a new, unselected group of students and their item responses were intercorrelated and factor analyzed. Much to our relief, anxiety and sensation seeking emerged as two distinct factors. All 15 items tentatively identified as sensation-seeking items loaded on one factor, and 15 of the 21 anxiety items from the AACL loaded on the second factor.

On the basis of this analysis we constructed the SSAST containing a 15-item, sensation-seeking state scale and a 15-item anxiety state scale. We decided to assess both states in the same test so that we could see how they interacted in predicting behavior in risky situations. Neary (1975) gave the SSAST to a new group of subjects in order to assess its reliability and validity. The subjects, students from an introductory psychology class, were tested on the trait SSS, and then given the SSAST form on five, weekly occasions in the classroom. A subsample of 55 males and 58 females drawn from the high, middle, and low ranges of the SSS trait scale were selected for further experiments. The subjects were brought into a room and given the SSAST after they had been told that they were about to be subjects in a hypnosis experiment. After taking the test, they were actually given the Harvard Group Hypnotic Susceptibility Test (HGHST), which yields a score of hypnotic susceptiblity based on responses to a series of graded suggestions. On another occasion the subjects were brought into another room and told that they were about to be subjects in a drug experiment. They were shown a bright orange pill (a placebo) and were told that the drug could produce "some strange effects, possibly hallucinations." To make the situation realistic, they were told that their physiological reactions would be monitored and the equipment was shown to them. They were then given the SSAST while the experimenter busied himself with "preparations" for the experiment. After they finished the SS and A state tests they were told that their participation was voluntary and were given a consent form on which to indicate their willingness or refusal to participate. This decision constituted the dependent variable in the experiment.

To Risk or Not to Risk

Before discussing the results of this study, I would like to explain the choice of hypnosis and drug-taking as experimental situations to test the behavioral validity of the state scales. Studies of willingness to volunteer for various kinds of experiments (Zuckerman 1974, 1978) have shown that hypnosis and drug experiments constitute two conditions where a rated willingness to participate correlates positively and significantly with the general sensation seeking trait in both males and females. Both kinds of experiments promise to produce new kinds of perceptual and affective experiences, but both also pose the risk of losing control. Our studies have shown that taking an unknown drug is seen as considerably riskier than being hypnotized. The responses in the Neary study bore this out; anxiety was significantly higher in the drug experiment than in either the hypnosis or the baseline conditions.

Sensation seekers would be expected to be attracted to both types of situations and the SS state should predict both hypnotizability and the decision to take the drug. A previous study (Zuckerman, Bone, Neary, Mangelsdorff, & Brusman, 1972) with the trait SSS showed that the trait measure could not predict hypnotizability. But since hypnotizability seems to be more related to states than to traits (Zuckerman *et al.*, 1967) the state SS scale might succeed where the trait scale could not. In the drug situation, where the risk is greater, anxiety state might also be crucial in the decision. Equally high levels of SS state would signal a readiness to take the risk, a high level of anxiety state should inhibit any desire to explore a new experience.

There is ample evidence that persons high on the trait SSS are willing to ingest all kinds of chemicals which promise new experiences, stimulation, or positive affect arousal. Studies by Segal (1976) and Singer, and Zuckerman *et al.* (1972) using college students, and studies of other populations by Kaestner, Rosen, and Appel (1977), Khavari, Humes, and Mabry (1977), and Kilpatrick, Sutker, and Smith (1976) have all shown that polydrug users, who experiment with many kinds of drugs, are high sensation seekers on all of the SS scales. I find it interesting that many of these sensation seekers from the early 1970s, who were ingesting any chemical that came down the pike, are now "into" natural health foods and are appalled by the idea of ingesting preservative chemicals or artificial flavorings. The difference probably is that salami loaded with sodium nitrate and red dye does not provide the kind of "trip" that made LSD worth the ride.

Relation between SS and A States

Table 1 shows the correlations between SS and A states in the neutral, hypnosis, and drug conditions. In the neutral classroom situations, there was no relationship between SS and A states in males and a low, negative relationship in females. The negative correlation between the states

Table 1. Correlations between Sensation-Seeking States and Anxiety States[a]

Occasions	Males	Females	All
Baseline 1	−.02	−.36[c]	−.25[c]
Drug Cond.	−.38[b]	−.57[c]	−.52[c]
Hyp. Cond.	−.26	−.40[c]	−.33[c]
$\bar{X}$ States	−.12	−.36[c]	−.25[c]

[a] From Neary (1975) and Zuckerman (1976b). Copyright 1976 by Hemisphere. Reprinted by permission. For the experimental group only (N = males 55; females 58).
[b] $p < .05$.
[c] $p < .01$.

increased somewhat in the hypnosis condition but increased even more markedly in the anxiety-inducing drug condition. The results suggest that as situations become appraised as riskier, the rise in anxiety results in a decrease of positive sensation seeking affect.

Prediction of Drug Decision

The predictions of the drug decision from trait SS and state SS and A scales are shown in Table 2. The trait SS scale could not predict either criterion. The state SS scale, obtained in the baseline, showed a low, positive correlation with hypnotic susceptibility. The state SS scale taken in the drug condition predicted the decision to take the drug, and hypnotic susceptibility as well. The state SS scale, taken in the hypnosis condition, predicted only hypnotic susceptibility. Baseline measured anxiety state did not predict either criteria. State anxiety measured in the drug condition correlated negatively with the decision to take the drug. State anxiety in the hypnosis condition did not correlate with hypnotic susceptibility or the drug decision.

Both SS and A states influenced the drug decision, the former positively, and the latter negatively. This interaction is shown in Table 3 which shows the percentages of subjects in each combination of high or low SS and A states who volunteered to take the drug. The highest percentage volunteering is found in the group high in SS state and low in A state, and the lowest percentage is found in the group low in SS and high in A, but it is

Table 2. Predictions of Drug Decision and Hypnotic Susceptibility[a]

	Prediction of drug decision[b]			Prediction of hypnotic susceptibility[c]		
Predictors	M	F	All	M	F	All
Trait SS	.11	.18	.16	.09	.25	.17
State SS-baseline 1	−.22	.01	−.08	.28[d]	.24	.26[d]
State SS-drug cond.	.28[d]	.26[d]	.30[e]	.29[d]	.47[e]	.37[e]
State SS-hyp. cond.	−.15	.08	−.01	.28[e]	.46[e]	.37[e]
State Anx, baseline 1	−.15	.07	−.03	−.11	.21	.07
State Anx, drug cond.	−.33[d]	−.33[d]	−.36[e]	−.14	−.08	−.11
State Anx, hyp. cond.	−.06	−.09	−.02	−.14	.01	−.07

[a] From Neary (1975) and Zuckerman (1976b), copyright 1976 by Hemisphere. Reprinted by permission.
[b] Point biserial correlations.
[c] Production moment correlations.
[d] $p < .05$.
[e] $p < .01$.

Table 3. Percentages of Subjects Volunteering to Take Drug in High and Low SS and A State Groups

Group		% Yes	% No	N
High SS	Low A	74	26	43
High SS	High A	71	29	14
Low SS	Low A	69	31	13
Low SS	High A	41	59	43

$\chi^2 = 10.89.$
$d.f. = 3, p < .05.$

really the latter group that accounts for the overall differences between groups.

Risk, Sensation Seeking, and Anxiety

The results from Neary's validity study suggested a model relating sensation seeking and anxiety affect arousal to risk, as appraised by the subjects. Figure 1 presents this model.

Novelty was assumed to vary with risk appraisal up to some point beyond which increased novelty does not necessarily relate to appraised risk. Things that we do very often, or familiar situations, are seldom rated as risky, except in the unusual case where one's daily activities are at the high-risk end of the continuum (e.g., a soldier who is engaged in daily combat). Beyond this case, there is probably some increase in appraised risk simply as a function of the uncertainty of the situation. However, there are certainly many situations which we have never encountered which we would not appraise as risky. I have never been to Toronto before this meeting, for instance, but I did not appraise the trip here as risky.

To assess this assumption, I devised 116 situations and had a small group of 31 subjects rate these situations for their "riskiness" and how much experience they had had with each situation. The correlation between novelty and risk appraisal was .56, which was highly significant even for this small group. However, a look at the scatterplot confirmed my supposition. The correlation was produced by the fact that there was no very familiar situations (experienced more than four times) which subjects rated as even moderately risky. But at the extreme novelty end (never experienced), there was absolutely no relationship to risk. None of our subjects reported having seen a flying saucer in the sky, but none of them felt it would be risky to

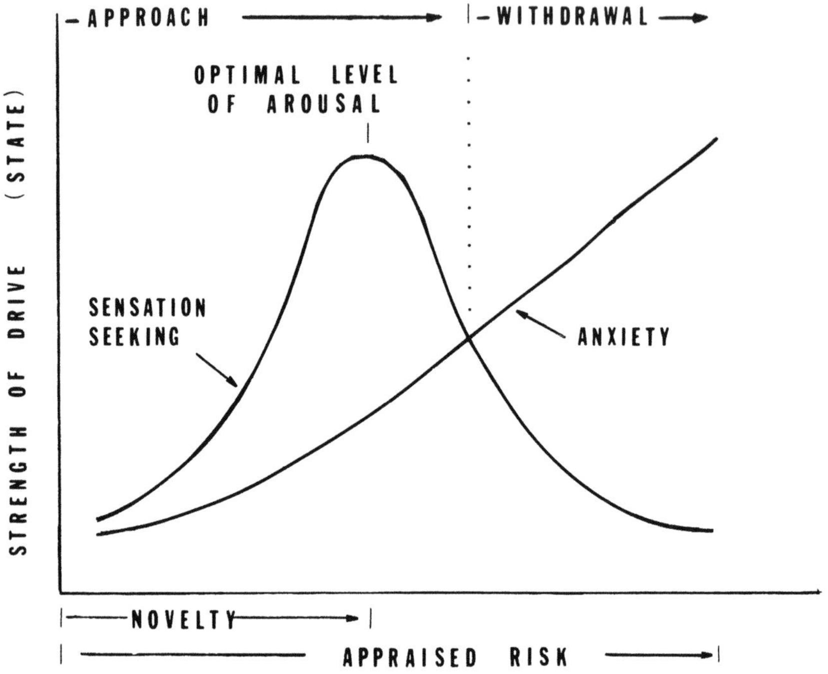

Fig. 1. Model for the relationship between appraised risk and sensation-seeking and anxiety states. Copyright 1976 by Hemisphere. Reprinted by permission.

have that experience. None of our subjects reported having taken heroin or being involved in a battle, but all regarded these as highly risky activities.

Since novelty seemed secondary to appraised risk, I decided to concentrate on the latter dimension, the theory being that anxiety increases in a linear fashion with appraised risk, while sensation-seeking state increases to some optimal level of arousal with appraised risk, but beyond that point, decreases. Having sex with an attractive stranger is more novel and riskier than having sex with one's usual partner, but it certainly does wonders for the sensation-seeking type of arousal. Of course, it also entails some increase in anxiety, and if the anxiety is stronger than the sensation-seeking, the outcome will be withdrawal from the situation. Our research (Zuckerman *et al.*, 1972; Zuckerman, Tushup, & Finner, 1976) has shown that high sensation seekers do engage in more varied kinds of sexual activity with more partners than do the lows.

Obviously, there must be individual differences in risk appraisal, otherwise, some people would never do the kind of things that other people regard as insanely risky. Illustrations of activities engaged in by some high sensation seekers are parachuting, sky diving, and scuba diving (even at the risk of encountering some undersirable fellow swimmers—sharks are not sensation seekers, they are just hungry. Many of us regard drugs as risky and would never ingest anything of that sort, but in every generation there are those experience seekers who ignore the physical, social, and legal risks entailed. And, of course, there are the more mundane types of disinhibition seeking that we see at parties.

A study was done to evaluate the relationship between risk appraisal and the trait of sensation seeking. Fifty situations, covering the risk dimensions from low to high, were chosen from the novel end of the items used in the previous study. The subjects, 96 males and 114 females from psychology classes, were given the trait SSS and asked to evaluate the degree of physical risk, mental risk, and punishment risk for each of the activities. The risk appraisals were totalled across the situations for each subject, and the risk appraisal scores were correlated with the SSS scores. The correlations were −.42 for males and −.40 for females. The results confirmed the hypothesis that high and low sensation seekers tend to evaluate risk differently.

However, differential risk appraisal may not account for all of the behavioral differences between high and low sensation seekers. It is possible that even when risk is appraised equally by both types, that the high sensation seeker experiences greater positive sensation-seeking affect and less anxiety than the low sensation seeker. In order to determine this relationship, I had to find situations varying in risk in which both highs and lows agreed on the riskiness. Fortunately, there was one subset of situations that met this criteria for both sexes, and another which did so for the males. Risk appraisal of travel situations, ranging from about to start a trip to Europe to about to blast off for the moon, did not correlate with trait sensation seeking in either males or females. Experimental situations, similar to the ones used by Neary, did not correlate with sensation seeking in males although they did show some low negative correlations in females.

These two situations were used in a new situation inventory. In this form, the subject was asked to rate how he or she would react if they were in the situations described by using an abbreviated form of the SSAST containing sensation-seeking and anxiety items.

Sixty males and 111 females were selected from the extreme ranges on the trait sensation-seeking scale and given the situation-response inventory in large groups. The detailed results of this study appear in a chapter in another book (Zuckerman, 1979b), so I will not go into great detail here. The results were similar for both travel and experimental situations. The main effects of situations and sensation-seeking trait were significant for both anxiety and sensation-seeking states. The main effect of sex was significant only for anxiety. The interactions between sensation-seeking trait and situations, and sex and situations were significant for both anxiety and sensation-seeking states in both sets of situations.

Let us examine the interactions between sensation-seeking trait and situations as shown in Figure 2. The three hypothetical situations are ranged along the abscissa in proportion to their rated risk value in the previous study. One set of ratings was made of how subjects felt at the time of taking the test. This situation (being involved in group testing) was assumed to be of minimal risk value. Overall, high sensation seekers report less anxiety and more sensation seeking affect in all situations. The differences are not significant in the current situation (taking the test in a group setting), and become larger and more significant as we move to the situations rated higher in risk. Note also that anxiety increases linearly with risk, while sensation-seeking state shows a curvilinear pattern in conformance with our model. However, the curvilinearity is more pronounced for the low sensation seekers than for the highs.

A significant triple interaction justifies breaking down the data for the sexes separately, and since risk appraisal is independent of sensation-seeking trait in males, it is particularly worth examining the male data. Figure 3 shows the SS and A states for the low and high SS trait males. In the low SS trait males the anxiety curve crosses and surpasses the SS state curve at a fairly low risk level. In the high SS trait males, the SS state is higher than the A state even at the highest risk levels, and, in contrast to the low SS

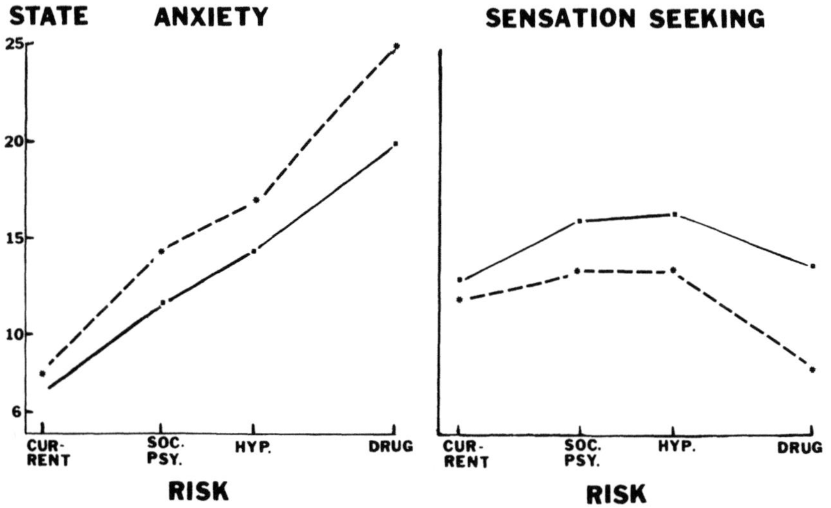

Fig. 2. Sensation-seeking (SS) and anxiety states in high and low (trait) sensation seekers. ■ = high SS trait; * = low SS trait. From Zuckerman(1979b). Copyright 1979, Plenum Press. Reprinted by permission.

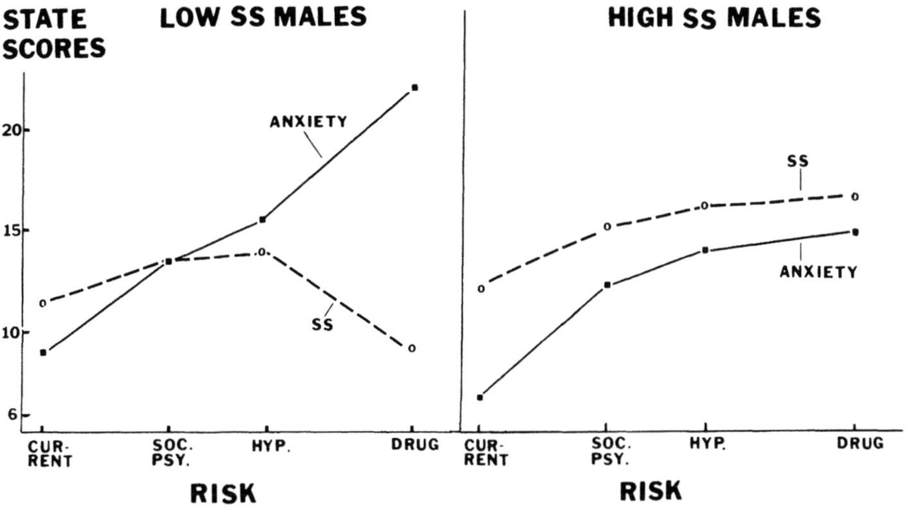

Fig. 3. Sensation-seeking and anxiety states in high and low sensation-seeking (SS) (trait) males. From Zuckerman (1979b). Copyright 1979, Plenum Press. Reprinted by permission.

trait males, SS state in the highs shows no decline, and A state shows no great increase in the risky drug experiment situation.

The results show why high sensation seekers are much more likely to use drugs, or take other kinds of risk, than the lows. Even when they see the situation to be risky, as do the lows, the high sensation seekers are likely to experience less anxiety and more positive, euphoric affect than low sensation seekers. In some ways, the manageable anxiety may enhance the positive sensation seeking affect since the two kinds of arousal may not be clearly discriminated. As long as the sensation seeker identifies his pounding heart as elation, rather than fear, he will not be deterred from taking the risk. But even if he senses some fear, the expectation of a rewarding new experience may outweigh the feared consequences. Thus, in any situation of high risk, there is a balance between two kinds of affective arousal, and the cognitive decision, or behavior which follows, will reflect this delicate balance, as was shown in Neary's (1975) study.

Performance and Affect

The classical Yerkes–Dodson (1908) law was translated into the optimal level of arousal or inverted U-shaped curve relating performance to levels of drive (Spence, 1964) or arousal (Hebb, 1955). Arousal and generalized drive are neutral as to the specific emotion or goal involved. Theoretically, there is no reason why Spence could not have used a test of joy or elation rather than anxiety in his learning studies. But we psychologists of the 1950s were a rather joyless lot.

A fundamental mistake in these eyelid conditioning studies was the use of a trait test of anxiety rather than a state measure taken at the time of the experiment. The findings were inconsistent because the relationship was a weak one depending upon persons scoring at the extremes of the scale. When unselected subjects were used, the correlation between trait anxiety and eyelid conditioning was about .2 for males only (Spence & Spence, 1964). Only subjects at the extremes of a trait are likely to be reliable in their state on a given occasion; and even at the extremes of the trait, the situation must be conducive to the arousal of the state. Perhaps that is why Spence used a dental chair in a semidarkened room to test his subjects. Researchers who used less threatening experimental conditions did not find the relationship between the Manifest Anxiety Scale and eyelid conditioning.

The question I want to raise is: do positive affect states predict performance as well as negative ones, and, if so, is the prediction in the same direction? A theory which makes no distinction between types of arousal suggests that positive and negative affect arousal should summate, and, therefore, both should correlate in the same direction with performance. A cognitive-emotion theory would predict that performance is in some part a function of attitudes or sets toward the task. A person who is telling himself, "I'm going to fail" is going to have negative affect arousal and such non-task-oriented cognitions will interfere with performance, confirming his self-fulfilling prophecy (Mandler & Sarason, 1952, 1953; Wine, 1971). But what happens to the confident person who tells himself, "I'm going to cream this test" and is also aroused, but in a more positive coping sense? Is the specific anticipation, or the arousal, the crucial factor?

A study recently completed by Carrol (1978) provides some answers to these questions, for he included measures of positive, as well as negative, affects in a study of the effects of stimulant and depressant drugs on high and low sensation seekers. He also included three performance tests: the Finger Tapping Test (FTT), the Pursuit Rotor (PR), and the Digit Symbol Substitution Test (DSST). The affect tests included the SSAST and the ZIPERS. The 32 subjects took the affect state tests followed by the performance tests on 7 occasions: once on a baseline day, prior to the experimental sessions, and before and after placebo, D-amphetamine, and diazepam treatments. The treatment days were one week apart, and the order of treatments was varied.

The effects of treatments and the sensation seeking trait variable are not of concern here. What I will present are the correlations between positive and negative affects from two tests and the immediate, subsequent performance on the three behavior tests for the seven occasions of testing.

Table 4 presents the correlations between the SSAST sensation seeking (SS) and anxiety (A) states and performance measures, and between the ZIPERS positive affect (PA) and anger-aggression-avoidance (AAA) states and performance. The correlations between positive and negative affect measures are also given in the table.

Looking first at the SSAST correlations with performance, we see that the correlations vary considerably from one testing to the next, and only 12 of the 42 correlations reach the .05 level of significance. What is remarkable is that all 21 of the correlations between SS state and performance are positive in direction, and 20 of 21 correlations of the A state with performance are negative. This could be explained by a high negative correlation between the two states, but, as we can see, the two states correlated significantly on only 2 of the 7 occasions of testing, and on only one of these, in the predepressant testing, was the correlation of substantial magnitude. In some cases, both states correlated significantly with a performance measure; one positively and one negatively. On the baseline occasion, for instance, the SS state correlated +.36 and the A state correlated −.35 with the score on the Digit Symbol Substitution Test. The multiple correlation of .53 means that taken together, the two states accounted for about 25% of the variance in performance. Similarly, in the same condition, the multiple correlation of the two states with the finger-tapping test was .50, again accounting for a quarter of the variance.

Looking at the two factors from the ZIPERS, we find 13 of the 42 correlations significant; 20 of the 21 correlations between the positive affect score and performance are positive in sign, and 15 of the 21 between the negative affect score and performance are negative. Positive and negative affect scores correlated negatively, and significantly, on five of the 7 occasions, but the correlations exceeded .4 on only two occasions.

Looking at the correlations between affect measures from the two tests, we can see that sensation seeking in the SSAST and positive affect in the ZIPERS correlate very highly on all occasions. Considering the magnitude and consistency of these correlations we can say that sensation seeking and positive affect are pretty much the same. While anxiety in the SSAST and the negative affect factor in the ZIPERS are also positively correlated, the magnitudes of the correlations do not allow for complete identification of the two variables. However, there is no question of their relatedness.

The data show that affect states are a significant factor in performance, although clearly not the only one. Ability, after all, may count for something. What is interesting is the consistent directionality of the affect-performance relationships. Sensation seeking positive affect is positively related to

Table 4. Correlations[a] *between Positive and Negative Affects and Subsequent Performance on Seven Occasions*

		Condition									
Per. Test	SSAST affect	Base line	Pre-placebo	Post-placebo	Pre-stim.	Post-stim.	Pre-depr.	Post-dep.	No. sig. r's/7	No. +r's	No. −r's
DSST[b]	SS[e]	36[i]	23	23	23	22	02	13	1	7	0
	A[f]	−35[i]	−16	−06	−13	−38[i]	−01	06	2	1	6
FTT[c]	SS	39[i]	43[j]	18	43[j]	25	31	21	3	7	0
	A	−29	−13	−09	−41[j]	−11	−27	−05	1	0	7
PRT[d]	SS	26	18	53[j]	21	06	35[i]	34	2	7	0
	A	−10	−21	−39[i]	−35[i]	−35[i]	−31	−16	3	0	7
SS *vs*	A	−03	−22	−18	−36[i]	−30	−56[j]	−21	2	0	7
	ZIPERS										
DSST	PA[g]	33	28	13	19	21	17	17	1	7	0
	AAA[h]	−40[i]	02	−35[i]	−26	−41[i]	06	25	3	3	4
FTT	PA	37[i]	35[i]	03	30	29	37	17	3	7	0
	AAA	−36[i]	−11	−13	−47[j]	−35[i]	−09	07	3	1	6
PRT	PA	24	06	24	15	−04	39[i]	33	1	6	1
	AAA	−30	14	−51[j]	−20	−19	−41[i]	10	2	2	5
PA *vs*	AAA	−35[i]	−36[i]	−30	−67[j]	−24	−44[i]	−30	4	0	7
SS *vs*	PA	71[j]	71[j]	69[j]	79[j]	83[j]	78[j]	74[j]	7	7	0
A *vs*	AAW	33	56[j]	31	44[i]	46[j]	54[j]	72[j]	5	7	0

[a] Decimals omitted, $N = 32$.
[b] Digit Symbol Substitution Test.
[c] Finger Tapping Test.
[d] Pursuit Rotor Tracking.
[e] Sensation Seeking State.
[f] Anxiety State.
[g] Positive Affect State.
[h] Anger-Aggression-Avoidance State.
[i] $p < .05$.
[j] $p < .01$.

performance and anxiety, and anger-aggression are negatively related to performance. These results suggest that the cognitive aspect, implied in the content of these affect measures, is more important than the arousal factor which is usually the same in direction, if not of the same magnitude, for both types of affect measures. We had some crude measures of arousal in these situations, namely, pulse and blood pressure taken by a nurse. There were few correlations between these measures and the affect measures, but most were positive for both types of affect, and almost all of the significant ones were positive in sign.

These results are not surprising if we consider the test anxiety literature which has increasingly emphasized the effects of anxiety cognitions, rather than arousal, on test performance (Spielberger, Anton, & Bedell, 1976). Some cognitively oriented behavior therapists, notably Meichenbaum (1972) have attempted to focus on the cognitive component of anxiety in the treatment of test anxiety, as well as other conditions.

The results showing a facilitory effect of positive affects on performance also have therapeutic implications. Perhaps there is some power to "positive thinking" and feeling. I am not advocating a psychology of joy, but if our treatments are capable of reducing negative affects, they also should be capable of increasing positive affects. These affects, however, may not appear magically when we reduce anxiety and inhibition. Such thinking is based on the bipolar fallacy of Freud. With due respect to the biologically based limits of sensation seeking tendency, we might consider directing our clients toward experiences which might enhance positive affect. I suspect many of us are doing so now, although we do not talk about it in published case reports. The exception to this trend are the sex therapists who use that epicurean, gourmet guide, *The Joy of Sex* (Comfort, 1972), and even borderline pornography, to direct their clients toward more positive arousal in sex. How about a book on the "joy of taking examinations," or "mountain climbing and parachuting for acrophobics," or "body-crush games for claustrophobics"? I am not being totally facetious, because I do believe that after anxiety is reduced to a tolerable minimum, positive affects can be powerful influences and may "innoculate" the patient against recurrences of anxiety.

References

Carrol, E. N. Sensation seeking and psychological reactions to drugs that stimulate and depress central nervous system arousal. Unpublished doctoral dissertation. University of Delaware, 1978.

Comfort, A. *The joy of sex*. New York: Crown, 1972.

Datel, W. E., & Guerjoy, H. Unpublished data. Personal communication, 1969.

Freud, S. Beyond the pleasure principle. In J. Strachey (Ed.), *The standard edition of the complete psychological works*. Vol. 18. London: Hogarth Press, 1961. (First German edition, 1920.)

Freud, S. *Civilization and its discontents*. J. Strachey (Trans.). New York: Norton, 1962. (First German edition, 1930.).

Gouax, C., Lamberth, T., & Friedrich, G. Affect and interpersonal attraction: A comparison of trait and state measures. *Journal of Personality and Social Psychology*, 1972, *24*, 53–58.

Gough, H. G., & Heilbrun, A. B. *The adjective check list manual*. Palo Alto, California: Consulting Psychologist Press, 1965.

Hebb, D. O. Drives and the CNS (conceptual nervous system). *Psychological Review*, 1955, *62*, 243–254.

Izard, C. E. *The face of emotion*. New York: Appleton-Century-Crofts, 1971.

Izard, C. E. *Human emotions*. New York: Plenum, 1977.

Kaestner, E., Rosen, L., & Appel, P. Patterns of drug abuse: Relationships with ethnicity, sensation seeking and anxiety. *Journal of Consulting and Clinical Psychology*, 1977, *45*, 462–468.

Khavari, K. A., Humes, M., & Mabry, E. Personality correlates of hallucinogen use. *Journal of Abnormal Psychology*, 1977, *86*, 172–178.

Kilpatrick, D. G., Sutker, P. B., & Smith, A. D. Deviant drug and alcohol use: The role of anxiety, sensation seeking and other personality variables. In M. Zuckerman & C. D. Spielberger (Eds.), *Emotions and anxiety: New concepts, methods and applications*. Hillsdale, N.J.: Erlbaum, 1976.

Mandler, G., & Sarason, S. B. A study of anxiety and learning. *Journal of Abnormal and Social Psychology*, 1952, *47*, 166–173.

Mandler, G., & Sarason, S. B. The effects of prior experience and subjective failure on the evocation of test anxiety. *Journal of Personality*, 1953, *21*, 338–341.

Meichenbaum, D. H. Cognitive modification of test anxious college students. *Journal of Consulting and Clinical Psychology*, 1972, *39*, 370–380.

Mellstrom, M., Jr., Cicala, G. A., & Zuckerman, M. General versus specific trait anxiety measures in the prediction of fear of snakes, heights and darkness. *Journal of Consulting and Clinical Psychology*, 1976, *44*, 83–91.

Mischel, W. *Personality and assessment*. New York: Wiley, 1968.

Neary, R. S. The development and validation of a state measure of sensation-seeking. Doctoral Dissertation, University of Delaware, 1975.

Neary, R. S., & Zuckerman, M. Sensation seeking trait and state anxiety, and the electrodermal orienting reflex. *Psychophysiology*, 1976, *13*, 205–211.

Nowlis, V. Research with the Mood Adjective Check List. In S. S. Tompkins & C. E. Izard (Eds.), *Affect, cognition and personality*. New York: Springer, 1965.

Patrick, A. W., & Zuckerman, M. An application of the state-trait concept to the need for achievement. *Journal of Research in Personality*, 1977, *11*, 459–465.

Patrick, A. W., Zuckerman, M., & Masterson, F. A. An extension of the trait-state distinction from affects to motive measures. *Psychological Reports*, 1974, *34*, 1251–1258.

Plutchik, R. *The emotions*. New York: Random House, 1962.

Segal, B. Personality factors related to drug and alcohol use. In D. J. Lettieri (Ed.), *Predicting adolescent drug abuse: A review of issues methods and correlates*. Washington, D. C.: U.S. Government Printing Office, Dept. of Health, Education and Welfare. Publication no. (ADM) 77-299, 1976.

Spence, K. W. Anxiety (drive) level and performance in eyelid conditioning. *Psychological Bulletin*, 1964, *61*, 129–139.
Spence, K. W., & Spence, J. T. Relation of eyelid conditioning to manifest anxiety, extraversion and rigidity. *Journal of Abnormal and Social Psychology*, 1964, *68*, 144–149.
Spielberger, C. D., Anton, W. D., & Bedell, J. The nature and treatment of test anxiety. In M. Zuckerman & C. D. Spielberger (Eds.), *Emotions and anxiety: New concepts, methods and applications*. Hillsdale, N.J.: Erlbaum, 1976.
Sullivan, H. S. *The interpersonal theory of psychiatry*. New York: Norton, 1953.
Ulrich, R. S. Anxiety reducing effects of built versus nature scenes. Paper presented at 9th annual meeting of Environmental Design Research Association. Tuscon, Arizona, April, 1978. (a)
Ulrich, R. S. Psycho-physiological effects of nature versus urban scenes. Unpublished report prepared for the Swedish Council for Building Research. February, 1978. (b)
Wine, J. Test anxiety and the direction of attention. *Psychological Bulletin*, 1971, *76*, 92–104.
Yerkes, R. M., & Dodson, J. D. The relation of strength of stimulus to rapidity of habit-formation. *Journal of Comparative and Neurological Psychology*, 1908, *18*, 459–482.
Zuckerman, M. The development of an affect adjective check list for the measurement of anxiety. *Journal of Consulting Psychology*, 1960, *24*, 457–462.
Zuckerman, M. Dimensions of sensation seeking. *Journal of Consulting and Clinical Psychology*, 1971, *36*, 45–52.
Zuckerman, M. The sensation seeking motive. In B. A. Maher (Ed.), *Progress in experimental personality research* (Vol. 7). New York: Academic, 1974.
Zuckerman, M. General and situation specific traits and states: New approaches to assessment. In M. Zuckerman & C. D. Spielberger (Eds.), *Emotions and anxiety: New concepts, methods and application*. Hillsdale, N.J.: Erlbaum, 1976. (a)
Zuckerman, M. Sensation seeking and anxiety, traits and states, as determinants of behavior in novel situations. In I. G. Sarason & C. D. Spielberger (Eds.), *Stress and anxiety*; Vol. 3. Washington, D.C.: Hemisphere, 1976. (b)
Zuckerman, M. Development of a situation-specific trait-state test for the prediction and measurement of affective responses. *Journal of Consulting and Clinical Psychology*, 1977, *45*, 513–523.
Zuckerman, M. Sensation seeking. In H. S. London & J. E. Exner (Eds.), *Dimensions of personality*. New York: Wiley, 1978.
Zuckerman, M. *Sensation seeking: Beyond the optimal level of arousal*. Hillsdale, N.J.: Erlbaum, 1979. (a)
Zuckerman, M. Sensation seeking and risk taking. In C. E. Izard (Ed.), *Emotions in personality and psychopathology*. New York: Plenum, 1979. (b)
Zuckerman, M., Bone, R. N., Neary, R., Mangelsdorff, D., & Brusman, B. What is the sensation seeker? Personality trait and experience correlates of the Sensation Seeking Scales. *Journal of Consulting and Clinical Psychology*, 1972, *39*, 308–321.
Zuckerman, M., & Lubin, B. *Manual for the Multiple Affect Adjective Check List*. San Diego, California: Educational and Industrial Testing Service, 1965.
Zuckerman, M., Lubin, B., Vogel, L., & Valerius, E. Measurement of experimentally induced affects. *Journal of Consulting Psychology*, 1964, *28*, 418–425.
Zuckerman, M., Persky, H., Eckman, K. M., & Hopkins, T. R. A multitrait multimethod approach to the traits (or states) of anxiety, depression and hostility. *Journal of Projective Techniques and Personality Assessment*, 1967, 31, 39–48.
Zuckerman, M., Persky, H., & Link, K. Relation of mood and hypnotizability: An illustration of the importance of the state versus trait distinction. *Journal of Consulting Psychology*, 1967, *31*, 464–470.

Zuckerman, M., Schultz, D. P., & Hopkins, T. R. Sensation seeking and volunteering for sensory deprivation and hypnosis experiments. *Journal of Consulting Psychology*, 1967, *31*, 358–363.

Zuckerman, M., & Schwartz, L. *Bibliography for the Multiple Affect Adjective Check List* (*MAACL*). San Diego: Educational and Industrial Testing Service, 1977.

Zuckerman, M., Tushup, R., & Finner, S. Sexual attitudes and experience: Attitude and personality correlates and changes produced by a course in sexuality. *Journal of Consulting and Clinical Psychology*, 1976, *44*, 7–19.

CHAPTER 5

Detecting the Dimensions of Depression

Behavioral Assessment in Therapy Outcome Research

Lynn P. Rehm

Department of Psychology
University of Houston
Houston, Texas

My intent in this chapter is to describe a series of psychotherapy outcome studies which we have conducted at the University of Pittsburgh. In doing so, however, I want to emphasize and make specific reference to the issues of assessing depression in its various aspects for the purposes of psychotherapy outcome research. In order to discuss the problems that arise in assessing depression, I will start out with a brief review of some current conceptions of the nature of depression which are relevant to assessment strategy. I will briefly discuss the symptomatology of depression and the broad spectrum of behaviors which it includes, I also want to comment on the current state of the art of methods currently used to assess depression. Given the variety of symptoms displayed by depressed persons, an assessment strategy needs to incorporate a variety of assessment modalities to adequately assess the disorder. The word "detecting" was used in the title of this paper not only for the purposes of alliteration, but to reflect the fact that, whereas there is some agreement as to the clinical phenomena of depression, the methods which have been devised to assess these phenomena have not been entirely successful.

Clinical Phenomena

Depression is usually assumed to be a clinical syndrome made up of a number of specific symptoms. The symptoms involved cover a wide range of response dimensions. The particular constellation of symptoms varies considerably from one depressed individual to another. While there is considerable general agreement regarding many of the symptoms of depression there is remarkable variability in the lists of symptoms attributed to depressive disorders by various clinical writers.

Sad affect is an obvious first symptom on a list of symptomatology of depression. Individuals who are depressed label their emotional state with terms such as depressed, sad, blue, down in the dumps, etc. While sad affect is usually expressed as part of a constellation of attitudes, beliefs, and behaviors, it can be identified as a separate dimension unto itself. Sad affect varies in degree or severity. At the normal end, degrees of sad affect are usually referred to as differences in normal mood; whereas, at the more severe end of the dimension, sad affect is a symptom of depression. It is notable, however, that sad affect is also a symptom of many other psychiatric and physical disorders as well. Nathan, Robertson, and Andberg (1969) found that the symptom of depressed affect is so universal among psychiatric patients that it does not significantly differentiate between depression and other psychiatric disorders. Thus sad affect is obviously not sufficient to discriminate the clinical disorder of depression. The concept of masked depression in psychiatry suggests that, indeed, sad affect may not even be a necessary condition for clinical depression.

A second class of symptoms of depression are the so-called *neurovegetative signs*. These include sleep disturbance (difficulty falling asleep, middle of the night and early morning awakening, or hypersomnia), loss of appetite (often with weight loss), loss of sexual interest, and a general loss of interest in formerly rewarding activities including work, hobbies, etc. These symptoms, by and large, form the basis for diagnosing clinical depression. It is, therefore, the breadth of the symptomatology that a given individual presents, which is used to define the psychopathological level of depression. Since these symptoms involve basic biological functions, the inference is often made that they have a physiological or biochemical basis. With the possible exception of sleep disturbance, where recent research has suggested sleep EEG patterns specific to particular depressive disorders, the physiological or biochemical basis for individual neurovegetative signs is largely an assumption. Behavioral analysis of these symptoms suggests that what is, in fact, being reported is a decrease in rate of certain classes of behavior (eating, sex, work, etc.) accompanied by a self-report of decreased satisfaction or reward from these behaviors. Pending more definitive physiological or biochemical findings, these symptoms will probably continue to be assessed as changes in overt-motor and verbal-cognitive behavior.

In addition to the neurovegetative signs there are other overt-motor signs and symptoms of depression. Ferster (1973) argues that rate of response should be considered the basic behavioral datum for depression. He argues that what is most characteristics of depression is the decelerated overt-motor behavior of the individual. It is generally agreed clinically that the verbal and nonverbal behavior of depressed persons is characterized by increases in latency and a decrease in frequency, rate, duration, and amplitude. The clinical observations of depressed persons note a lack of initiatives, retardation in movement, slowness in responding, minimal answers to questions, lack of expressivity, and diminished speech volume. While these are common clinical observations about the nature of depression, there is some question as to whether retardation is true of all types of depression. While there have been many attempts to develop subtypes of depression, the recent interest in the typology of unipolar versus bipolar depressions (Winokur, 1973) seems to have a fairly solid empirical basis. Two types of depression are differentiable in terms of family history, drug response, age of onset, and symptomatology. Bipolar depressions in their depressed phase are typified by behavioral retardation, whereas unipolar depressions are more typically agitated in their overt behavior. While agitated versus retarded depression does not overlap strictly with the unipolar-biploar differentiation, this classification schema highlights the variability of behavior which is classed as depressed. It also should be pointed out that while there is some empirical evidence that the motor behavior of agitated depression is indeed increased, it may be that these depressed individuals are still manifesting deficits in certain functionally significant behaviors. That is, these individuals also may be disrupted in their work and leisure behavior. They may show deficits in the effectiveness of this behavior. Retardation, however, continues to be the most generally assumed behavioral characteristic of depression.

The cognitive symptomatology of depression is particularly complex and perplexing. Beck (1972, 1974) argues that cognitive dysfunction is the essential feature of depression. For Beck depression can be defined by the cognitive triad of a negative view of the self, a negative view of the world, and a negative view of the future. More typical clinical lists of symptoms would include low self-esteem, excessive guilt, pessimism, and hopelessness. Beck argues that these cognitive symptoms merely reflect more basic cognitive distortions, that is, dysfunctions in cognitive processing. Not only do depressed persons manifest negative attitudes and beliefs about self, world, and future, but they also process information about the world in ways which lead to these conclusions. Beck talks about such forms of distortion as *selective abstraction* whereby individuals attend to negative elements of their experience. It seems reasonable to draw the conclusion that the complexity of cognitive dysfunctions in depression go well beyond simple elaborations of a basic sad affect. The cognitive symptomatology of depression seems to affect the way in which depressed individuals perceive the world, process information about it, and develop attitudes and beliefs toward it.

It can be seen that the symptomatology of depression reflects a broad spectrum of behavior. Symptoms of depression are manifested across many response systems, across many situations, and at several stages of processing experience. Assessment methodologies need to reflect this diversity.

Assessment Methods

The self-report inventory has long been the major format for assessing depression as it has been for assessing other forms of psychopathology. Levitt and Lubin (1975) list 23 scales which have been used to assess depression in the research literature. These scales vary considerably in their format, rationale, and psychometric specification. For the purposes for our own research, we have employed two depression scales primarily: the MMPI-D scale and the Beck Depression Inventory (Beck, Ward, Mendelsohn, Mock, & Erbaugh, 1961). While these scales do cover a variety of cognitive symptoms beyond sad affect, it is important to point out that if indeed the clinical symptomatology of depression includes cognitive distortion, then self-report instruments should probably not be taken as the primary source of data about overt behavior in depression. They should be taken as primary data about cognitive and/or affective states.

At this point, physiological assessment of depression is not practical for therapy outcome research. There are no generally accepted physiological signs of depression as physiology is usually assessed. Recent research has pointed to sleep EEG patterns specific to depression (Kupfer & Foster, 1972) and recent research on facial EMG assessment also seems to show some promise (Schwartz, Fair, Salt, Mandel, & Klerman, 1976). However, at this point, both methodologies are in the experimental stage.

A third general methodology for assessing depression has been the use of clinical ratings. There is some dispute as to the utility of these techniques. On the one hand, it is argued that only an experienced clinician can make accurate judgments as to the severity of a given individual's symptoms (cf. Costello, 1978). It has been argued on the other hand that clinician ratings based on interview materials simply interpose an additional source of subjective bias in evaluating a symptom (cf. Rehm, 1976). The most freqeuntly used clinician rating scales for assessing depression have been the Hamilton Rating Scale (Hamilton, 1960) and the Raskin Scale (Raskin, Schulterbrandt, Reatig, & Rice, 1967). The Hamilton asks for ratings on 17 symptom categories whereas the Raskin involves ratings on three broad dimensions. Both result in a total score used to assess severity of depression.

Another kind of clinician rating methodology is represented by the Schedule for Affective Disorders and Schizophrenia (SADS) (Endicott & Spitzer, 1977). The SADS is a structured interview on the basis of which clinicians make diagnostic distinctions based on Research Diagnostic Criteria (Spitzer, Endicott, & Robins, 1978). Diagnostic decisions are made on the basis of clinical judgments concerning the presence or absence of specific symptom criteria. Exclusion criteria are also part of the SADS. In our research program, we have used the Hamilton and Raskin scales as outcome measures and a simplified version of the SADS interview as a part of our subject selection procedure.

Perhaps the most problematic and least-developed assessment methodology in depression has been the attempt to assess the overt-motor behavior of depressed individuals by either direct observational or mechanical recording methodologies. At this point there have been a number of research studies investigating overt activity among depressed individuals, but little has developed in the form of standardized assessment methods. Williams, Barlow, and Agras (1972) have described an observational methodology whereby the behavior of depressed inpatients is observed using a time-sampling procedure. Behavior is coded into a relatively simple set of categories. The method is limited to use with inpatients. Some recent research attempts have been aimed at direct mechanical recording of activity level of depressed persons (Kupfer, Weiss, Foster, Detre, Delgado, & McPartland, 1974; O'Hara & Rehm, 1978). Kupfer *et al.* have used miniaturized movement counters worn on the wrist by depressed individuals. O'Hara and I used simple pedometers. Evidence to date has suggested only moderate correlations between activity level and mood.

The most frequent methodology used for assessing overt behavior of depressed persons is the activity schedule. While a variety of *ad hoc* activity schedules have been used by various researchers, the best-developed instrument is the MacPhillamy and Lewinsohn (1971) Pleasant Events Schedule. The instrument asks individuals to indicate the frequency of occurrence of 320 specific pleasant events in a given period of time and to indicate the degree of pleasantness of each event. *Activity level*, *reinforcement potential*, and *obtained reinforcement* scores are derived from the sums of the two scales and their summed crossproduct. The instrument is used in a 30-day retrospective manner and as a day-to-day checklist. Both intrasubject and intersubject correlations with depressed mood have been demonstrated. Although it is a self-report methodology and thus subject to possible cognitive distortion, the specificity of the items suggests that the report may indeed be accurately representative of a broad range of functionally significant behavior. More recently, Lewinsohn and his colleagues have developed an Unpleasant Events Schedule (Lewinsohn & Amenson, 1978) to parallel the Pleasant Events Schedule. Our research program has used an abbreviated version of the Pleasant Events Schedule and our own Unpleasant Events List as a pre- and posttherapy assessment measure.

Activity schedules have their utility in assessing major activity events on a day-to-day basis outside the lab. Other methodologies have attempted to assess more detailed aspects of depressed behavior by direct observation in the lab. Categories of nonverbal behavior, such as eye contact, smiling, arm, leg, and head movements, have been assessed in various studies (e.g., Ranelli & Miller, 1977; Waxer, 1974, 1976; Youngren & Lewinsohn, 1977). In specific studies these measures have differentiated between depressed and nondepressed individuals. Paralinguistic behavior has also assessed, particularly in a series of studies conducted by Peter Lewinsohn and his colleagues (Libet, Lewinsohn, & Javorek, 1973; Youngren & Lewinsohn, 1977). By and large Lewinsohn's research has suggested that measures, which could be described as assessing speech activity level, differentiate between depressed and other individuals. In particular, measures of frequency of speech initiation, speech rate, and speech latencies have differentiated depressed and nondepressed subjects. Certain verbal content measures have also been found to differentiate depressed and nondepressed individuals. McLean, Ogston, and Grauer (1973) collected half-hour tape recordings of discussions between identified depressed patients and their spouses, and counted positive and negative references. Improvement on these measures was found with psychotherapy.

Our research program has employed methods for coding various classes of content (nonverbal, paralinguistic, and verbal) from several different circumstances. We have coded verbal interaction among depressed subjects in group therapy sessions, responses to standard questions from each subject individually in the group sessions, and segments of individual interviews conducted with depressed subjects before and after therapy. It is these methods I want to expand on these methods, in particular, and comment on them later with regard to our therapy outcome studies. In general, we have followed an assessment strategy for thereapy research which measures multiple response dimensions and employes multiple methodologies.

The Self-Control Model of Depression

Before describing the specific therapy studies which we have carried out, I would like to describe the model of depression which we have been using as a framework for our research (Rehm, 1977). The beginnings of this research program go back a few years to a time when I, and several graduate students, became interested in the possibilities of investigating depression from a behavioral orientation. In attempting to review the literature at the time, we looked at clinical accounts of depression, experimental studies, and theoretical accounts. In all instances we were struck by the diversity and pervasiveness of depressive symptomatology. This diversity seems to be reflected in the nature of current models of the disorder. It was our impression that each model tends to identify a particular phenomenon as the core of depression and see the other phenomena as secondary elaborations or epiphenomena. Lewinsohn's (1974) behavioral model suggests that depression arises because of insufficient reinforcement occasioned by either a deficient environment, lack of capacity for reinforcement, or a lack of social skills to obtain reinforcement. A lowered rate of behavior is seen as the primary symptom and cognitive symptoms are perceived as secondary elaborations of the basic dysphoria which results form lowered activity level. Beck (1972, 1974), on the other hand, views cognitive symptoms as primary in depression and, in almost diametric contrast to Lewinsohn, views the overt behavioral symptoms of depression as secondary consequences of distorted cognitions. While Beck's theory focuses on negativity of depressed cognitions, Seligman's model (1974, 1975) focuses on cognitions regarding people's control over their environment. Each of these models appeared to us to offer particular insights into the nature of depression, but seemed almost mutually exclusive in their foci. We felt that there was a need for a larger framework within which to relate these various aspects of depression. It would be desirable to have a model which would allow us to relate these different variables to one another in order to establish a fruitful program of research and therapy.

Such a model, we felt, should also be able to interrelate cognitive and overt behavioral variables via some specified mechanism or process. Given the phenomena of depression as reviewed above, it would also seem necessary for such a model to be able to incorporate three broad sets of variables. First, it should include some form of dealing with input variables, that is, the strategies by which the organism seeks information about the environment by attending to and perceiving events. Secondly, the model should, in some form, incorporate processing or mediation variables, that is, how does the organism process information, make inferences and evaluations, and develop attitudes and beliefs about self and the world? Thirdly, such a model should, in some way, incorporate output variables, that is, ways in which the organism translates attitudes and beliefs into overt behavior through behavior plans, choices, or strategies based on understanding of the environmental contingencies. It has been our perception that Kanfer's behavioral model of self-control (Kanfer, 1970, 1971; Kanfer & Karoly, 1972a,b) provides an example of just such a model.

Kanfer has outlined a three-phase model to account for the ways in which people are able to bridge delays in reinforcement (to resist temptation or to persist toward a goal in the face of adversity). He suggests that under circumstances in which individuals perceive a lack or loss of expected reinforcement, they initiate the three-phase process as a self-regulatory feedback loop functioning to optimize longterm reinforcement. The first phase of the model is self-monitoring whereby individuals attend to their own behavior and its antecedents and consequences as a form of information gathering relevant to instituting behavior change. In the second, or self-evaluation phase of the model, individuals evaluate the obtained information in comparison to an internal standard. In a slight revision of Kanfer's original model, we have suggested that during this phase other inferential processes occur as well. While individuals make inferences about the nature of their performance, they also make inferences about the conditions of that performance. Specifically they make attributions with regard to the causes of their behavior and the outcomes achieved. In our revision of the model, individuals compare more internally-attributed behavior to a standard. According to the model, individuals set standards for positive and/or negative self-evaluation. Behavior which exceeds the positive standard is deemed commendable; behavior which falls short of the negative standard is deemed condemnable. In the third phase of the model, self-reinforcement, the evaluation is translated into an effect on overt behavior. Here Kanfer adopts a reinforcement model as a mechanism for explaining the translation of cognitive evaluation into behavioral self-control. Behavior judged to be commendable is self-rewarded, that is, reinforcement is administered by individuals to themselves, contingent on the positively-evaluated behavior. Similarly behavior can be self-punished.

Thus Kanfer's is an instance of the type of model for which we were looking. The self-monitoring phase of the model accounts for input processes and suggests individual differences in skills in the way in which individuals self-monitor. For example, individuals may selectively attend to different classes of feedback. The self-evaluation phase of the model suggests certain mechanisms of information processing or mediation, and individual differences may exist in the nature of standard-setting or of attributional styles. The self-reinforcement phase of the model attempts to account for output variables where processed information is translated into behavior. In this instance, the hypothesized mechanism is a simple reinforcement process whereby the probability of a response is increased or decreased by self-reinforcement.

The status of this model is somewhat in question in light of the continuing controversy in the literature over self-control concepts, in particular over the idea of self-reinforcement (cf. Catania, 1975; Goldiamond, 1976). While alternative formulations may evolve to account for the manner in which individuals translate evaluation processes into behavior, it is our feeling that the basic three-phase division serves as a utilitarian model not only for describing self-control behavior, but also for accounting for certain forms of psychopathology, depression in particular. There may be individual differences, styles, or skills involved in the manner in which individuals self-control at each of the three phases. Therefore there can be maladaptive styles, deficiencies, or deficits at each of these phases, and these maladaptive styles, deficiencies, or deficits may provide a model for certain forms of psychopathology.

Since we have employed self-control as a model for depression, we have hypothesized that individuals may show different combinations of deficits in each of the three phases (Rehm, 1977). We have proposed six specific deficits to account for the symptomatology of depression. In the self-monitoring phase, we have asserted that individuals who are depressed have a tendency to monitor aversive as opposed to pleasant events in their environments. This assertion has parallels in Beck's concept of selective abstraction and in Ferster's (1973) argument that depressed individuals expend excessive effort in avoiding punishment as opposed to seeking reward. Selective attention to aversive events can be assessed in three ways: (1) distribution of time in attending to aversive as opposed to positive events (Roth & Rehm, 1978); (2) accuracy in monitoring aversive versus positive events associated with one's own behavior (e.g., Roth & Rehm, 1978); and (3) memory for aversive versus positive events (e.g., Buchwald, 1977; DeMonbreun & Craighead, 1977; Nelson & Craighead, 1977; Wener & Rehm, 1975).

The second hypothesized deficit is a tendency to monitor the immediate as opposed to the delayed effects of their behavior. In general, the model predicts that depressed persons would have difficulty in behavior which would be controlled by delayed reinforcement only. The model suggests that the behavior of depressed persons would be virtually identical to normals under conditions of immediate control by environmental events. The model, therefore, predicts that the first behaviors which would show a decrease in frequency or rate in depression would be those which were formerly under the control of delayed reinforcers. Only as depression becomes much more severe, and perhaps clinically significant, would deficiencies begin to be evident in behaviors which are ordinarily under more immediate control. Ferster (1973) argues that much behavior which seems to be under immediate control is in fact organized in a hierarchial fashion under some longterm goal. Generally this deficiency in response to delayed reinforcement is a consequence of poor self-control skills. Although we have proposed that this tendency is related to a self-monitoring deficit, empirical evidence here is virtually nonexistent (cf. Rehm & Plakosh, 1975).

The third deficit proposed in depression occurs in the self-evaluation phase. Depressed individuals are assumed to have a tendency to set stringent self-evaluative criteria; they recognize few successes and many failure. Clinically, depressed persons are seen as being perfectionistic and sensitive to failure and criticism.

The fourth deficit proposed by the model concerns the self-attributional behavior of depressed persons. Depressed persons make attributions of causality which reduce or minimize positive self-evaluation. They make attributions which are consistent with negative expectations about themselves and the world. Specifically, depressed persons tend to attribute success to external, unstable, and specific factors, and they tend to attribute failure to internal, stable, and general factors. They may also overgeneralize failure experiences. In this regard, our model is consistent with Seligman's recent revision of his learned helplessness model (cf. Abramson, Seligman, & Teasdale, 1978). We differ from that model in the extent to which we see perceptions of controllability as necessarily the core of depression. In our model self-attribution acts as a moderator variable on the self-evaluation process. Internally attributed success or failure is given a greater weight than externally attributed success or failure.

The fifth and sixth deficits in depression asserted by the self-control model occur in the self-reinforcement phase. Depressed persons tend to engage in low rates of self-reward and high rates of self-punishment. Self-reward and self-punishment supplement externals reinforcement in determining rates of behavior in normal and depressed individuals. Self-reward and self-punishment have been found to be relatively independent of one another (Kanfer, Duerfeldt, & LePage, 1969). Research evidence consistent with these postulated deficits has been obtained by Rozensky, Rehm, Pry, and Roth (1977) and by Roth, Rehm, and Rozensky (1978).

In our view, the model accounts for the symptomatology of depression. From the self-control framework, the symptoms of depression are seen as reflecting deficits or maladaptive styles at various phases of self-control. That is, the perceptual distortions and pessimism of depression reflect deficits in self-monitoring, the low self-esteem and helplessness reflect self-evaluation and self-attribution deficits, and the decreased rates of adaptive behavior reflect the consequences of low rates of self-reward and high rates of self-punishment.

The model is seen as integrating mechanisms identified by other models. For instance, some of Beck's (1972) ideas concerning cognitive distortion and Seligman's (1975) ideas regarding self-attributions and helplessness fit well into this framework. The model is seen as supplementing Lewinsohn's model in that it suggests deficits in self-reinforcement as equivalent, or as supplemental, to deficits in external sources of reinforcement. The model provides a basis for interrelating the symptoms and concepts of depression. Even though it assumes that individuals may manifest different combinations of self-control deficits, and thus display different combinations of depression symptoms, there is an underlying relationship between the phases of the model and thus between deficits in depression. For example, the model would suggest that negative self-monitoring would be likely to produce negative self-evaluations regardless of standard setting. Stringent self-evaluative criteria would produce low rates of self-reward and high rates of punishment, regardless of usual habits with respect to magnitude or frequency of self-reward of self-punishment. Thus, different specific deficits could lead to the same resulting reductions in overt behavior.

In that the deficits are somewhat independent, the model also provides a framework for assessing the effects of various etiological factors on specific deficits. That is, the model would suggest that each deficit might have its own etiology. Factors, such as experience with noncontingent aversive stimulation, might effect self-attributional style and might or might not have an additional affect on self-monitoring behavior. Stringency of criterion setting might be influenced primarily by early modeling experiences. The model thus has the potential for integrating information about a variety of etiological factors in depression. The model provides a framework for research on depressive psychopathology, and in addition, we have used it as a framework for devising a depression psychotherapy program.

Therapy Program

The therapy program which we have devised using this model as an outline has been assessed in three outcome studies. To date approximately 80 depressed women have received some form of the self-control therapy program in our clinic. A fourth study is presently underway involving another 33 subjects. The self-control therapy techniques have been structured as a therapy package or program. The program is administered in a group format with groups normally numbering from 6 to 8 persons. It is relatively structured and involves presentation and discussion of self-control concepts of depression. It is didactic in that elements of the program aim at modifying the subjects' understanding of the nature of their behavior. There are discussions and exercises to assure that the concepts are acquired, and behavioral homework assignments instigate change in behavioral performance based on the self-control principles. Thus the aim of the program is both cognitive and overt-behavior change. In the three studies we have completed, the program is presented in 6 or 7 1½-h group sessions, weekly.

While there have been some revisions and additions as the research program has progressed, the basic order of presentation has been essentially as follows. Successive two week phases of the program emphasize training in each of the phases of self-control (i.e., self-monitoring, self-evaluation, and self-reinforcement, respectively). In the first session, subjects are given a general overview of the program and are introduced to two concepts: (1) that mood is a function of behavior; and (2) that depressed persons may monitor negative, unpleasant, or aversive behavior excessively. After discussing the relevance and application of these principles to the presenting problems of each individual in the group, homework assignments are made. Subjects are given positive activity self-monitoring logs. Positive activities are defined as behaviors which are rewarding in themselves or which may produce reward in the long run. To facilitate the monitoring, subjects are given a Positive Activities List to be used as a checklist or guide in learning to recognize these events. The list consists of 25 classes of positive activities (e.g., "playing a sport or game," or "discussing an interesting or amusing topic"). Subjects record a one-line description of each of their day's positive activities on the logs and indicate the item on the Positive Activities List which corresponds most closely to that activity. In addition, subjects are asked to rate their mood each day on an 11-point scale from zero ("worst or most miserable day ever") to 10 ("best day ever").

Session II, and all subsequent sessions, begins, with a check-in procedure in which clients' homework assignments are reviewed and problems and successes are discussed. In the second session, subjects are guided through a paper-and-pencil exercise in which they graph their week's daily activity and mood ratings. This exercise is used to reinforce the concept of the relationship between mood and activity. Discussion focuses on reactions to monitoring positive activities as a way of validating the tendency in depression to monitor negatively. During the session subjects are also given an exercise aimed at helping them discriminate between the immediate and delayed positive and negative effects of any given behavior. The homework assignments for the coming week are to continue these same self-monitoring logs with the addition of an assignment to record the positive delayed effects of their positive activities for one week only.

Session III introduces the self-evaluation procedure with the presentation of a rationale stressing the importance of realistic goal-setting. Subjects are asked to select a class of behaviors from their monitoring records which they feel they would like to increase. They are given a worksheet and guided by the therapist in defining goals in behavioral terms. They are instructed that their goals should be stated in a positive manner and should be operationally defined. An example of such a goal would be: "increasing social interactions with neighbors." Each goal is further broken down into a series of operationally-defined subgoals (e.g., "call a neighbor and invite her over for coffee"). The homework assignment is to continue self-monitoring all positive activities with particular emphasis on those which were defined as subgoals.

Session IV begins with a review and revision of the goal setting worksheets. Also a self-attribution exercise is introduced where subjects are taught to identify their attributions with regard to recent instances of success and failure. The rationality of their attributions is questioned and they are encouraged to consider less helpless styles of attribution.

In Session V, the rationale and principles of self-reinforcement are presented and subjects are helped to construct self-managed programs to reinforce their subgoal activities. Subjects fill out "Reinforcement Menus" consisting of easily self-administered positive activities. Point values are assigned to these rewards and to subgoal activites. A point system is thus established by which subjects earn points for working on their goals and cash them in for self-reinforcement menu items.

In Session VI, the self-reinforcement assignment and principles are reviewed and adjustments are made in the point system. Another self-reinforcement exercise is introduced in this session in which subjects develop a list of positive self-statements which they are then to read following the accomplishment of each subgoal behavior during the following week.

The seventh session consists of a general review of the program. Subjects are encouraged to continue using the self-control procedures and extra copies of self-monitoring logs and other forms are handed out.

Subjects in all of our studies have been depressed women, recruited through announcements in the news media. We chose to work with female subjects for two reasons: (1) data suggests greater incidence of depression among women in the population; and (2) to expedite research by having more homogeneous therapy groups. Recruiting announcements made it clear that subjects were being offered therapy for depression under the auspices of a research program and were subject to a three-step screening process. First, subjects were screened on the phone to confirm that they were not presently in any other form of treatment, and to assure that they understood the nature of the program and its requirements. Secondly, subjects came in for a session of psychometric assessment at which time they signed an informed consent form and filled out a battery of self-report instruments. Subjects with Minnesota Multi-Phasic Personality Inventory (MMPI) depression scores greater than 70 who met other MMPI criteria aimed at excluding subjects whose problem was primarily anxiety rather than depression, were invited to a second screening session in which they were individually interviewed. In the first two studies, this interview was relatively informal and was aimed at clarifying depressive symptomatology and excluding psychosis or immediate suicidal crises. In all instances, subjects who did not meet the criteria were aided in finding appropriate referral resources. In our most recent studies we have used a more structured interview to assure that subjects met Research Diagnostic Criteria for Major Affective Disorder (Spitzer *et al.*, 1978). The interview, an abbreviated form of the SADS (Endicott & Spitzer, 1977) also excluded subjects who evidenced bipolar depression or who fell into a number of other diagnostic categories including anxiety reaction, schizophrenia, alcoholism, Briquet's snydrome, and others. Thus, although the subjects were analog subjects in the sense of being recruited volunteers, they were clearly of clinical severity, and met clinical depression criteria. The mean depression score for subjects in these studies has been well over 80 *T* scores on the MMPI-D and above 20 on the Beck Depression Inventory. Both means suggest a moderate to severe range of depression. Subjects have ranged in age from 18 to 60, with a mean in the early 30s. A wide range of socioeconomic classes and living situations have been represented.

Therapy Research

I would like to present the design and a general summary of the results of each of our first three studies. Then I will go back and discuss more specifically the types of assessment measures that we have employed, and their success, or lack of success, in detecting depression and its change. In the first study, a dissertation by Carilyn Fuchs (Fuchs & Fehm, 1977), our earliest version of the self-control package was compared to a nonspecific group therapy program and a waiting list control. Two therapists each saw one self-control and one nonspecific therapy group. In general the results of this study indicate that the self-control program was significantly more effective than either the nonspecific therapy program or waiting list. Nonspecific therapy was better than the waiting list condition on most measures. Significant differences were found on self-report measures of depression and on certain measures of overt activity level. Differences were also reflected on some experimental measures of self-control behavior, all of which were self-report in format.

There have been suggestions in the literature that depressed persons suffer from deficiencies in social skills and in particular, assertiveness skills. In the second study (Rehm, Fuchs, Roth, Kornblith, & Romano, 1978) the self-control program was compared to a behavioral social skills training program. Male–female pairs of therapists each saw one group in each condition. In general, results of this study indicated that the social skills subjects improved more in measures of social skills, the self-control subjects improved more on measures of self-control, and in addition the self-control subjects improved more than the social skills subjects on measures of depression. In fact the self-control subjects improved to a degree comparable to the self-control subjects in the first study, whereas the social skills subjects, improved to a degree comparable to the nonspecific therapy subjects in the first study. We concluded from the study that, whereas certain depressed subjects may lack social skills, self-control therapy seems to be a better overall strategy for ameliorating depressive deficits.

Our third study (Rehm, Kornblith, O'Hara, Lamparski, Romano, & Volkin, 1978) was an attempt to begin a disassembly strategy. That is, we attempted to compared conditions which eliminated various aspects of the program in an attempt to identify the contribution of the different program elements. There were five conditions in this study. A waiting list condition was compared to a self-montioring only condition, a self-monitoring plus self-evaluation condition, a self-monitoring plus self-reinforcement condition, and a full package including self-monitoring, self-evaluation and self-reinforcement. Two therapists saw one group in each of the four conditions. The results of this study have been quite puzzling to us. In general, we found that any one of the therapy conditions was more effective than the waiting list, but there were no clear-cut patterns of differences between the experimental conditions. The degree of therapy effectiveness was less in this study than in the two previous studies. I will discuss the implications we have drawn from this outcome at the end of this paper.

I would like to turn to a more detailed discussion of the specific kinds of measures that we have used in these three studies. First let me comment on the self-report instruments that we have used. Our primary measures of depression consistently have been the MMPI-D scale and the Beck Depression Inventory. These have clearly differentiated the self-control program from control conditions. In the first two studies, the self-control program was significantly more effective than any of the other conditions. In addition it is notable that when pre- and posttherapy scores were categorized simply into depressed range versus normal range, significant changes and significant differences were still obtained (i.e., subjects changed to a clinically significant degree). In the third study, the degree of change was not as great as in the first two. The experimental groups were significantly better than the waiting list on the Beck Depression Inventory but not on the MMPI-D at posttest. Overall we conclude that we have been dealing with a clinically significant degree of depression and, in general, have been fairly effective in ameliorating at least the subjective manifestation of depression.

Mention should also be made of the fact that we have been attempting to assess model-specific self-control behaviors in these studies. A self-control questionnaire which we have been developing has shown significantly greater improvement for self-control subjects in all three studies. This made it a particularly interesting contrast in the second study where taped situation test behavioral measures of assertion yielded greater improvement for the social skills subjects. Thus both therapies were validated by model-specific assessment measures.

Clinician rating methods were employed only in the third study where we had an extensive interview on which to base the ratings. Pre- and posttherapy interviews were conducted by master's-level interviewers who were trained in the use of the Hamilton and Raskin scales plus a Global Assessment of Severity scale. In addition to the interviewers, videotapes of interviews, which were edited to conceal whether they were pre- or posttests, were viewed by doctoral-level psychologists who made independent Hamilton, Raskin, and Global Assessment of Severity ratings. On all three scales, the interviewers found greater improvement in all experimental subjects than in waiting-list subjects. While the clinicians' ratings were highly correlated and in the same direction, they did not reach statistical significance. The interviewers were not entirely blind as to subject condition, that is, it was obvious which subjects were waiting-list subjects. They may have unconsciously biased their ratings in favor of the experimental groups. It should be noted that both interviewers and clinician raters clearly differentiated depressed subjects from a group of normal subjects, and their ratings were quite reliable and correlated fairly well with other measures of depression.

As a first approximation to assessing overt behavior of our subjects, Pleasant Events Schedules were administered at pre- and posttest. The Pleasant Events Schedules in general have shown greater improvement for the self-control condition across studies. The activity level measures showed greater improvement for the self-control condition in the first and second studies, whereas the reinforcement potential measure was significant in the third study. The Unpleasant Events List administered only in the third study did not produce any significant differences.

Observational measures of depression have varied across the three studies. In the first study, we used a simple measure of group activity level. Videotapes of a leaderless ten minute segment of the first and last therapy sessions were analyzed for verbal activity level (number of contributions by each person) and for response elicitation (number of persons who responded to or spoke after each subject). Self-control subjects increased more in activity level after therapy than did nonspecific therapy subjects.

In the second study, we videotaped a segment of the first and last therapy sessions during which subjects were asked to say something about themselves and their moods over the last few weeks. Eight measures of either nonverbal behavior (eye contact), paralinguistic behavior (speech duration, loudness rating, expressivity rating), and verbal content (positive self-references, positive other-references, negative self-references, negative other-references) plus an overall depression rating were scored for each person from the videotapes. Three measures significantly differentiated improvement of self-control versus social skills subjects at posttest. Social skills subjects improved more in terms of decreases in negative self-references and negative references to others (both verbal content measures), and showed greater improvement on a global rating of depression.

In our third study, we used videotapes of our pre- and posttherapy interviews as the source of a behavior sample. Our rationale was that the interview has traditionally been a source for behavioral observations. Clinicians have made observations of nonverbal and paralinguistic behavior in an unsystematic way for years and have used these observations as a partial basis for making diagnostic differentiations. Therefore, it seemed a logical and important situation within which to develop systematic and objective behavioral observations.

We expanded our coding system in this study drawing as we had in the past from clinical and experimental literature descriptive of the overt behavior of depressed persons. We scored five categories of nonverbal behavior: (1) head movements; (2) body movements; (3) arm movements; (4) smiles; and (5) duration of gaze (eye contact). We scored six categories of paralinguistic behavior: (1) loudness rating; (2) expressivity rating; (3) average log latency of response to the first five questions; (4) duration of speech during the first five minutes of the interview; (5) word count; and (6) speech rate.

As a test of the validity of our measures we also videotaped fifteen normal women in the same structured interview. Pretherapy, posttherapy, and normal subject tapes were given code numbers and randomly mixed for rating by teams of undergraduate raters. Three raters coded each behavior and reliabilities were very good.

None of these behavioral observation measures significantly differentiated among experimental conditions in analyses of covariance of posttherapy scores with pretherapy scores as covariate. This included comparisons of all therapy conditions versus the waiting-list control. This result was cast in a new light, however, when we compared pretherapy tapes of our depressed subjects to the tapes of our normal subjects. Only two measures, loudness ratings and frequency of smiles, significantly differentiated these two groups. Depressed subjects were quieter and smiled less often. Two other measures approached statistical significance, expressivity and duration of gaze. Depressed subjects tended to be rated as less expressive and established less eye contact. Thus it appears that most of the behaviors which we observed were not really measuring dimensions on which depressed persons deviate from normal, at least, not in this context.

By way of concluding, I would like to make some comments on behavioral assessment of depression and on therapy with this disorder. The development of methods for the assessment of the overt-motor aspects of depression is important not only to therapy outcome research but to our understanding of depressive psychopathology in general. In our research program, we have made several attempts to assess depressive behavior in different contexts. Some of the dimensions we have assessed have covaried with other standard measures of depression. Many others have not. Significant differences between depressed and nondepressed groups seem few and far between when their behavior is observed in the laboratory. Lewinsohn's (Libet *et al.*, 1973; Youngren & Lewinsohn, 1977) pioneering work on observational measures of depression has similarly found relatively few differences. Given the clinical importance attributed to the concept of psychomotor retardation in depression, it is puzzling why detecting differences is so difficult. There are several possible solutions to this puzzle. First, it may be that we have not as yet identified the relevant dimension. Perhaps psychomotor retardation is not best assessed by measuring speech rate or duration. Perhaps, instead, we should be assessing specific, functionally important behaviors like question-asking or initiating conversations, which may be important in a given individual's interpersonal relationships. A second possibility is that we are missing important differences by failing to discriminate between individuals who deviate from the norm in opposite directions. For instance, we may need to separate agitated depressions and look at their activity level differently. The third possibility is that situational factors are obscuring our attempts at assessment. Libet *et al.* (1973) found differences in depressive behavior between group therapy and home situations. One hypothesis generated by the self-control model is that deficits in overt behavior associated with depression would be found only in those situations in which immediate external control is minimized.

Thus, perhaps the interview dyad, although it has traditionally been the basis for clinical behavioral observations, is a poor situation for attempting to detect behavioral deficits in depression because, in a dyad, the social cues from the interviewer elicit verbal behavior at a fairly controlled rate. Perhaps group situations, where the contribution of each individual member is less directly cued, would be better. Certainly, the best assessment situation would be one in which external demands were entirely minimized.

Let me end on a more optimistic note by saying that at this point depression appears to be clearly amenable to treatment by methods which combine cognitive and behavioral methods. Our self-control program has been shown to be effective in three studies even though in the third study the effective components were not clearly identified and the magnitude of the effect was less. The self-control program has been demonstrated to be effective in terms of self-report measures and on some measures of overt behavior. Other studies have also used self-control procedures in various ways in treating depression. Hilford (1975) has reported some success using a simple self-control program with depressed inpatients. Jackson (1972) reported a case study in which a self-control program was devised for a depressed woman, and a number of other published case studies have used self-control techniques (Johnson, 1971; Mahoney, 1971; Todd, 1972; Vasta, 1976; Tharp, Watson, & Kaya, 1974). Recent studies by Aaron T. Beck and his colleagues and others have shown his cognitive-behavior therapy methods to be effective in several different depressed populations (Rush, Beck, Kovacs, & Hollon, 1977; Rush, Khatami, & Beck, 1975; Shaw, 1977; Taylor & Marshall, 1977). While the effective elements of these therapies have not been isolated, the combination of cognitive and behavioral strategies together appears to be important in dealing with the spectrum of symptoms which comprise depression. The effectiveness of the overall methods has been fairly well established, and now we need to develop a better understanding of the specific mechanisms which produce the effect. Further refinements in the assessment of depression, particularly of its overt behavioral aspects, will contribute to this research process.

References

Abramson, L. Y., Seligman, M. E. P., & Teasdale, J. D. Learned helplessness in humans: Critique and reformulation. *Journal of Abnormal Psychology*, 1978, *87*, 32–48.

Beck, A. T. *Depression: causes and treatment*. Philadelphia: University of Pennsylvania Press, 1972.

Beck, A. T. The development of depression: A cognitive model. In R. M. Friedman & M. M. Katz (Eds.), *The psychology of depression: Contemporary theory and research*. New York: Wiley, 1974.

Beck, A. T., Ward, C. H., Mendelsohn, M., Mock, J., & Erbaugh, J. An inventory for measuring depression. *Archives of General Psychiatry*, 1961, *4*, 561–571.

Buchwald, A. M. Depressive mood and estimates of reinforcement frequency. *Journal of Abnormal Psychology*, 1977, *86*, 443–446.

Catania, A. C. The myth of self-reinforcement. *Behaviorism*, 1975, *3*, 192–199.

Costello, C. G. A critical review of Seligman's laboratory experiments on learned helplessness and depression in humans. *Journal of Abnormal Psychology*, 1978, *87*, 21–31.

DeMonbreun, B. G., & Craighead, W. E. Distortion of perception and recall of positive and neutral feedback in depression. Cognitive Therapy and Research, 1977, *1*, 311–329.

Endicott, J., & Spitzer, R. L. *A diagnostic interview: The Schedule for Affective Disorders and Schizophrenia*. Paper presented at the annual meeting of the American Psychiatric Association, Toronto, May 1977.

Ferster, C. B. A functional analysis of depression. *American Psychologist*, 1973, *28*, 857–870.

Fuchs, C. Z., & Rehm, L. P. A self-control behavior therapy program for depression. *Journal of Consulting and Clinical Psychology*, 1977, *45*, 206–215.

Goldiamond, I. Self-reinforcement. *Journal of Applied Behavior Analysis*, 1976, *9*, 509–514.

Hamilton, M. A rating scale for depression. *Journal of Neurology, Neurosurgery and Psychiatry*, 1960, *23*, 56–61.

Hilford, N. G. Self initiated behavior change by depressed women following verbal behavior therapy. *Behavior Therapy*, 1975, *6*, 703.

Jackson, B. Treatment of depression by self-reinforcement. *Behavior Therapy*, 1972, *3*, 298–307.

Johnson, W. G. Some applications of Homme's coverant control therapy: Two case reports. *Behavior Therapy*, 1971, *2*, 240–248.

Kanfer, F. H. Self-monitoring: Methodological limitations and clinical applications. *Journal of Consulting and Clinical Psychology*, 1970, *35*, 148–152.

Kanfer, F. H. The maintenance of behavior by self-generated stimuli and reinforcement. In A. Jacobs & L. B. Sachs (Eds.), *The psychology of private events: Perspectives on covert response systems*. New York: Academic, 1971.

Kupfer, D. J., & Foster, F. G. Interval between onset of sleep and rapid eye movement sleep as an indicator of depression. *Lancet*, 1972, *2*, 684–686.

Kanfer, F. H., & Karoly, P. Self-control: A behavioristic excursion into the lion's den. *Behavior Therapy*, 1972, *2*, 398–416. a

Kanfer, F. H., & Karoly, P. Self-regulation and its clinical application: Some additional conceptualizations. In R. C. Johnson, P. R. Dokecki, & O. H. Mowrer (Eds.), *Socialization: Development of character and conscience*. New York: Holt, Rinehart & Winston, 1972. b

Kanfer, F. H., Duerfeldt, P. H., & LePage, A. L. Stability of patterns of self-reinforcement. *Psychological Reports*, 1969, *24*, 663–670.

Kupfer, D. J., Weiss, B. L., Foster, F. G., Detre, T. P., Delgado, J., & McPartland, R. Psychomotor activity in affective states. *Archives of General Psychiatry*, 1974, *30*, 765–768.

Levitt, E. E., & Lubin, B. *Depression: Concepts, controversies and some new facts*. New York: Springer, 1975.

Lewinsohn, P. M. A behavioral approach to depression. In R. M. Friedman & M. M. Katz (Eds.), *The psychology of depression: Contemporary theory and research*. New York: Wiley, 1974.

Libet, J., Lewinsohn, P. M., & Javorek, F. *The construct of social skill: An empirical study of several measures on temporal stability, internal structure, validity, and situational generalizability.* Unpublished manuscript, University of Oregon, 1973.

MacPhillamy, D., & Lewinsohn, P. M. *The Pleasant Events Schedule.* Unpublished manuscript, University of Oregon, 1971.

Mahoney, M. J. The self-management of covert behavior: A case study. *Behavior Therapy,* 1971, *2,* 575–578.

McLean, P. D., Ogston, K., & Grauer, L. A behavioral approach to the treatment of depression. *Journal of Behavior Therapy and Experimental Psychiatry,* 1973, *4,* 323–330.

Nathan, P. E., Robertson, P., & Andberg, M. M. A systems analytic model of diagnosis: IV. The diagnostic validity of abnormal affective behavior. *Journal of Clinical Psychology,* 1969, *25,* 235–242.

Lewinsohn, P. M., & Amenson, C. S. Some relationships between pleasant and unpleasant mood-related events and depression. *Journal of Abnormal Psychology,* 1978, *87,* 644–654.

Nelson, R. E., & Craighead, W. E. Selective recall of positive and negative feedback, self-control behaviors, and depression. *Journal of Abnormal Psychology,* 1977, *86,* 379–388.

O'Hara, M. W., & Rehm, L. P. Self-monitoring, activity levels and mood in the development and maintenance of depression. *Journal of Abnormal Psychology,* 1979, *88,* 450–453.

Ranelli, C. J., & Miller, R. E. *Nonverbal communication in clinical depression.* Paper presented at the meeting of the Eastern Psychological Association, Boston, April 1977.

Raskin, A., Schulterbrandt, J., Reatig, N., & Rice, C. E. Factors of psychopathology in interview, ward behavior, and self-report ratings of hospitalized depressives. *Journal of Consulting Psychology,* 1967, *31,* 270–278.

Rehm, L. P. Assessment of depression. In M. Hersen & A. S. Bellack (Eds.), *Behavioral assessment: A practical handbook.* Oxford: Pergamon, 1976.

Rehm, L. P. A self-control model of depression. *Behavior Therapy,* 1977, *8,* 787–804.

Rehm, L. P., & Plakosh, P. Preference for immediate reinforcement in depression. *Journal of Behavior Therapy and Experimental Psychiatry,* 1975, *6,* 101–103.

Rehm, L. P., Fuchs, C. Z., Roth, D. M., Kornblith, S. J., & Romano, J. A comparison of self-control and social skill treatments of depression. *Behavior Therapy,* 1979, *10,* 429–442.

Rehm, L. P., Kornblith, S. J., O'Hara, M. W., Lamparski, D., Romano, J. M., & Volkin, J. *An evaluation of major elements in a self-control therapy program for depression.* Paper presented at the annual meeting of the Association for the Advancement of Behavior Therapy, Chicago, November 1978.

Roth, D. R., & Rehm, L. P. *Relationships between selective attention, selective memory and depression.* Manuscript submitted for publication, 1978.

Roth, D., Rehm, L. P., & Rozensky, R. A. *Self-reward, self-punishment and depression.* Manuscript submitted for publication, 1978.

Rozensky, R. A., Rehm, L. P., Pry, G., & Roth, D. Depression and self-reinforcement behavior in hospitalized patients. *Journal of Behavior Therapy and Experimental Psychiatry,* 1977, *8,* 35–38.

Rush, A. J., Khatami, M., & Beck, A. T. Cognitive and behavior therapy in chronic depression. *Behavior Therapy,* 1975, *6,* 398–404.

Rush, A. J., Beck, A. T., Kovacs, M., & Hollon, S. Comparative efficacy of cognitive therapy and pharmacotherapy in the treatment of depressed outpatients. *Cognitive Therapy and Research,* 1977, *1,* 17–38.

Schwartz, G. E., Fair, P. L., Salt, P., Mandel, M. R., & Klerman, G. L. Facial muscle patterning to affective imagery in depressed and nondepressed subjects. *Science,* 1976, *192,* 489–491.

Seligman, M. E. P. Depression and learned helplessness. In R. J. Friedman & M. M. Katz (Eds.), *The psychology of depression: Contemporary theory and research*. New York: Winston-Wiley, 1974.

Seligman, M. E. P. *Helplessness: On depression, development and death*. San Francisco: Freeman, 1975.

Shaw, B. F. Comparison of cognitive therapy and behavior therapy in the treatment of depression. *Journal of Consulting and Clinical Psychology*, 1977, *45*, 543–551.

Spitzer, R. L., Endicott, J., & Robins, E. Research diagnostic criteria: Rationale and reliability. *Archives of General Psychiatry*, 1978, *36*, 773–782.

Taylor, F. G., & Marshall, W. L. Experimental analysis of a cognitive-behavioral therapy for depression. *Cognitive Therapy and Research*, 1977, *1*, 59–72.

Tharp, R. G., Watson, D. L., & Kaya, J. Self-modification of depression. *Journal of Consulting and Clinical Psychology*, 1974, *42*, 624.

Todd, F. T. Coverant control of self-evaluative responses in the treatment of depression: A new use for an old principle. *Behavior Therapy*, 1972, *3*, 91–94.

Vasta, R. Coverant control of self-evaluations through temporal cueing. *Journal of Behavior Therapy and Experimental Psychiatry*, 1976, *7*, 35–38.

Waxer, P. Nonverbal cues for depression. *Journal of Abnormal Psychology*, 1974, *83*, 319–322.

Waxer, P. Nonverbal cues for depth of depression: Set versus no set. *Journal of Consulting and Clinical Psychology*, 1976, *44*, 493.

Wener, A. E., & Rehm, L. P. Depressive affect: A test of behavioral hypotheses. *Journal of Abnormal Psychology*, 1975, *84*, 221–227.

Williams, J. G., Barlow, D. H., & Agras, W. S. Behavioral measurement of severe depression. *Archives of General Psychiatry*, 1972, *27*, 330–333.

Winokur, G. The types of affective disorders. *Journal of Nervous and Mental Disease*, 1973, *156*, 82–96.

Youngren, A. A., & Lewinsohn, P. M. *The functional relationship between depression and problematic interpersonal behavior*. Unpublished manuscript, University of Oregon, 1977.

CHAPTER 6

Consequences of Increasing the Functional Impact of Internal Emotional Stimuli

T. D. Borkovec

Department of Psychology
The Pennsylvania State University
University Park, Pennsylvania

and

J. B. Grayson

Department of Psychology
University of Iowa
Iowa City, Iowa

Traditional clinical psychology has long emphasized the importance of assisting clients with emotional problems to "get in touch with their feelings" in an effort to resolve these problems. Classic learning theory applications to clinical phenomena have viewed such a process as far less relevant to the therapeutic endeavor, relative to an emphasis on changing environment–response relationships. Recent research suggests, however, that the learning position has perhaps disregarded some fundamentally important dimensions of emotional behavior which are quite deducible from learning theory on the one hand, and yet, may be analogous to some of the outcomes, if not the goals or methods, of the traditional approaches. Specifically, internal stimuli (cognitive and physiological) are very much a part of the functional environment of the individual and probably represent fundamental units of the feeling states of concern to traditional therapy. As response-produced cues, they may provide some of the most important stimuli entering into relationships with emotional responses and, consequently, represent critical variables for the modification of emotional disorders. Certainly the emergence of cognitive behavior modification (e.g., Meichenbaum, 1974) rests upon such a position and has heralded an increased attention to the critical role of cognition in mediating maladjustment and modification within the field of behavior change research.

The present chapter will describe our recent research on two classes of internal stimuli which appear to be importantly involved in the maintenance and modification of anxiety: imagery and physiological responses. Even though we originally had very different purposes in conducting the various studies to be described, in retrospect, a common theme emerged from their respective outcomes. Manipulations which increase or decrease the individual's awareness of ongoing internal processes have significant consequences for modification of the emotional behaviors related to those processes. Although this statement seems intuitively obvious, we do not think behavior therapy researchers have paid close enough attention to its implications. It must be remembered that, even in a classic learning context, objective presentation of stimuli does not guarantee functional exposure to those stimuli. Thus, if exposure to imaginal stimuli is crucial to desensitization or flooding therapy or if awareness of physiological responses is crucial to relaxation or biofeedback procedures, then events which interfere with or facilitate the subject's awareness and/or processing of that information will critically influence the effect of those procedures on the targeted emotional behavior.

This chapter will describe two research programs: (1) the influence of expectancy and relaxation on the extinction of fear responses to imaginal phobic stimuli; and (2) the influence of relaxation on diffuse, general tension. Each section will begin with a description of our original reason for investigating the particular manipulation. In each case, we will conclude that the effects of the manipulations may be mediated by increases or decreases in functional exposure to the internal stimuli and that therapeutic or contratherapeutic consequences of such variation in degree of exposure depend upon the nature of those internal stimuli and their role in mediating the problem behavior.

Increasing Functional Exposure to Phobic Imagery via Expectancy and Relaxation

The concept of client expectation of improvement has had a stormy history in the literature. Correlational research by Goldstein and others (e.g., Goldstein, 1960; Goldstein & Shipman, 1961; Piper & Wogan, 1970) in the 1960s suggested a relationship between expectancy and outcome, while demonstrations of the power of placebo effects in medicine and clinical psychology (Frank, 1961; Shapiro, 1971) argued convincingly for the causative role of therapeutic expectation in the behavior change process. Yet, experimental manipulations of expectancy in the context of behavior therapy outcome investigations during the late 1960s and early 1970s have produced equivocal outcomes (Lick & Bootzin, 1975). Based on this literature, our own earlier conclusions were that demand characteristics, inherent in the instructional manipulation of expectancy, more parsimoniously explain the occurrence of an "expectancy" effect on therapeutic outcome and that, in agreement with demand research (e.g., Bernstein, 1973), such effects were limited to very mild anxiety problems (Borkovec, 1973). To date, no adequate demonstration of the causative role of expectancy in behavioral change has been reported, and some writers even question the heuristic value or logical possibility of pursuing the construct (e.g., Wilkins, 1973). We are still faced, however, with periodic reports of dramatic "placebo" effects exemplified, for example, by faith healing and the frequent documentation of significant, though less dramatic, effects among placebo conditions in clinical outcome studies. Such reports suggest the potential value of continuing the attempt to demonstrate unambiguously an expectancy effect independent of demand and to isolate the mechanisms of such an effect. Successful completion of such a program would result in replacing the terms *placebo* and *expectancy* with specific laws of behavior, instead of relegating those constructs to the realm of "nonspecific factors."

The first two studies described below involved a typical expectancy manipulation (presence or absence of therapeutic instructions) superimposed on repeated exposures to imaginal fear stimuli. The reason for including that variable was to test our earlier hypothesis that if expectancy simply involves demand characteristics (i.e., discriminative stimuli for display of nonfearful behavior regardless of level of experienced fear), then an expectancy manipulation would have no effect on a target behavior involving a strongly elicited physiological component of fear (Borkovec, 1973). It was assumed that reduction in the physiological fear component was a prerequisite to the secondary influence of other external manipulations such as demand, reinforcement incentives, etc. If expectancy does have an influence independent of demand, that influence must somehow directly contribute to the reduction of the physiological fear component. This hypothesis stemmed from research on two different target behaviors. Mildly fearful snake phobics have been found to be markedly influenced by demand and to display little physiological reaction in response to snake exposure. Social phobics on the other hand are relatively uninfluenced by demand and show large increases in physiological activity during social interactions

(Borkovec, Stone, O'Brien, & Kaloupek, 1974). While speech anxiety has also been characterized by high levels of physiological activity (Borkovec, Wall, & Stone, 1974; Singerman, Borkovec, & Baron, 1976), the effects of demand on this target had not yet been assessed in a pre-posttest design. Since both of the experiments below involved treatment of speech anxiety, the opportunity was thus available to examine the demand effects inherent in the expectancy manipulation on this target. In addition to this primarily methodological concern, we maintained a hope that expectancy might be found to interact with therapy and provide a basis for identifying its potential role, independent of demand, in the therapeutic process.

The first experiment (Grayson & Borkovec, 1978) assessed the subjective and physiological effects of repeated exposure to phobic scenes. Between pre- and posttest public speaking tasks, speech phobic subjects imagined fear scenes under one of three imagery conditions and under either positive or neutral expectancy conditions. All subjects visualized the same phobic scenes for 20-second durations, but the three imagery conditions differed in terms of whether the subjects then visualized responding to the depicted situations with competence, excessive anxiety, or avoidance during the subsequent 20 seconds. Three phobic scenes and their response elaborations were each presented three consecutive times.

The effects of response elaboration conditions during the treatment process, the central concern of this investigation, were quite limited. Subjects imagining competent performance showed significantly greater reductions in subjective fear across scenes and over repetitions of each scene relative to the anxious and avoidance imagery groups. However, imagery condition had no effect on heart rate during the visualization treatment.

The interesting outcome of this study came from the effects of expectancy. As we had hypothesized, expectancy had no effect on posttest subjective, behavioral, or physiological fear measures. We did not anticipate, however, that expectancy would significantly influence both subjective and physiological measures during treatment, nor that its effects on these variables would parallel a process previously identified in the literature to be of significance to fear reduction. Subjects in the positive expectancy condition reported greater fear to the first presentation of each scene and lesser fear to the third presentation of the scene, relative to the neutral expectancy subjects on each of the three scenes. Thus, the former group showed greater initial reactivity and greater reduction in subjective fear. Indeed, the neutral expectancy group displayed very little change in fear over repetitions of each image.

A simple demand interpretation of the above outcome is readily available. Subjects who think they are receiving therapy may assume that fear should decline over repeated presentations and their reports simply express that belief. Heart rate is not so easily controlled, however. While modulation of cardiovascular activity in response to demands has been demonstrated for lengthy trials of heart rate control tasks (Bergman & Johnson, 1971), instructions to increase heart rate are ordinarily much more effective than instructions to decrease rate. Furthermore, the likelihood of systematic declines in heart rate due to voluntary control is fairly remote in the context of the brief visualization periods of our study. Our positive expectancy subjects did show such declines, however. Heart rate for these subjects was greatest during the first presentation of each scene, decreased during the life of each scene (from phobic scene presentation to response elaboration to a postimagination period), and declined over repetitions of each scene. The neutral expectancy group showed no systematic change within or across either the scenes or their repetitions. Thus, heart rate closely paralleled the results of the subjective fear measure: greater initial reactivity, and greater reductions over scene repetitions among positive expectancy subjects. These effects were uninfluenced by type of imagery condition and were unrelated to vividness ratings of the scenes.

The importance of the above results is that greater initial reactivity and habituation across repetitious presentations of feared stimuli have been identified as characteristic of effective fear reduction in earlier investigations. Lang, Melamed, and Hart (1970), for example, have reported that such a pattern during systematic desensitization was significantly related to outcome improvement. Lader and Mathews (1968) have found that rate of Galvanic Skin Response (GSR) habituation to repetitive neutral stimuli is inversely related to level of physiological activity. In the latter study, complex phobias were associated with lower habituation rate and higher physiological level, while specific phobia and no-phobia subjects showed, respectively, increasingly greater habituation and lower overall level. Furthermore, in the Lang *et al.* (1970) report, synchrony of reported fear with physiological activity also related to outcome improvement. The pattern of subjective and physiological data for the positive expectancy subjects in our study thus suggests the presence of optimal conditions for fear extinction.

Why positive expectancy should produce such an effect is not altogether clear. Lang (1977) has recently proposed a reformulation of imagery effects which stresses an information processing analysis. His model suggests that presented material will have an emotional impact to the extent that the subject completely processes important elements of the image (especially assertions inherent in the image that are related to the subject's response to the situation, rather than the simple symbolic representation of the concrete stimulus situation) ordinarily employed, for example, in desensitization therapy. Within this context, we may speculate that subjects in the positive expectancy condition may have: (1) more completely processed the presented scenes, although such processing did not empirically relate to the vividness of the imagery; or (2) processed the scene in a manner which provided greater exposure to the response elements rather than the stimulus elements of the image. In either case, we would argue that functional exposure to the feared situation was facilitated under positive expectation and/or mitigated under neutral expectation. Whether this effect reflects an underlying motivational variable or some other process remains undetermined.

Our speculation is, of course, somewhat premature. Even though the pattern of response in the positive expectancy group mimicked that found by earlier research to relate to outcome improvement, no posttest effects due to expectancy were found. Either the process induced by expectancy was not the same as that characterizing fear extinction, or the process was not complete enough to find expression in changes in fear behavior. The latter interpretation is defensible since only one session involving only three images was employed. However, we were encouraged to find a during-therapy effect on both subjective and physiological variables. For the first time, it appeared that expectancy, independent of demand, may have an influence on a process of fundamental importance to fear reduction.

Our second study allowed us to replicate the above effects and to assess the influence of expectancy on treatment process and outcome during more extensive therapy. Again, our principal concern was with a different issue. Initiated by Davison (1968) numerous studies have attempted a component analysis of systematic desensitization in order to test Wolpe's (1958) counterconditioning principle (cf. Borkovec & O'Brien, 1976). Procedurally, these studies are essentially assessing whether or not contiguous relaxation facilitates fear extinction during the presentation of imaginal fear scenes. Due to a variety of methodological problems (e.g., preponderant use of small animal phobics, inadequate control conditions, and the general absence of physiological dependent measures), unambiguous conclusions cannot be drawn from the extant research.

Using socially anxious subjects and continuous heart rate monitoring during pre- and posttesting, our first attempt to address this question again with what we thought was a more adequate design, provided some support for the facilitative role of relaxation to the desensitization process (O'Brien & Borkovec, 1977). This support was limited to posttest heart rate, however, and the absence of physiological recording during treatment precluded an examination of the during-therapy effects of relaxation on the fear extinction process. Consequently, we replicated O'Brien's effort, comparing his conditions in the treatment of speech anxiety and obtaining heart rate measures during therapy (Sides, 1978). Speech phobics were randomly assigned to desensitization (hierarchy exposure plus relaxation), noncontiguous relaxation (hierarchy exposure during the first half of the session, relaxation training during the last half), exposure only, and no-treatment. Positive and neutral expectancy conditions were established within each treatment condition; one practice session and four treatment sessions were administered. Hierarchy exposure for all three treated conditions involved 16 items with four scenes employed in each of the last four treatment sessions. Exposure followed Paul's (1966) criteria of two 10-second presentations per scene with additional temporally graded re-presentations any time anxiety was experienced by the subject. Vividness and fear ratings on 7-point scales were obtained after each presentation. Ten-second heart rate samples were taken just before scene presentation, during the verbal presentation of each scene, and during the visualization period subsequent to presentation. Heart rate change scores (presentation minus pre-item periods and visualization minus pre-item periods) were calculated to reflect heart rate response to the images.

The expectancy manipulation once again allowed a test of our hypothesis that such a factor has no influence on desensitization outcome as long as the target problem was characterized by a substantial physiological component of the fear response, and as long as demand was the only operative factor. This time, however, we were anxious to see whether we could replicate Grayson's results which suggested expectancy effects on the physiological fear component itself.

Several significant results emerged from analyses of the pre-posttest and during-treatment measures, only some of which can be summarized here. As predicted, expectancy had virtually no main effect on the numerous physiological, subjective, and behavioral outcome measures, nor did it interact with treatment condition on those variables. Like social anxiety, speech anxiety was thus uninfluenced by the demand characteristics inherent in expectancy instructions. Systematic desensitization produced significantly greater reductions in subjective fear from pretest to posttest exposure to the public speaking task, as compared to the other three conditions. The treatment effect was marginally significant on the heart rate measure. While desensitization did produce lower heart rate during the posttest than no-treatment, much to our surprise, the two hierarchy exposure conditions without relaxation displayed even greater reductions. Thus, relaxation contiguous with hierarchy presentations facilitated subjective fear elimination, but did not influence physiological outcome.

Analyses of the during-therapy measures yielded the most interesting and potentially important findings. Vividness was found to be a function of the interaction of treatment, scene number, and repetitions of each scene. Specifically, vividness was very high in desensitization to both first and last presentations of each of the 16 scenes, while the two exposure conditions without contiguous relaxation resulted in more variable and generally declining vividness over scenes, especially on the first presentation of each scene. In exact replication of Grayson's study, expectancy interacted with repetitions regardless of treatment condition on fear ratings. Subjects in positive expectancy showed higher initial fear to the first presentation and greatly reduced fear to the last presentation of each image, while neutral expectancy subjects showed no change across repeated presentations.

More remarkable were the changes that occurred in heart rate reactions to the phobic images due to treatment and expectancy factors. Since Grayson's study involved only one session and Sides's investigation included four sessions of exposure treatment, we initially analyzed her first session alone. During the presentation period, subjects in positive expectancy displayed large reactions to the first presentation of an image and markedly reduced reactions to the last presentation, while neutral expectancy subjects showed virtually no heart rate change to either presentation. This result is an agreement both with the fear ratings and with Grayson's subjective and heart rate data. Overall analysis of the four sessions revealed that the expectancy effect disappeared completely during the remaining three sessions. Whatever the role of expectancy may be in imaginal fear processes, its influence is thus short-lived.

Grayson's heart rate analyses involved only the visualization period and did not include a presentation period analogous to that described above. We fully expected to find his effect on Sides's visualization data but did not. Analyzing Session 1 alone, we did find a significant repetition interaction of heart rate reaction to visualizing the phobic images. Both exposure conditions without contiguous relaxation displayed the Grayson effect: greater reaction to the first presentation and marked reduction in reaction to the last presentation of each image for positive expectancy, and no reaction to either presentation for neutral expectancy. The significant interaction with treatment was due to the performance of the desensitization groups. Regardless of expectancy condition, greater initial reaction and habituation characterized desensitization. Thus, the Grayson effect occurred for conditions similar to his (absence of relaxation during exposure) and did not occur when relaxation was contiguous with exposure. Again, however, the influence of expectancy occurred only during the first session and disappeared over subsequent sessions.

The last piece of data completing this mosaic involved a significant treatment by scene by repetition effect on visualization heart rate over all four sessions. Desensitization resulted in substantial reaction to the first presentation of the first image, reductions in reaction across repetitions of each image, and declining initial reactions to the consecutive hierarchy images. Heart rate for the other two exposure conditions was far more variable, involving fewer systematic changes reflective of an extinction process.

Despite the complexity of the above findings, we think they fit together very well, and we will now attempt to provide an interpretation which has perhaps important implications for the role of both expectancy and relaxation in imaginal fear reduction therapies.

Though most expectancy effects on outcome measures in the literature probably reflect a simple demand influence, some process, inherent in expectancy and separate from demand, significantly contributes to the processing of inputs related to feared stimuli in such a way that fear reduction is facilitated. Evidence for greater processing and habituation under positive expectancy instructions stems from the remarkably consistent results of the Grayson and Sides studies. Greater processing is reflected in both self-report and heart rate reactions to initial presentation of a phobic image, though greater habituation is revealed in declines in both response systems over repeated exposure to the same image.

We still have no evidence for what the underlying mechanism of this effect may be. We did find some major limitations of the effect. First, the phenomenon is seen in self-report responses over several sessions, but is revealed in heart rate only during the first session. Second, regardless of the fact that the expectancy effect may relate to fundamentally important fear reduction processes in imaginal exposure, it is insufficient to influence therapeutic outcome. The latter restriction is probably a function of the former.

In summary, when a target behavior relatively impervious to demand influence is employed, expectancy has no direct outcome effect due to demand and a therapy process effect which: (1) is not due to demand; (2) appears to be important for fear reduction; but (3) is too short-lived to find expression in ultimate fear reduction. It is interesting to note that dramatic placebo effects exemplified in drug research and faith healing cases often occur rapidly and immediately and less commonly emerge over extended applications. Expectancy may then be a very powerful cognitive/attitudinal variable, but significant effects may be limited by the brevity of its influence. If our speculations regarding its role on fear process in imaginal exposure procedures are correct, its effects fit well with existing extinction principles and their explanation does not require much further elaboration beyond those principles. Our only addition is that the expectancy effect is due to the influence of the manipulation on the degree of functional exposure to the feared stimulus.

How to increase the potency or duration of the expectancy effect remains an important research question. Perhaps reemphasis of the expectancy instructions at the beginning of each session, for example, might have prevented the mitigation of the phenomenon. It is clear, however, that other manipulations (e.g., presence of relaxation) can have exactly the same influence on imaginal fear process as those induced by expectancy and that influence is far more persevering. Specifically, even though the expectancy effect was found during the Grayson study and the first session of the Sides study, the latter investigation found that: (1) the presence of relaxation during imaginal exposure can override the influence of expectancy on heart rate during that first session; and (2) the presence of relaxation results in greater initial heart rate reaction, and greater decline in reaction within and across repetitions of phobic images over several sessions of treatment. Furthermore, the imagery process effects of contiguous relaxation did find expression in the self-report outcome measures, in contrast to the lack of outcome effects due to expectancy. The absence of a facilitative relaxation effect on heart rate outcome was unexpected, and suggests the complexity of the process responsible for generalization from imaginal to real-life exposures to the feared situation (cf. Mathews, 1971).

Despite these differences, we will hypothesize that the roles of both expectancy and contiguous relaxation in imaginal exposure treatments are similar and that both result in an increase in functional exposure to the feared stimuli, thus facilitating the extinction process. Wilson and Davison (1971) have offered a similar hypothesis for the role of incompatible responses in extinction procedures on the basis of their review of relevant animal research. It remains unclear whether expectancy and contiguous relaxation share the same underlying mechanism to produce their similar effects. In agreement with Mathews's (1971) speculation regarding the role of relaxation in desensitization process, relaxation contiguous with hierarchy exposure was found in Sides's study to promote greater vividness of the images than exposure without relaxation. Thus, relaxation may facilitate extinction by increasing the clarity of the images and thereby increasing functional exposure to the feared stimuli. Neither of the above studies found expectancy to be related to vividness. Consequently, the expectancy effect may be mediated by some other information processing event.

In an attempt to further understand the information processing aspects of imaginal phobic exposure, Grayson (1978) has recently examined physiological responding to neutral and phobic scenes in light of Sokolov's (1963) neuronal comparator model. His model proposes that the introduction of any stimulus can result in either an orienting response (OR) or a defensive response (DR), depending upon the nature of that stimulus. For purposes of the present discussion, we will only concern ourselves with the DR.

A DR is produced by exposure to intense stimulation, such as electric shock or very loud white noise. Rather than habituating to repeated exposure, the DR may actually increase. The work of the Laceys (cf. Lacey & Lacey, 1974) and others has suggested that the DR represents an avoidance or rejection of environmental stimuli on a perceptual level. Early research of the DR involved the use of unconditioned stimuli (e.g., shocks, loud white noise) to produce DRs. However, Hare (Hare, 1973; Hare & Blevings, 1975) has found DRs in response to phobic slides by phobic subjects, while they do not occur in nonphobic individuals. Thus, the presence or absence of DRs may serve as a useful indicant of the degree of functional CS exposure to feared stimuli and the effectiveness of repeated exposure to such stimuli. Evidence already exists that procedures resulting in the inhibition of DRs lead to greater habituation than those that do not when using unconditioned stimuli (Gersh, 1978).

In order to determine the utility of the DR to anxiety and imagery research, Grayson presented randomly ordered speech-related and neutral scenes to a group of public speaking phobics. The scenes were presented in a written form via a slide projector, and each trial consisted of a rest period, presentation period, and visualization period. Using second-by-second change heart rate as a physiological indicant of DRs, Grayson found that only the speech scenes resulted in DRs during the visualization period.

In light of this test result and our earlier findings concerning the effects of expectancy and relaxation upon habituation, we might hypothesize that the latter manipulations lead to greater functional CS exposure and habituation by inhibiting the development of DRs. Further research in our lab will focus on this hypothesis.

The above discussion of relaxation effects focused on its role as a component in the systematic desensitization treatment of phobic anxiety. The reviewed data suggested that relaxation increases the functional impact or processing of imagery, possibly through increased image clarity, thereby resulting in: (1) increases in cardiovascular response to initial presentations of phobic imagery; (2) decreases in initial reactions to increasingly fear-producing images; and (3) extinction of the physiological fear component during repeated exposure to the phobic scenes. While these results are quite in accord with Wolpe's (1958) reciprocal inhibition principle as well as with the facilitated extinction models of Lader and Mathews (1968) and Wilson and Davison (1971), our own view places less stress on autonomic conditions felt to be optimal for fear reduction by these earlier models, and emphasizes the role of relaxation in facilitating the processing of imagery information. Thus, the variables of interest to us are approaching more closely to Lang's (1977) information processing analysis of phobic imagery. Notice that the history of theorizing regarding relaxation's role in desensitization is quite brief, with most of the relevant research being conducted in the late 1960s to the present. The effects of relaxation on other response systems has been a topic with a far longer history, and it is to that tradition we shall now turn.

Increasing Functional Exposure to Physiological Responses via Relaxation

Since its original development by Jacobson (1938) in the early 1900s, progressive relaxation has been operationally defined by two procedures: tension-release of gross muscle groups throughout the body and directed attention to the resultant sensations. The purpose of muscle tension-release was to provide the client with repeated opportunities to observe the occurrence of tension signals, their specific location, and intensity. The primary goal of these two operations was to create a skill of discriminating tension levels in the skeletal system and, ultimately, of identifying even very mild tension signals, so that the client could eliminate all unnecessary tension. The indirect by-product of such a procedure was the general reduction of sympathetic activity and the elicitation of a parasympathetic state of relaxation. In attempting to produce a brief relaxation response for use as a reciprocal inhibitor of anxiety during one-hour desensitization sessions, Wolpe markedly abbreviated the relaxation procedure. The primary ingredients (tension-release and internal attention-focusing) remained. However, emphasis was placed not so much on providing the client with a habitual relaxation response. Rather, muscle tension-release was employed because reduced muscle activity presumably could be better achieved for a brief period of time by first tensing muscles before releasing them than by simply allowing the body to remain quietly reclined without activity. At any rate, practice of either Jacobson's method or Wolpe's abbreviated procedure could potentially result in a usable, adaptive relaxation skill as long as the client engaged in extensive practice and application to daily living circumstances, and both techniques emphasized muscle tension-release and physiological attention-focusing to promote the development of that skill.

Examples of the use of the relaxation response as the sole or primary treatment of emotionally related disorders have been replete in the medical and psychological literature for several decades. Wolpe's incorporation of the procedure into a more complex package quickly captured the interest of modern behavior therapy researchers. With a recent emphasis within behavior therapy on self-control rather than therapist-control during the 1970s, a renewed interest in the therapeutic use of relaxation by itself has emerged. Whatever disorders have been so treated (e.g., asthma, insomnia, hypertension, tension headaches, anxiety neurosis), assumptions are made that the problem involves excessive physiological activity, and that learning to identify increases in that activity, and to reduce the activity, will be therapeutic.

Thus, increasing the functional impact of physiological responses has long been one of the major goals of relaxation training, in marked contrast to our recent appreciation of relaxation as a method for increasing the functional value of phobic imagery. Greater awareness of internal events mediating emotional behavior may or may not eventuate in a therapeutic outcome, however. Simply increasing one's awareness of physiological activity may actually result in an exacerbation of a problem mediated by excessive physiological arousal, unless the client is simultaneously taught to deal effectively with the arousal. A classic example of this possibility is provided by cardiac neurosis. A client with this problem is ill-advised to learn detection of subtle changes in heart action, unless previously established coping skills have been provided.

The preceding discussion sets the stage for a description of our recent research efforts on the treatment of general tension. Distinct from the circumscribed phobias discussed earlier, general tension is characterized by a chronic response of subjective tension throughout the day, perhaps elicited by major stressors in the life of the individual but relatively unmodulated by daily activities or the occurrence of specific environmental stimuli. As such, the maintaining conditions for the problem may well reside within the individual in the form of cognitive and/or physiological response styles. Given these assumptions, clinical treatment of such cases would focus on providing cognitive, behavioral, and physiological methods of dealing with extant major stressors and/or maladaptive approaches to living. Relaxation training would seem to be part of a reasonable treatment strategy in this context.

Our own "high tension" subjects have been selected on the basis of indicating on a questionnaire that they experience tension (nervousness, anxiety, feeling "uptight," being physiologically overaroused) during 50% or more of each day, that this tension is moderate to severe in intensity, and that they consider the tension to be a problem in their daily living. The pervasiveness of this problem is aptly documented by the fact that 21% of our college samples report this degree of tension and that 77 million prescriptions for benzodiazepine antianxiety agents were filled by retail pharmacies in 1972 alone (Greenblatt & Shader, 1974).

Since we initiated this program only recently, we do not know very much about general tension. Pilot work by Grayson in our lab began with the construction of 50 items referring to behavioral, physiological, and cognitive response categories commonly reported by high tension subjects in describing their tension on an open-ended questionnaire. The 50-item measure was then administered to new samples of high- and low-tension subjects. Half of the subjects were given a true-false format with instructions to indicate which reactions occurred when they were tense. The remaining subjects rated each item on a 5-point scale with instructions to rate each reaction in terms of how frequently they noticed the reaction during a typical day. On both forms, high-tension subjects obtained significantly higher scores on each response category than low-tension subjects. Thus, general tension is reflected in behavioral, physiological, and cognitive response channels. Furthermore, O'Brien's (1978) recent pilot work found his 31 high-tension subjects to obtain significantly greater scores ($p < .004$) than 29 low-tension subjects on several measures: the Trait Scale of the State-Trait Anxiety Inventory (Spielberger, Gorsuch, & Lushene, 1970), the Social Avoidance and Distress Scale (Watson & Friend, 1969), the Test Anxiety Scale (Sarason, 1957), the Achievement Anxiety Test (Alpert & Haber, 1960), and the Irrational Beliefs Test (Jones, 1969), and marginally ($p < .08$) greater scores on Paul's (1966) Personal Report of Confidence as a Speaker. The only measure failing to distinguish the two groups was the State Scale of the State-Trait Anxiety Inventory, suggesting that response bias did not account for the differences found on the other measures. Thus, our simple criteria for selecting high-tension subjects seem to possess substantial concurrent validity and identify a sample of people who certainly are anxious under a variety of circumstances.

Three outcome investigations employing progressive relaxation training (Borkovec & Hennings, 1978; Borkovec, Grayson, & Cooper, 1978) and a study involving a brief relaxation manipulation (R. Grayson, 1978) have been completed so far with this population. The first experiment, a 2×2 design, focused on a methodological concern: whether type of demand (positive versus neutral) or type of no-treatment condition (waiting-list versus informed control) would influence four weeks of baseline recording of daily tension levels. Positive demand subjects were told that the self-monitoring involved in baseline recording would actually have a therapeutic effect, while neutral demand subjects were given no such suggestion. Waiting-list subjects were informed that their treatment would begin in four weeks, while informed control subjects were explicitly told that they were a no-treatment comparison condition and would not receive treatment. Neither of the above factors nor their interaction influenced baseline tension levels. Thus, reported tension appears to be impervious to demand characteristic effects, unlike snake phobias (Bernstein, 1973) and moderate sleep disturbance (Steinmark & Borkovec, 1974). Four sessions of relaxation training administered to the waiting-list group over the two subsequent weeks produced a significant reduction in tension level relative to the informed control group. Seven month follow-up reports indicated maintained improvement among treated subjects and maintained baseline levels of tension among untreated subjects. General tension thus appears to be readily modified by brief relaxation training, even though tension levels will remain high over a substantial number of months if left untreated.

The next two experiments initiated our attempt to isolate the critical procedure components in the progressive relaxation treatment of general tension. Since muscle tension-release and physiological attention-focusing represent the two operations of the technique, a 2 × 2 design involving the presence or absence of each operation provides the cells necessary for a component analysis of its active ingredients. In the second experiment, high-tension subjects were randomly assigned to progressive relaxation (tension-release with physiological attention-focusing), no-tension-release relaxation with physiological attention-focusing, and waiting-list no-treatment. In the no-tension-release condition, subjects were instructed to concentrate on the pleasant feelings of relaxation occurring in inactive muscles while the therapist verbalized the very same indirect suggestions of warmth, relaxation, heaviness, etc. employed in the progressive relaxation condition. Thus the two relaxation conditions were procedurally identical with the single exception of the presence or absence of muscle tension-release. Nine sessions of treatment were administered over a five-week period. To control for unlikely, though possible, demand effects and very likely placebo effects, treated subjects were given counterdemand instructions (i.e., they were told not to expect improvement until after the seventh session of treatment). Analysis of daily tension level reports during the counterdemand period indicated the superiority of progressive relaxation over no-treatment, while the no-tension-release condition fell between the other two groups and did not differ significantly from either. Relative to no-tension-release subjects, progressive relaxation subjects did practice their procedure at home significantly more often, and more quickly achieved a subjective state of deep relaxation during training sessions. Five-month follow-up reports indicated further improvement for both treated conditions, although the progressive relaxation group reported greater success in eliminating tension and continued to report more frequent practice of the technique. Interestingly, analysis of numerous physiological measures (heart rate and variability, frontalis EMG, and five derived measures of respiration) obtained during three of the training sessions revealed virtually no treatment condition effects, even though data were included from the no-treatment subjects who attended physiological assessment sessions at those times under self-relaxation instructions. However, success at reducing physiological activity during the session, irrespective of the method used, was correlated with reduction in daily tension level.

Once again, it appeared that progressive relaxation was an effective means of promoting both immediate and long-term improvements in general tension. Muscle tension-release seemed to contribute somewhat to its efficacy and definitely to both its efficiency and its likely continued employment. So far, so good. We were not prepared for the results of the final outcome investigation.

The third study compared progressive relaxation to no-treatment and its other component control condition: muscle tension-release without physiological attention-focusing. The latter condition involved tension-release procedures identical to those of progressive relaxation. Between tension cycles, however, subjects were instructed to focus on pleasant images presented by the therapist rather than on physiological sensations. Only four treatment sessions were administered, the first three under counterdemand instructions.

Much to our surprise, not only was tension-release relaxation without physiological attention-focusing significantly superior to progressive relaxation during counterdemand, but the latter condition actually showed an increase in daily tension level over those three weeks relative to no-treatment. Thus, muscle tension-release was associated with reductions in subjective discomfort as in the earlier experiments, but only if attention was directed away from the physiological sensations. This outcome is difficult to interpret, given the positive effects of progressive relaxation found in the first two studies, unless we assume that a subset of tense subjects exist for whom increased awareness of physiological activity in general and relaxation sensations in particular exacerbates the problem. In these cases, as in cardiac neurosis, physiological responses may serve as conditioned stimuli for anxiety.

Several additional results from the subjects employed in the third study as well as the outcome of a final investigation lend some credence to this otherwise contra-intuitive hypothesis. At the same time that the third tension study was conducted, a group of sleep-disturbed subjects received training under the same treatment conditions. Following the treatment period, subjects from both problem types participated in a postassessment session involving a variety of tasks and measures. Sequentially, this assessment included an adaptation period, a time estimation task, a heart rate perception task, and a stress task involving preparation and presentation of speech. Physiological measures were obtained throughout the session, and several subjective report scales were administered subsequent to the speech task. These data along with subjective measures during training sessions were analyzed to evaluate the main, and interaction, effects of problem type and treatment condition, and thus provided an opportunity to evaluate application effects of the two relaxation conditions and to compare the tension sample to another problem group unrelated to general tension. Physiological attention-focusing in combination with tension-release was found to produce greater awareness of heart activity, lower heart rate during a rest period prior to the speech task, and lower respiration rate during speech preparation. Thus, directed attention to physiological sensations during tension-release relaxation was associated with reduction in physiological activity and an increase in its perception, relative to tension-release relaxation without physiological attention-focusing and no-treatment. Such has been the clinical lore surrounding relaxation. Problem type was also a significant factor on several measures. Tension subjects reported higher levels of anxiety than sleep disturbed subjects at the beginning of each training session, and greater increases in respiration rate in anticipation of the speech task and during its preparation period. Thus, higher subjective discomfort and a predisposition to react to stress with increased physiological activity characterized this group. Finally, subjective anxiety in response to the speech stressor was greater for tension subjects in the progressive relaxation condition relative to relaxation without physiological attention-focusing, while the reverse was true for the sleep disturbed subjects. Since progressive relaxation did result in increased awareness of internal cues and decreased physiological activity, the increases in subjective discomfort and physiological activity among tension subjects supports the notion that either general physiological sensations or relaxation-produced cues can elicit anxiety in this group.

The final study conducted by R. Grayson (1978) provided the most compelling data regarding the possibility that focused attention on physiological sensations may result in increased tension among high tension subjects. High- and low-tension subjects were given four consecutive cycles of tension-release relaxation on one hand and forearm, and four cycles of no-tension-release relaxation on the other hand and forearm, both under instructions to focus on the relaxation sensations. Order of administration of the two types of relaxation in this within-subject design was counterbalanced. Forearm EMG from each arm and frontalis EMG were monitored continuously. While a variety of results emerged, effects on frontalis EMG are of greatest interest to the present discussion. High-tension subjects showed an increase in frontalis tension over the four training cycles, regardless of the presence of absence of tension-release of hand and forearm muscles or the order in which the two types of relaxation were administered. Low-tension subjects displayed little EMG change over cycles when tension-release relaxation preceded no-tension-release training and reductions in EMG over cycles when no-tension-release training preceded tension-release.

Thus, directed attention to physiological events may facilitate tension reduction among non-tense individuals, but results in increasing tension levels among high-tension subjects.

Obviously, it is incumbent on us to identify what subject characteristics are associated with our hypothetical subset of tense people for whom either increased awareness of physiological cues in general, or relaxation sensations *per se*, serve as conditioned stimuli for anxiety reactions. Even the above statement suggests two potential subtypes, with the former exemplified, perhaps, by cardiac neurosis. The possible existence of the latter subtype is supported on the basis of both clinical experience as well as animal learning literature.

Our own clinical experience has been shared by numerous colleagues. Cases involving pervasive anxiety or general tension rarely benefit from progressive relaxation training. Three such cases treated by the first author displayed the following phenomenon during relaxation. They began to move about and become restless halfway through the relaxation session. Postquestioning revealed they were becoming relaxed until a growing, vague feeling of apprehension occurred during treatment. In each case, progressive relaxation was abandoned and relaxation via pleasant imagery produced more beneficial results.

Denny (1976) has recently reviewed a series of provocative experiments from his animal lab which establish the following points. Subsequent to termination of aversive stimuli, two temporally sequential, internal processes occur (relief and relaxation). Manipulation of the occurrence of these states during avoidance learning or fear extinction leads to predictable variations in response rates. Most importatly, if shock is paired with incipient relaxation cues occurring during the extinction of a conditioned fear response, subsequent number of trials to extinction is markedly increased. Thus, relaxation-produced cues can clearly become conditioned, internal stimuli for anxiety. Denny extrapolates from these data to suggest that a history of such conditioning experiences may provide an explanation for pervasive anxiety cases. He concludes that treatment based on this model would involve maintaining the anxiety level of the client until relaxation inevitably occurs and repeated exposure to relaxation-produced cues takes place. The surprising outcome of our third experiment suggests tension-release relaxation with pleasant imagery may also be effective. Muscle tension-release produces physiological relaxation. Directing the client's attention away from those anxiety-provoking sensations and toward non-anxiety-provoking internal stimuli (e.g., pleasant imagery) has two potential effects: (1) a well-established relaxation skill is acquired over the several sessions of training without intense exposure to anxiety-provoking stimuli which might otherwise undermine the training, and (2) numerous, less intense exposures to the relaxation-produced cues no doubt occur during the course of training, providing a graduated extinction paradigm.

Conclusion

Remaining within the basic context of learning theory, it is possible to consider the effects of constructs like expectancy and relaxation in terms of their influence on the perception of internal stimuli related to the maintenance of emotional behavior. In phobic imagery, both expectancy and relaxation appear to increase the degree of functional exposure to the feared stimuli, thus facilitating extinction effects. While relaxation does result in a skill capable of reducing physiological response to stress, there well may be a subset of generally anxious subjects for whom increased awareness of physiological events or, indeed, of relaxation cues may lead to greater anxiety. Thus, increasing our client's awarness of internal, emotionally related events will very much influence the course of change in emotional disturbance, sometimes by bringing them into closer contact with the therapeutic process, but at other times by exacerbating the problem unless we can provide adequate, additional treatment in anticipation of such occurrences.

ACKNOWLEDGMENT

Research cited in this paper was supported by NIMH Grant MH27484 awarded to the first author. Appreciation is expressed to Jeri Sides, Kris Cooper, Bill Hennings, and Rebecca J. Grayson whose contribution and commitment to the laboratory program have made this paper possible.

References

Alpert, R., & Haber, R. N. Anxiety in academic achievement situations. *Journal of Abnormal and Social Psychology*, 1960, *61*, 207–215.

Bergman, J. S., & Johnson, H. J. The effects of instructional set and autonomic perception on cardiac control. *Psychophysiology*, 1971, *8*, 180–190.

Bernstein, D. A. Behavioral fear assessment: Anxiety or artifact? In H. Adams & P. Unikel (Eds.), *Issues and trends in behavior therapy*. Springfield: Charles C Thomas, 1973.

Borkovec, T. D. The role of expectancy and physiological feedback in fear research: A review with special reference to subject characteristics. *Behavior Therapy*, 1973, *4*, 491–505.

Borkovec, T. D., & Hennings, B. L. The role of physiological attention-focusing in the relaxation treatment of sleep disturbance, general tension, and specific stress reaction. *Behaviour Research and Therapy*, 1978, *16*, 7–20.

Borkovec, T. D., & O'Brien, G. T. Methodological and target behavior issues in analogue therapy outcome research. In M. Hersen, R. M. Eisler, & P. M. Miller (Eds.), *Progress in behavior modification*. New York: Academic, 1976.

Borkovec, T. D., Stone, N. M., O'Brien, G. T., & Kaloupek, D. G. Evaluation of a clinically relevant target behavior for analogue outcome research. *Behavior Therapy*, 1974, *5*, 504–514.

Borkovec, T. D. Wall, R. L., & Stone, N. M. False physiological feedback and the maintenance of speech anxiety. *Journal of Abnormal Psychology*, 1974, *83*, 164–168.

Borkovec, T. D., Grayson, J. B., & Cooper, K. M. Treatment of general tension: Subjective and physiological effects of progressive relaxation. *Journal of Consulting and Clinical Psychology*, 1978, *46*, 518–528.

Davison, G. C. Systematic desensitization as a counterconditioning process. *Journal of Abnormal Psychology*, 1968, *73*, 91–99.

Denny, M. R. Post-aversive relief and relaxation and their implications for behavior therapy. *Journal of Behavior Therapy and Experimental Psychiatry*, 1976, *7*, 315–322.

Frank, J. D. *Persuasion and healing*. New York: John Hopkins Press, 1961.

Gersh, F. S. *The incremental stimulus intensity effect: An exploration of its mediating processes*. Unpublished doctoral dissertation, University of Iowa, 1978.

Goldstein, A. P. Patient's expectancies and nonspecific therapy as a basis for (un)spontaneous remission. *Journal of Clinical Psychology*, 1960, *16*, 399–403.

Goldstein, A. P., & Shipman, W. G. Patient expectancies, symptoms reduction, and aspects of the initial psychotherapeutic interview. *Journal of Clinical Psychology*, 1961, *17*, 129–133.

Grayson, J. B. *The elicitation and habituation of orienting and defensive responses in phobic imagery and the incremental stimulus intensity effect*. Unpublished doctoral prospectus, University of Iowa, 1978.

Grayson, J. B., & Borkovec, T. D. The effects of expectancy and imagined response to phobic stimuli on fear reduction. *Cognitive Therapy and Research*, 1978, *2*, 11–24.

Grayson, R. *Effects of relaxation with vs. without muscle tension-release on muscle activity of low and high tension subjects*. Unpublished honors thesis, University of Iowa, 1978.

Greenblatt, D. J., & Shader, R. I. Drug therapy: Benzodiazepines. *The New England Journal of Medicine*, 1974, *291*, 1011–1015.

Hare, R. D. Orienting and defensive responses to visual stimuli. *Psychophysiology*, 1973, *10*, 453–464.

Hare, R. D., & Blevings, G. Conditioned orienting and defensive responses. *Psychophysiology*, 1975, *12*, 289–297.

Jacobson, E. *Progressive relaxation*. Chicago: University of Chicago Press, 1938.

Jones, R. G. A factored measure of Ellis' irrational belief system, with personality and adjustment correlates. (Doctoral dissertation, Texas Technological College, 1968). *Dissertation Abstracts International*, 1969, *29*, 4379B–4380B. (University Microfilms No. 69–6443)

Lacey, B. C., & Lacey, J. I. Studies of heart rate and other bodily processes in sensory motor behavior. In P. A. Obrist, A. H. Black, J. Brenner, & L. V. Dicara (Eds.), *Cardiovascular psychophysiology: Current issues in response mechanisms, biofeedback, and methodology*. Chicago: Aldine, 1974.

Lader, M. H., & Mathews, A. M. A physiological model of phobic anxiety and desensitization. *Behaviour Research and Therapy*, 1968, *6*, 411–421.

Lang, P. J. Imagery in therapy: An information processing analysis of fear. *Behavior Therapy*, 1977, *8*, 862–886.

Lang, P. J., Melamed, B. G., & Hart, J. A. A psychophysiological analysis of fear modification using an automated desensitization procedure. *Journal of Abnormal Psychology*, 1970, *76*, 220–234.

Lick, J., & Bootzin, R. Expectancy factors in the treatment of fear: Methodological and theoretical issues. *Psychological Bulletin*, 1975, *82*, 917–931.

Mathews, A. M. Psychophysiological approaches to the investigation of desensitization and related procedures. *Psychological Bulletin*, 1971, *76*, 73–91.

Meichenbaum, D. *Self-instruction and the therapeutic modification of self-statements or cognitive-hyphen-behavior therapy*. Paper presented at the 8th Annual Convention of the Association for the Advancement of Behavior Therapy, Chicago, November 1974.

O'Brien, G. T. *A component analysis of the semantic content of self-statements in the cognitive-behavioral treatment of general tension in college students*. Unpublished doctoral prospectus, University of Iowa, 1978.

O'Brien, G. T., & Borkovec, T. D. The role of relaxation in systematic desensitization: Revisiting an unresolved issue. *Journal of Behavior Therapy and Experimental Psychiatry*, 1977, *8*, 359–364.

Paul, G. L. *Insight vs. desensitization in psychotherapy*. Stanford: Stanford University Press, 1966.

Piper, W. E., & Wogan, M. Placebo effect in psychotherapy: An extension of earlier findings. *Journal of Consulting and Clinical Psychology*, 1970, *34*, 447.

Sarason, I. G. Test anxiety, general anxiety, and intellectual performance. *Journal of Consulting Psychology*, 1957, *21*, 485–490.

Shapiro, A. K. Placebo effects in medicine, psychotherapy, and psychoanalysis. In A. E. Bergin & S. L. Garfield (Eds.), *Handbook of psychotherapy and behavior change*. New York: Wiley, 1971.

Sides, J. K. *The contribution of relaxation and expectancy to the fear reduction effects of imaginal, graded exposure to fear stimuli*. Unpublished honors thesis, University of Iowa, 1978.

Singerman, K. J., Borkovec, T. D., & Baron, R. S. Failure of a "misattribution therapy" manipulation with a clinically relevant target behavior. *Behavior Therapy*, 1976, *7*, 306–313.

Sokolov, Y. N. *Perception and the conditioned reflex*. Oxford: Pergammon, 1963.

Spielberger, C. D., Gorsuch, R. L., & Lushene, R. E. *STAI manual for the State-Trait Anxiety Inventory*. Palo Alto: Consulting Psychologists Press, 1970.

Steinmark, S. W., & Borkovec, T. D. Active and placebo treatment effects on moderate insomnia under counter demand and positive demand instructions. *Journal of Abnormal Psychology*, 1974, *83*, 157–163.

Watson, D., & Friend, R. Measurement of social-evaluative anxiety. *Journal of Consulting and Clinical Psychology*, 1969, *33*, 448–457.

Wilkins, W. Expectancy of therapeutic gain: An empirical and conceptual critique. *Journal of Consulting and Clinical Psychology*, 1973, *40*, 69–77.

Wilson, G. T., & Davison, G. C. Process of fear reduction in systematic desensitization: Animal studies. *Psychological Bulletin*, 1971, *76*, 1–14.

Wolpe, J. *Psychotherapy by reciprocal inhibition*. Stanford: Stanford University Press, 1958.

CHAPTER 7

Cognitive Ethology

Assessing the Streams of Cognition and Emotion

Donald Meichenbaum and Lynda Butler

Department of Psychology
University of Waterloo
Waterloo, Ontario, Canada

The relationship between cognition and emotion has been considered from a number of viewpoints. For example, Averill (1974) has explored this relationship in a historical, philosophical, and legal framework, while Plutchik (1978) has considered it from an evolutionary vantage point. The intent of the present chapter is to consider the complex relationship between cognition, emotion, and behavior from yet another perspective: that of assessment.

In order to introduce our present concerns and to illustrate how the streams of emotion, cognition, and behavior may interact, consider the following incident that was recently experienced by the senior author. Although this anecdote is somewhat long, it nicely illustrates many of the points to be made in this chapter. Moreover, we suspect that the thrust of our argument will remain with you longer because of its telling. The anecdote involves the senior author's attempt to put his four children (ages two to ten) to bed. Since his wife had gone out before dinner, this was to be a solo effort. The task was rather straightforward: tidy up after dinner, give baths, help with homework, read stories, and so on. All these duties were, hopefully, to be completed prior to nine o'clock because father had a hidden priority: to watch *I Claudius* on television. (As this anecdote heats up, and the opportunities for catharisis increase, it becomes necessary to switch to the personal case.)

The events began rather pleasantly, with a bath after dinner for two-year-old Danny. While I was bathing Danny—A most delightful and enjoyable time for both father and son—ten-year-old Lauren asked if I could help her find her ruler. My response was to encourage independence training, posing questions about where she had seen the ruler last, and so on. Lauren's request for the ruler will take on added significance as the story unfolds. So far, so good!

With the two-year-old in bed, the next task was to see that four-year-old David had a bath. Fortunately, eight-year-old Michelle volunteered to give David a bath, an invitation I readily accepted. While I was cleaning up in the kitchen, I heard David running back and forth in the tub and immediately had a flood of "catastrophizing" images of his falling and hurting himself. Concerned, I raced up the stairs to stop him. As I opened the bathroom door, the door knob smashed into the eye of Michelle, who was drying herself. "Oh no, what have I done?," I thought as I attended to Michelle's eye.

David, however, continued to run in the tub. I yelled at him, in what I judged a controlled manner (i.e., loud enough to get him to stop, but not loud enough to wake Danny). My exhortation to stop nevertheless startled David, which resulted in his falling, swallowing water, and beginning to choke. Given David's past history with croup, my sense of alarm was now heightened.

At this point, Lauren innocently arrived on the scene and asked if I had found her ruler yet. I exploded. "What, your ruler! Don't you see what has happened? Chaos has broken out"! With these words, of course, the two-year-old awakened.

Anyone who is a parent has experienced many similar situations. As parents know, you sort these things out. You put ice on the eye of the eight-year-old; you put the two-year-old back to bed; you comfort the four-year-old; and you never do find the ruler for the ten-year-old. By this time, it was little after nine o'clock; at least, I thought, I'd catch most of my television program. With scotch in hand, I collapsed in front of the television set, at which point Michelle called from her bed for a drink. Feeling very badly about what had happened to her eye, I decide to take a glass of grape juice up to her. Yes, as you guessed, she spilled the juice all over herself and the bed. As I surveyed this latest catastrophe, I kept firmly in mind that a general concern of mine is not to hit my children in anger. I also reflected, as philosophically as I could, that I would read the book instead of watching *I Claudius* on television.

When my wife returned home and asked me how everything went, I sighed wearily, "Fine, someday you'll read about it in some paper I write. I don't have the energy at this moment to relive it."

This anecdote illustrates several points about the complex relationship between cognition, emotion, and behavior (besides providing the senior author with a medium for communicating with his wife). For example, we would point out that within a very short period of time a whole host of emotions were experienced in rapid succession by the senior author—from the heights of love and joy in sharing, through anxiety and parental concern, to eventual deep frustration, exasperation, and anger. Most theories of affect highlight one emotion (such as depression, anxiety, or anger), focusing upon that emotion as central and ignoring the rapid fluctuation in feelings that was evident in this example and in many other real-life situations.

We would also argue that one should consider cognition and emotion as two closely related, ongoing, changing streams of experience that interact with one another and affect overt behavior in subtle and complex ways. For example, the senior author's hearing his son running back and forth in the tub elicited an orienting response and a state of physiological arousal that was quickly accompanied by a flood of "catastrophizing" images, which, in turn, further impacted on physiology, emotion, and behavior. Underlying concerns or values (for example, the senior author's concern not to hit his children in anger, or his hidden priority of television-viewing) also affected his emotional state and behavior in a variety of ways.

It is clear that the task of untangling the subtle and complex relationships between cognition, emotion, and behavior requires, as a first step, sophisticated assessment procedures designed to tap the respective streams of cognitive and affective experience. We have chosen to summarize these assessment procedures under the heading of *cognitive ethology.* Like the ethologist who follows the pattern of overt behavior (e.g., the interaction of a female bird and its young), noting fixed action patterns, looking for releasing stimuli and the like, we wish to develop procedures to capture the flow of cognitions and affect, and their complex interrelationships. Perhaps a more appropriate example is the ethologically-oriented investigator who studies the developmental relationship between a mother and her child. This researcher develops a category system for mother behaviors and a category system for child behaviors, and then examines the transactional and interactional nature of these respective streams of behavior in an analysis of sequential probabilities in the mother-child behavior matrix. We are proposing that a similar strategy (albeit *intra*personal rather than *inter*personal) may be helpful in studying the interaction between cognition and affect. One purpose of this paper—over and above the therapeutic value it has clearly provided the senior author—is to consider the host of assessment procedures that are subsumed under the heading of cognitive ethology.

Before we consider specific assessment procedures, one other set of points has to be made with regard to this anecdote. The first point is that an overly simplistic view of the relationship between cognition and emotion has pervaded the literature. One can find theorists, researchers, and practitioners arguing for a direct causal relationship between cognition and affect, with the direction of causality usually being viewed as cognition (e.g., irrational beliefs, negative self-statements, "catastrophizing" images), causing certain affective states (e.g., anxiety, depression) as well as more enduring emotional disorders. This approach is evident in the work of Albert Ellis (1962) or the therapy suggestions of Aaron Beck (1970), as well as in experimental studies where the research strategy is one of altering the individual's cognitions via the emission of certain self-statements, and then examining the resultant changes in affect (e.g., Velten, 1968; Strickland, Hale, & Anderson, 1975; and others). Our intention is not to denigrate the important contribution of cognition to emotion, but to argue that the notion that cognitions *cause* emotion is too one-sided, too simplistic to capture the flavor of what is really going on. An analogy to this point of view might be found in the developmental studies that, at one time, focused only on the impact of parents on children, while failing to consider the reciprocal impact of children on parents. The call of the present paper is for bidirectionality—the view that affect can cause changes in cognition and vice versa. Going back to our favorite anecdote, one can readily imagine the ways in which the senior author's feelings of anxiety, anger, fatigue, and so on impacted on the nature of his cognitions and vice versa. The realtionship between cognition and emotion becomes even more complicated if one considers the proprioceptive (facial and bodily) cues as well as the hormonal and physiological changes which affect one's feelings and thoughts (see, e.g., Izard, 1971; Saarni, 1978; and others). Moreover, one's cognitions and affects frequently have interpersonal consequences, in terms of other individuals' behavioral or emotional reactions in particular interactions, an aspect of the question which has received insufficient attention in the literature on cognition and emotion. At a broader level, Averill (1977) highlights the fact that cultural meanings or values also affect the relationship between cognition, emotion, and behavior; recall, for example, my desire or concern not to direct physical aggression toward my children, although the expression of anger seemed acceptable. We would argue that studies that examine emotion in the laboratory, essentially, are taking a snapshot which captures only one element of a rich, ongoing movie.

One other example, this time from the clinical domain, highlights further the need for caution in drawing causal inferences about the relationship between cognition and affect. Beck (1970) reported a clinical case involving a female college student who was quite depressed and anxious, apparently as a result of a phobia about walking around campus in the evening. Beck was able to determine that this student's avoidance behavior resulted from her fear of being attacked, and possibly, raped. She had a set of images about attack and rape that Beck suggested caused her emotional disturbances. Beck's proposals are consistent with the notion of a direct causal relationship between cognition and emotion; there is, however, some danger is drawing such a conclusion based upon clinical material. What we do not know in this instance is what the likelihood is that other female undergraduates have similar concerns and images, which, in their cases, lead to less emotional upset and appropriate problem-solving cautionary behaviors rather than to anxiety, depression, and phobic avoidance behaviors. Finding a friend to go out with, planning one's schedule so as to avoid potentially dangerous areas in the evening, reminding oneself of the security resources which exist on campus, and so on, all represent entirely different cognitions, behaviors, and feelings that may follow from that same set of images. What we are suggesting here (and what we have discussed elsewhere in greater detail: Meichenbaum & Butler, in press; Meichenbaum, Butler, & Joseph, in press) is that it is not the image *per se* but the personal meaning which the individual attaches to that image that determines the particular relationship between specifc cognitions, emotional reactions, and behaviors in a given situation. To return to the examples we cited, perhaps those females who do not become immobilized by fear of rape, as did Beck's patient, have an overriding concern to appear competent or independent in the handling of such situations, or are able to view such risks as relatively small negative possibilities in the context of a fulfilling life; in other words, they may tend to attach some broader meaning to the situation which mediates the relationship between cogniton, emotion, and behavior in a coping or problem-solving direction. A somewhat similar notion has been offered recently by Lazarus, Kanner, and Folkman (in press), who argue for the necessity of understanding the nature of the cognitive themes associated with various emotions. Their suggestion is that when negatively-toned emotions arise, the theme will likely involve the appraisal of the situation as harmful or threatening, or an appraisal of the individual as lacking in some important aspect of the ability to manage it. While the notions of cognitive themes and that of meaning systems differ in some respects, they are similar in positing the need for a level of analysis which extends beyond the examination of specific cognitions and emotional states. We shall return to this and other more "heady" issues later; let us now turn our attention to the more mundane question of how we may go about assessing the flow of cognitions, and how these cognitions relate to emotional states and behavior.

Cognitive Ethology

The assessment of the stream of consciousness, or the concern with introspection has a long history that we will not consider at this time (see

Cacioppo & Petty, 1978; Ericcson & Simon, 1978; Hurlburt, 1976; Kendall & Korgeski, in press; Pope & Singer, 1978; for some relevant accounts of this history). Instead, our focus will be on itemizing the variety of different ways that have been employed to assess the ongoing streams of cognition and emotion. This description will not be exhaustive, but rather illustrative, and we will highlight along the way a number of methodological and conceptual problems associated with these procedures, especially the issue of the individual's accessibility to cognitive processes and the veridicality of cognitive self-report.

Cognitive etholgy is our term for the variety of measurement techniques that are employed to describe the content, frequency, and patterning of cognitions (self-statements, images, appraisals, expectancies, etc.) that may reflect or engender different affective states and contribute to individual differences in performance in a variety of situations. The assessment techniques include such procedures as interviews, questionnaires, think-aloud protocols, videotape reconstruction, thought sampling, thought-listing procedures, and others. We would point out that each of these procedures has its own strengths and weaknesses, and that a multimethod assessment procedure will be needed to determine if common patterns of ideation accompany emotion and contribute to inadequate preformance across a variety of tasks and settings. One can group the various cognitive assessment devices in terms of when they are administered: either following performance, accompanying performance, or preceding performance. We shall consider them in that order. Because the field is potentially so large, we plan to focus upon a single target problem: that of social and evaluative anxiety, in order to illustrate how the various cognitive assessment procedures may help to throw some light upon the complex relationship between cognition, emotion, and behavior.

The role of cognitions as a contributor to social anxiety is captured by Dan Greenburg and Marcia Jacobs (1966), whose humorous book, *How to Make Yourself Miserable*, provides innumerable examples of negative self-referrent ideation reflecting or engendering dysphoric affect and interfering with interpersonal relations. We particularly liked one cartoon involving a couple who, while being intimate in an idyllic country scene, entertained the following set of thoughts: a passing bird could soil their heads; a passing airline could jettison its septic tank on their car or persons; a rabid herring could leap out of the stream and attack their toes; their companion could suddenly realize how boring they were; and so forth. This rather far-fetched account of a romantic afternoon undoubtedly gone awry contains, nevertheless, more than an element of truth. We will review below evidence that indicates that such negative, self-referrent ideation is an important correlate of anxiety states, and it interferes with performance in a variety of situations.

Cognitive Assessment Following Performance

Several different approaches have been developed to tap the flow of subjects' cognitions in postperformance assessment. These postperformance assessment procedures include questionnaires, thought listing, videotape reconstruction, and interviews. In each case, the investigator must recognize the inherent methodological and interpretative problems that such postperformance reports offer. One of the obvious problems is that the investigator who uses such postperformance cognitive assessment procedures cannot determine if the subject actually *had* such thought while performing a task or engaging in an interaction, *or* whether the answers to the postperformance questionnaire or interview merely represent a postperformance rationalization of cognitive processes (i.e., the thoughts they *likely* had in the situation). Perhaps it is best to view such postperformance self-reports as examples of "availability heuristics" as described by Tversky and Kahneman (1973). As Tversky and Kahneman indicate, availability is a useful concept in explaining such self-reports, on the assumption that frequent events are typically easier to recall and to imagine than infrequent events. Reliance on availability can lead to error, however, because availability also depends on such factors as saliency or recency that are often unrelated to true frequency. For example, Loftus (1975) found that eyewitnesses to an accident incorrectly remembered seeing a stop sign one week after the event if they had been asked about a stop sign immediately after the event (and correctly replied "no"). Apparently, subjects can confuse an event representation created by a question with an event representation created by observation. Thus, in using postperformance assessment procedures, the investigator may be changing, by means of the questions asked, the subject's self-observation about his or her own thoughts.

Put simply, the postperformance account of what one thought (or must have thought) while performing some task may represent an "availability heuristic". The postperformance self-report may reflect the greater ease of generating relevant instances, regardless of whether the event, or those specific thoughts, had actually occurred. The cognitive ethologist who uses postperformance reports will thus have difficulty distinguishing between whether the subject's self-report reflects an inference process or a veridical account of the ongoing process. As will be noted below, other assessment procedures that precede and accompany performance will be necessary in the interpretation of the postperformance self-reports.

Moreover, the cognitive ethologist must recognize that a good deal of behavior is automated or "scripted" to use Abelson's (1978) term, or "mindless" to use Langer's (1978) and Thorngate's (1976, 1977) phrase. From this point of view, it is possible that subjects may not have, or at least, may be unaware of, ideation (i.e., self-statements and images) accompanying the performance of some highly familiar task such as an interpersonal interaction. (Are we indeed able, upon instructed recall, to reconstruct our thoughts in such situations?) Alternatively, the affect generated by a situation may result in suppression of cognitive processing at the level of personal awareness (as in the defence mechanism of denial) or at the level of interpersonal report (the familiar phenomenon of social desirability). Thus, in the instances where the subject is unable to report cognitions during a preceding task, it is extremely difficult with postperformance assessment procedures to untangle absence of thought due to highly automated processing from more affectively-laden occurrences of defensive denial or socially desirable responding.

Despite the problems in both availability and veridicality of such self-report data, we can still question whether post-performance self-reports are useful in helping us understand individual differences in the nature of performance, and moreover, in understanding the relationship between cognition and emotion. Let us examine several recent experiments on social anxiety with this issue in mind.

Postperformance Questionnaire

In trying to understand the nature of social anxiety, Schwartz and Gottman (1976) conducted a task analysis of the cognitive and behavioral deficits of individuals who were low in social assertiveness. They identified groups of low-assertive and high-assertive individuals and conducted multiple assessments in order to discern the role which cognitive factors might play in the affect disturbance and behavioral deficit. They found that low-assertive individuals did not differ from their more assertive counterparts with regard to knowledge of what was an appropriate response on an assertiveness questionnaire, nor did the two groups differ in the behavioral expression of assertion in a "safe," role-playing situation (that is, showing a friend how to handle specific assertive situations). If both groups knew *what* to do and, moreover, *could* perform in certain circumstances, then what was the nature of the low-assertive individuals' deficit? The answer was provided by a third experimental condition, in which Schwartz and Gottman asked their subjects to role-play assertive behaviour in a situation approximating real-life (the subject was to imagine being personally confronted with an unreasonable request). In this condition, the low-assertive group manifested deficient assertive behaviour.

In an attempt to understand why high- and low-assertive subjects differed in the real-life role-playing situation, Schwartz and Gottman asked subjects to indicate on a self-statement questionnaire how frequently "positive" as opposed to "negative" self-statements had characterized their thought processed during the preceding assertiveness situations. A negative self-statement was a thought which a previsous sample of people had indicated would cause them to be socially anxious and reduce the likelihood of their behaving assertively; for example, "I was worried about what the other person would think about me if I refused." Positive self-statements were those statements previously rated as increasing the likelihood of assertive behavior; for example, "I was thinking that I was perfectly free to say no."

Schwartz and Gottman found that moderate- and high-assertive subjects reported having experienced significantly more positive than negative self-statements in the role-playing situations, whereas low-assertive subjects did not differ in the number of positive and negative self-statements they reported. It appeared that while high-assertive individuals had a positive orientation and usually little doubt in their minds as to the appropriateness of their actions, low-assertive subjects, in contrast, could be characterized as experiencing an "internal dialogue of conflict" in which positive and negative self-statements competed against one another and interfered with interpersonal behavior.

Recently Halford (1979), using a self-statement checklist similar in format to that of Schwartz and Gottman, also found that it discriminated between subjects who differed in level of social anxiety. The low-assertive, socially anxious subjects in this study reported having experienced significantly more negative self-statements during a social role-playing situation than did the high-assertive, low anxious subjects. It should be pointed out that the data discussed above merely reflect a correlation between the incidence of negative self-statements, the amount of affect disturbance (as reported on self-report scales and manifested on measures of nonverbal and verbal behaviors), and the degree of ineffective interpersonal behavior. One cannot, however, draw conclusions about the functional relationships between affect, cognition, and social behavior from such data. Such studies only provide a beginning framework; more pieces, culled from other cognitive assessment procedures, must be offered to explain social anxiety and the complex interrelationships between cognition, affect, and behavior in social situations.

A somewhat different research strategy, designed to explicate the functional relationships between cognition, affect, and behavior, has used a training paradigm, where treatment is designed to alter the individual's negative self-statements and images with resultant changes in affect and behavior. For example, Glass, Gottman, and Schmurak (1976) successfully used cognitive modeling therapy, and Halford (1979) used cognitive restructuring therapy to directly alter socially anxious clients' cognitions with resultant changes in affect and behavior. It should be noted that the assessments of affect were largely confined to self-report measures and behavioral observations. Clearly more process measures of affect, as well as of cognition, are needed. But these training studies do suggest an intimate relationship between cognition and emotion, as well as the possibility of a directive role for cognition.

An important caveat must be offered concerning the nature of the conclusions that can be drawn from such training studies, however. It is important to recognize that even though one can alter subjects' cognitions with resulting changes in affect and behavior, one cannot conclude that cognition plays such a directive role in the natural occurrence of social anxiety. In short, there are two sides to the coin. On the one side, we may be able to use cognition to change affect and behavior; on the other side, we cannot then infer from such change or treatment studies that cognition plays such a directive functional role in the natural occurrence of social anxiety.

A related point is that when we consider the relationships between cognition and emption, it is naive to expect a directive influence of one process over the other. Negative self-statements can as easily be seen as engendered by or reflective of physiological or emotional arousal, as they can be viewed as the cause of such arousal. In fact, the process is most likely a circular one. In studying the complex relationship between cognition and emotion, our objective should be to note how the two processes of emotion and cognition affect each other over time. Going back to our ethological example of the mother and child relationship, one may question whether it makes sense to say that the behavior of one member of the pair (mother or child) causes the behavior of the other. Instead, the researcher's task is to describe and determine the reliability of the sequence of such interactions. The same logic may be applied to the relationship between cognition and emotion.

Finally, it should be noted that a number of investigators have successfully adopted Schwartz and Gottman post-performance questionnaire procedure to assess subjects' cognitions. Even though we cannot be sure if subjects actually had such thoughts during performance, their endorsement of particular self-statements (or availability heuristics) does appear to be a highly sensitive discriminator, or correlate, of affect disturbance and inadequate performance. It is likely that such endorsements of postperformance "inferences" about one's behavior play an important role in acting as a self-fulfilling prophecy for future performance. Thus, the postperformance appraisal (explanation, rationalization, or what have you) may, in actuality, be a statement about expectancies for future performance. Postperformance assessment from the vantage point of the experimenter may reflect a *pre*performance assessment from the viewpoint of the subject.

Thought Listing

A somewhat different assessment procedure, designed to tap subjects' postperformance cognitions, is a thought-listing procedure. A recent study by Cacioppo, Glass, and Merluzzi (1979) nicely illustrates the use of this procedure with socially anxious male subjects. Cacioppo *et al.* identified high- and low-socially-anxious subjects by means of Watson and Friend's (1969) Social Avoidance and Distress Scale, and then prepared subjects for an interaction with an unfamiliar female. The subjects' self-statements during a waiting period were later assessed by means of a thought-listing procedure. The thought-listing procedure asked the subject to list on a page (one thought per box) everything that went through his mind about the upcoming discussion. The subjects were only given 2.5 minutes to record their thoughts, with the expectation that this short time period would pull for dominant thoughts. Afterwards, the subjects were asked to rate each thought in terms of whether it was "favorable toward yourself," "unfavorable toward yourself," or "neither favorable nor unfavorable toward yourself." Similar ratings of the subjects' thoughts were made by raters who were blind to the subjects' level of social anxiety. Cacioppo *et al.* found that high-anxious subjects spontaneously generated more negative self-statements, and when evaluating themselves, considered themselves significantly less potent and less active than did low-socially-anxious men.

The finding that the socially anxious subjects in this study perceived themselves as less potent and competent is consistent with the results of a postperformance assessment by Curran, Wallander, and Fischetti (1977), who divided both high- and low-socially-anxious subjects into high- and low-social-skill groups on the basis of overt behavior in a simulated social interaction. On a postperformance questionnaire, Curran *et al.* asked subjects to rate the skill level of their social behavior in the experimental situation. It was found that high-anxious/high-skill subjects underestimated their own skill in comparison to blind judges' ratings, while high-anxious/low-skill subjects accurately assessed their own performance relative to the judges' ratings. Whatever the skill level of their social behavior, however, social anxiety occurred only when subjects *appraised themselves* as socially unskilled (i.e., incapable of dealing effectively with the situation) or as being under social threat.

The thought-listing studies and the self-statement assessment studies both suggest a close relationship between the content of the subjects' ideation and their social anxiety, but not always between cognition, emotion, and social behavior. In some instances, negative self-statements reflect realistic perception of an actual skill deficit (i.e., one may indeed be boring one's mate), but in other instances the internal dialogue reflects a systematic negative bias in self-evaluation which is not necessarily translated into social behavior. The important point to note, however, is that in attempting to understand the nature of socail anxiety (or, for that matter, any affective disturbance), it is essential to include some assessment of cognitive processes related to the situation.

Videotape Reconstruction

Still another procedure that has been employed to assess the role of cognitions in evaluation anxiety is videotape reconstruction. The procedure involves videotaping the subject while he or she is engaged in some task and then having the subject watch the videotape, attempting to *reconstruct* his or her feelings and thoughts at the time as accurately as possible. The advantage of the videotape procedure is that the experimenter can reproduce for the subject the situational context in an attempt to facilitate more veridical recall. Once again, however, we cannot determine to what degree subjects are *re*constructing or merely constructing the flow of ideation and emotion as they watch themselves on the videotape. But, as with the other postperformance measures, we can ask, do such (re)constructions help to explain individual differences in affect and performance, and do they help in the prediction of future behavior? The answer is an encouraging "yes". Three recent studies have used the postperformance videotape reconstruction procedure—with test-anxious subjects (Hollandsworth, Glazeski, Kirkland, Jones, & van Norman, 1978), with socially anxious subjects (Smye, 1977), and with subjects experiencing experimentally-induced pain (Genest, Turk, & Meichenbaum, 1977). For example, Hollandsworth *et al.* assessed the internal dialogue of female test-anxious subjects. Immediately after testing, subjects viewed their videotape with an experimenter and (re)constructed what they were thinking and feeling as they worked on the test. In addition to assessing the subjects' internal dialogue by means of this videotape reconstruction procedure, Hollandsworth *et al.* monitored the subjects' physiological reactions during testing. As was expected, they found that high-test-anxious subjects engaged in more task-irrelevant thinking and negative rumination than did low-anxious subjects. Interestingly, the low-anxious subjects showed more physiological arousal than did the high-anxious subjects, but they described their arousal on the Alpert-Haber (1960) scale as facilitative rather than debilitative anxiety. Thus, in the Hollandsworth *et al.* study, it did not appear to be the level of physiological arousal *per se* that had a debilitating impact on test performance, but rather how the subjects viewed the arousal they experienced. The point to be highlighted about the Hollandsworth *et al.* study is not the findings *per se* (although they are interesting), but rather the use of a research strategy which attempted to assess the stream of ideation as tapped by videotape reconstruction, as well as the actual flow of autonomic arousal and personal interpretations of that arousal. We would suggest that more research is needed that attempts to capture the flow of the streams of cognition, emotion, and behavior and examines the sequential interdependencies between these streams of experience over time.

It is also clear that a good deal of research is needed which compares the various postperformance assessment procedures in order to determine the degree of "method variance" in the assessment procedure. Many other postperformance techniques could be included in such method studies, including interviews, imagery replays with accompanying reconstruction, and others. As we have suggested, since each of these procedures has its own strengths and weaknesses, one should not have much confidence in results that use only *one* procedure. Instead, a similar pattern of ideation and its impact on affect and behavior must emerge across the various assessment procedures if we are to identify "fixed action patterns" and "releasing stimuli," to once again use the ethology analogy. When we reconsider introspection, we must do so with a degree of methodological and theoretical sophistication that was not available to our "structuralist" forefathers. We have the advantage of a generation of research on demand characteristics, response sets, sequence analysis, and multitrait, multimethod assessment that we can bring to bear on the study of our subjects' cognitions.

Concurrent Cognitive Assessment

The focus of the discussion of cognitive assessment thus far has been on inquiring about subjects' cognitions after the fact, namely, in postperformance assessment. Two alternative time-honored procedures that involve concurrent assessment of cognitions are the "think-aloud" and "private-speech" techniques.

The think-aloud procedure has been recently reviewed in some detail by Ericcson and Simon (1978) and will not be considered in detail here because of space limitations. Simply, in the think-aloud procedure, the experimenter asks the subject to verbalize all the thoughts and feelings he or she has while doing a task. Subjects are usually give some training in producing such protocols and, needless to say, the impact of such training on the think-aloud protocols that subjects produce bears investigation in its own right.

It is important to recognize that not all tasks lend themselves to such think-aloud analyses. Some tasks that are so dependent upon imagery (such as mental rotation tasks) may be inappropriate for a think-aloud procedure that focuses on language. Second, it is important to recognize that when we ask subjects to think aloud we are changing the process of the performance of the task to some degree; that is, asking subjects to focus on their thought processes (by thinking aloud) may have an important impact on their concurrent or subsequent task-related behaviors. Moreover, one should not equate language with thought. Obviously, one can think faster than one speaks, and a good deal of editing is likely to occur in such think-aloud productions. But, as in the case of the postperformance questionnaire, we can still learn a good deal about individual differences and styles of information processing and their relationship to emotion and behavior. For example, Henshaw (1978) used a think-aloud procedure to examine high- and low-creative subjects' problem-solving styles while taking tests. The high-creative subjects differed from the low-creative individuals, not only in the frequency of certain categories of thought, but also in the patterning or sequence of their thoughts and behaviors. Following every major category of verbal behavior, high-creative subjects were significantly more likely than low-creative subjects to emit facilitative cognitive mediation and expressions of positive affect ("What else can I do;" "Just try to think of possibilities;" "Hey, I'm pretty good at this"), and less likely to become silent. (It is important to recognize that the expression of such facilitative mediation is frequently accompanied by a good deal of affect, highlighting the necessity of listening to audio- or videotapes while scoring the think-aloud transcripts in order to classify utterances correctly.) In contrast, the low-creative individuals in the Henshaw study produced significantly more inhibitive ideation reflecting a negative attitude toward their own personalities or abilities, their task strategy or solution, the task itself, or the experiment as a whole. Expressions of negative affect included frustration, anger, and boredom.

Interestingly, facilitative positive mediation functioned similarly in both the high- and low-creative groups, especially during the first five minutes of a ten-minute task, while inhibitive negative ideation functioned differently over time in the two groups. Both the high- and low-creative individuals came up with good responses at the outset of the task, but over the course of the task, both affect and cognitions changed in a negative direction for the low-creative individuals. Similar results have been offered by Goor and Sommerfeld (1975), who also used a think-aloud procedure with high- and low-creative individuals. The potential of such a think-aloud assessment has also been noted recently by Diener and Dweck (1978), who found differences in the think-aloud protocols of children who differed in attributional styles. The "helpless" children (as identified by a self-report locus of control scale) differed dramatically from "nonhelpless" children in the style of their thoughts and affect while doing a problem-solving task.

Closely related to the think-aloud procedure is a *thought sampling* or *task interruption* procedure. In this method, the experimenter attempts to sample the subject's "stream of consciousness" either in the laboratory or *in vivo* by signaling the subject at variable intervals to record their ideation (see Hurlburt, 1976, for a description of the thought-sampling procedures, including the use of remote control beepers). The task-interruption procedure is used in two ways: (1) the experimenter interrupts the subjects, for example, while taking an examination and asks subjects to indicate what thoughts they were just having by means of either free recall or a recognition task requiring endorsement of certain classes of ideation (see Bruch, 1976); or (2) the subjects, on their own, indicate when they have certain classes of thoughts (such as task-irrelevant thoughts) by pressing one of several telegraphic keys. For example, Antrobus and Singer (1964) had subjects engage in a vigilance task, and the subjects were to indicate whenever their ideation wandered and in which direction by pressing buttons that corresponded to different thought content areas.

The final concurrent assessment procedure to be noted is the subject's *spontaneous production of private speech* (i.e., speech that is not intended for a listener). Children between the ages of three and five emit sufficient private speech to permit the developmental study of cognition and its relationship to affect (e.g., smiles) and performance (e.g., puzzle-solving competence). One can, for example, analyze the data sequentially, determining the probabilistic relationship between certain classes of private speech (e.g., self-directive verbalization) and the other streams of behavior, such as task proficiency, and affect expression, such as smiles (see Goodman, 1978, for an example of such research). A forthcoming volume by Zivin (1979) on private speech, as well as a recent paper by Meichenbaum and Goodman (1979), discuss the potential uses of private speech data.

Our intent in this section was simply to familiarize the reader with the wide range of procedures available to the cognitive ethologist for tapping the stream of consciousness concurrent with performance, as well as to discuss briefly methodological pitfalls and research strategies for assessing the complex interrelationships between cognition, emotion, and behavior using these procedures. Let us now turn to our final group of assessment procedures, those that assess preperformance cognitions.

Cognitive Assessment Preceding Performance

As is perhaps self-evident, entire chapters could be written on the strengths and weaknesses of each of the cognitive assessment procedures we have discussed thus far. This observation applies as readily to the cognitive assessment procedures that precede performance. Included under this heading is a wide range of self-report assessment devices: interviews, task-related projectives, cognition-specific assessment questionnaires, such as those designed to tap attributions and expectancies, and so forth. Staying with the theme of social and evaluative anxiety, let us illustrate some of the ways in which such cognitive assessment procedures have been employed.

Mahoney and Avener (1977) used *interviews* and *preperformance questionnaires* to study thirteen male gymnasts who were competing in the final trials for the U.S. Olympic team. They found that the athletes' self-report of their anticipated self-statements and images under conditions of competition differentiated the successful gymnasts from those who failed to make the Olympic team. The better gymnasts tended to be more self-confident, and they "tended to use their anxiety as a stimulant to better performance. The less successful gymnasts seemed to arouse themselves into near panic states by self-verbalizations and images which belied self-doubts and impending tragedies" (p. 140).

A similar set of findings with socially anxious subjects was offered by Fiedler and Beach (1978). They secured ratings from women on the likelihood of various behavioral alternatives occurring in specific hypothetical assertive situations. They found that expectancies about consequences following a proposed behavioral act more adequately explained unassertiveness and social incompetence than did the subjects' behavioral repertoires. Fiedler and Beach's results are consistent with the data and arguments put forth by Bandura (1977) about the important influence of expectancies on interpersonally competent behavior.

Elsewhere (Meichenbaum and Butler, in press; Meichenbaum, Butler, & Joseph, in press); we have reviewed other cognitive assessment measures of social and evaluative anxiety. If one considers the data emerging across preperformance, concurrent, and postperformance measures with high socially and test-anxious subjects, an interesting pattern is evident. An examination of high- versus low-anxious individuals' internal dialogues reveals that the thinking processes of high-anxious individuals tend: (a) to be self-oriented rather than task-oriented, which serves to deflect attention from the task at hand; (b) to have a basic orientation that is negative (often "catastrophizing") rather than positive and coping, which serves to deflate motivation; and (c) to have an automatic, stereotyped, "run-on" character, which has the effect of escalating rather than controlling anxiety. Meichenbaum, Hensahw, and Himel (in press) have even suggested that a common pattern of ideation contributes to poor performance in diverse achievement or stress situations. The absence of a problem-solving set (i.e., viewing a stressor, task, or social situation as a problem to be solved) seems to lead to inadequate performance in many different situations. Self-referent ideation and all that goes with it also may contribute to disturbances in affect that interfere with performance. The picture that seems to be emerging is that the nature of an individuals' cognitions has an important impact on both emotion and behavior.

Similarly, however, one may ask how affect impacts on the bridge between cognition and behavior. The data suggest that emotion may put stress upon ongoing cognitive activity and interfere with the adoption and maintainance of the needed problem-solving set. Cognitive activity becomes negative and nonfacilitative, and escalates subjective and physiological arousal. A cycle is established whereby affect, cognition, and behavior all interact and feed upon each other. Affect may lead to certain negative cognitions that result in inadequate performance, which in turn leads to further emotional arousal and a further escalation of the content of the cognitions, which further interferes with performance, and so forth. This pattern was evident in the initial anecdote offered at the outset of this paper.

Units and Levels of Analysis

The thrust of the argument thus far has been to highlight the intimate transactional relationship between cognition, affect and behavior, and to illustrate the variety of assessment techniques available to study cognition and emotion. The impression offered is that one should unitize and categorize the subject's cognitions, and in a type of matrix sequence analysis determine the functional relationship between such cognitive units and other streams of affect or behavior. One issue that must be considered, however, is whether focusing on specific self-statements and images (in terms of both frequency and pattern analysis) represents the best approach. Or put in other words, should we be preoccupied with such limited units of response or should we focus, instead, on larger units of analysis? For example, Henshaw, in the think-aloud study discussed earlier, analyzed subjects' protocols by means of a Markovian chain analysis, in terms of the conditional probabilities of the sequence of specific categories of thoughts (facilitative, inhibitive, etc.) and silences that characterized high- and low-creative subjects. Such sequential analysis of the flow of ideation and behavior produces data which are quite rich and detailed. But is this the best way to proceed?

Another interesting way to examine such think-aloud protocols, or for that matter cognitions as assessed by other means, is to use clinical judges. Clinical judges could be asked to read the complete think-aloud protocol, or interview, or private speech protocol, and rate it for styles of thinking. One could ask judges to use Q-sort techniques to evaluate cognitions collected across tasks, settings, and time.

It is being suggested that at this point in the development of cognitive ethology we should leave open the question of the best unit of response to employ, and we should be interested in comparing the utility of various methods of analysis (e.g., sequence probabilistic analyses versus clinical ratings). We are reminded of a recent clinical case involving a client who was phobic about crossing streets. He would debate whether to cross or not, in a type of debit-credit basis. It turned out the client was an accountant by profession and this ledger-style thinking extended to every sphere of his life, especially when he experienced intense affect. The recognition that he was engaging in this thinking style further exacerbated the accompanying emotion and often led to total behavioral debilitation. Focusing only on the content of the client's thinking in one situation may miss the larger stylistic qualities of his behavior that Shapiro (1965) has described.

An issue which is related to the question of the appropriate unit of analysis is the issue of the most appropriate level of analysis. In our introductory comments, we commented that in order to understand fully the relationship between cognition, emotion, and behavior, one must consider some construct such as meaning system or current concerns. We have discussed the history and need for the concept of cognitive structures elsewhere (Meichenbaum, 1977; Meichenbaum & Butler, in press; Meichenbaum, Butler, & Joseph, in press). For the present purposes let us simply illustrate the generative role such meaning systems may play in influencing the cognition–emotion–behavior linkage. Staying with our example of social and evaluation anxiety, Wine (in press) has summarized data that indicate that a constant and overriding concern for high-test-anxious subjects is: "How am I being evaluated?" This general concern about evaluation may arise for different reasons, we would suggest, since the test situation may hold a somewhat different meaning for each individual. For some individuals an evaluative situation may represent a concern over loss of control, a fear of being overwhelmed by anxiety and the consequences this anxiety could entail; while for someone else evaluation may reflect a concern for gaining esteem from authority figures or peers; and for still another individual, evaluation may reflect an opportunity to gain professional or personal success. We would suggest that it is the individual meaning (or the network of personal concerns or motivations), surrounding evaluation that will influence the content of the subject's cognitions and accompanying affect in such situations. For the high evaluation-anxious subject a variety of (negative) concerns around evaluation will lead to the expectation that he or she is being negatively evaluated and a set of self-statements and images while performing that will be task-irrelevant and of a negative self-referent quality. Such self-statements or internal dialogue may represent a "final common pathway" that describes all high-anxious individuals, but the intensity and patterning of the individual's emotions will be influenced by the meaning system or concerns that are brought to bear in that situation. In fact, the process may be circular, in that the intensity of one's emotion (amount of fear, anxiety) may influence which concerns (i.e., primarily negative or inhibitive versus positive or facilitative) will prevail. Thus, emotions may impact on cognitions in terms of the specific automatic thoughts that are experienced and the particular meaning systems that are activated in the situation.

Wine (in press) argues that subjects who are low test-anxious have qualitatively different concerns and cognitions from high test-anxious subjects. It is not that the low test-anxious subjects are positively preoccupied with talking to themselves about how wonderful they are, but as Wine notes, rather, their contents of consciousness reflect the current concerns of the demands of the situation and meeting these demands. Thus, the cognitions of the low-anxious individuals vary situationally and reflect a problem-solving set. Under these circumstances, physiological arousal is viewed as facilitative, as being "turned on" (or at least, as aversive but controllable), and attention is directed to situational demands. Thus, emotion impacts upon cognition and behavior differently depending upon the subject's meaning system and current concerns.

The nature of one's meaning system and current concerns influence the way the situation will be perceived and chunked, and this in turn will influence emotional arousal. In the anecdote offered earlier, the senior author's general concern (e.g., the desire not to hit his children) as well as his immediate current concern or hidden priority (i.e., the desire to watch a specific television program) helped to determine whether a specific set of behaviors would be viewed as a provocation, and whether a specific emotional reaction and certain behavioral consequences would be elicited. While his emotions were influenced by his personal concerns, however, the intensity of his emotional state(s) may have determined which current concern or meaning system was actually called into play. Thus emotions can serve to organize experience. This bidirectional process is evident at several levels of analysis, with emotional arousal not only influencing specific thoughts, images and problem-solving capacities, but also impacting on the nature of one's predominant meaning systems or concerns.

It is being argued that to fully understand the relationship between cognition and affect it is necessary to recognize that there are different levels of cognitions, ranging from specific automatic thoughts or images to cognitive-affective schema or meaning systems. A complete explication of the relationship between cognition and emotion will have to consider these various levels.

Perhaps one other example of current concerns will illustrate this complex relationship. The example comes from the work of a sociologist, Keiser (1969), who conducted a study of a Chicago street gang. Keiser, in observing and interviewing the gang members, found that a major dimension underlying their behavior was the assessment of risk in social situations. The gang members divided such situations into two categories of rather colorfully labeled events: (1) high-risk activities (for example, "humbugging," "gangbanging," "wolf-packing," and "hustling"); and (2) other activities ("gigs," "games," "sets," and "pulling jive"). It was in the former set of risk activities that one earned peer acceptance (earned one's "rep," displayed "heart," or showed one was no "punk"). Thus, acceptance by one's peers in the gang represented a current concern that influenced how situations were perceived (i.e., in terms of risk) and how affect (i.e., anxiety, anger, pride) was experienced in the street situation. To understand the relationship between affect, cognition, and behavior for this street gang, we would suggest, it is necessary to understand the central role that a "risk-taking" meaning system plays.

The preceding discussion of assessment methods and the proper units and levels of analysis is likely to raise the hackles (if not the cognitions) of many. One persistent concern that the cognitive ethologist must consider is the accessibility and veridicality of self-reports in general. It is with a slightly more detailed consideration of these issues that we will end this chapter.

Accessibility and Accuracy of Verbal Reports

Self-reports of psychological processes have long been suspect. This suspicion has been most recently articulated by Nisbett and Wilson (1976) and by Nisbett and Bellows (1977), who reviewed a considerable amount of research which they purport indicates that self-reports are often based upon presuppositions or "*a priori* theories" about the causal links between stimuli and responses. Nisbett and his colleagues tend to view an individuals' self-reports as post-hoc rationalizations for his or her behavior rather than a veridical reflection of experience.

Nisbett and Wilson (1976), in considering the accuracy of self-report data, draw a distinction between the individual's access to "private facts" versus the individual's access to "mental processes." Under "private facts," Nisbett and Wilson include the individual's knowledge of (and ability to accurately report) the focus of his or her attention, sensations, emotions, evaluations, and plans). Where subjects do most poorly, according to Nisbett and Wilson, is in situations where they are asked questions about their "mental processes." Instead of searching memory, the argument runs, subjects tend to use *a priori* theories about their cognitive processes in the situation. In considering Nisbitt and Wilson's review, it is important to recognize that the studies they review used assessment procedures that were quite feeble in comparison to the range of techniques described in the present chapter. A similar criticism of the Nisbett and Wilson argument has been offered by Ericcson and Simon (1978) and by Smith and Miller (1978). Such factors as a prolonged time lag between the task and the cognitive inquiry, or the use of assessment procedures that probed minimally or did not employ good retrieval cues, would all underestimate the usefulness of the assessment of subjects' "mental processes." We wonder what the Nisbett and Wilson data would look like if they employed videotape reconstruction procedures, think aloud protocols and detailed post-performance questionnaires, or better yet, a combination of these methods.

But let us reluctantly give Nisbett and Wilson the benefit of the doubt, that cognitive retrieval under certain conditions may indeed be minimal. For example, in a hypothetical experiment that is typical of the studies that Nisbett and Wilson might cite, consider a social psychologist who wishes to study jury behavior. The experiment is arranged so that the social psychologist manipulates the attractiveness of the witnesses for the defense or the prosecution, and then examines the effect of this manipulation on the jurors' behavior. When subjects are asked about the reasons why they voted "innocent" (i.e. in the direction of the attractive witness), they do not offer the attractiveness of the witness as an explanation or otherwise hint at the independent manipulation that interests the social psychologist. Nisbett and Wilson present many variations on this experimental theme, and on this basis, question the value of subjects' reports. The question remains, however: what should we conclude from such studies and what are the implications for cognitive assessment? We have already questioned the adequacy of the assessment of the subject's report in such experimental studies and wonder if the assessment procedures described above would yield the same conclusions. But beyond this, even if the subject's report did not match the explanation held by the social psychologist (i.e., attractiveness), the subject's account or inference may prove a useful explanation and predictor of his or her future behavior. In short, although one must be cautious in tapping subjects' reports of their cognitions, the conclusions that such reports are of little value or nonveridical is indeed premature. Subjects may behave in light of their *a priori* theory, and it may be that from the vantage point of understanding the relationship between cognition and affect this is of paramount importance.

Finally, it is à propos to conclude this discussion by repeating some observations offered by Epstein (1979) at the last Erindale conference on communication and affect. Epstein acknowledged, and we would concur, that self-report data have certain limitations, but that this is true of other sources of objective data as well, including psychophysiological and behavioral data. To quote Epstein:

> It [self-report] is easily obtained, can efficiently include long periods of self-observation, and can provide data on inner states that cannot be obtained by any other means. If self-report were to be abandoned, it would not be possible to study the content of dreams, fantasies, thoughts, and the subjective experience of emotions. It should be considered that, for some purposes, it is not even important to assume that self-report is veridical, but only that it reveals the construals of people. (Epstein, 1979, p. 51)

The cognitive ethology approach described herein is designed to illuminate the limitations and advantages of a self-report methodology.

References

Abelson, R. Scripts, Paper presented at one meeting of the Midwestern Psychological Association, Chicago, May 1978.

Alpert, R., & Haber, R. Anxiety in academic achievement situations. *Journal of Abnormal Social Psychology*, 1960, *61*, 207–215.

Antrobus, J., & Singer, J. Visual signal detection as a function of sequential task variability of simultaneous speech. *Journal of Experimental Psychology*, 1964, *68*, 603–610.

Averill, J. An analysis of psycho-physiological symbolism and its influence on theories of emotion. *Journal of Theory of Social Behavior*, 1974, *4*, 147–190.

Averill, J. Anger. Paper presented at the *Nebraska Symposium on Motivation*, 1977.

Beck, A. Cognitive therapy: Nature and relation to behavior therapy. *Behavior Therapy*, 1970, *1*, 184–200.

Bandura, A. Self-efficacy: Towards a unifying theory of behavior change. *Psychological Review*, 1977, *89*, 189–215.

Bloom, B., & Broder, L. *The problem solving processes of college students.* Chicago: University of Chicago Press, 1950.
Bruch, M. *Type of cognitive modeling, observers' imitation of modeled strategies, and modification of test anxiety.* Unpublished manuscript, Bradley University, 1976.
Cacioppo, J., Glass, C., & Merluzzi, T. *Self-statements and self-evaluations: A cognitive-response analysis of social anxiety.* Unpublished manuscript, Notre Dame University, 1979.
Cacioppo, J., & Petty, R. *Inductive techniques for the assessment of cognitive response.* Unpublished manuscript, University of Notre Dame, 1978.
Curran, J., Wallander, J., & Fischetti, M. The role of behavioral and cognitive factors in the maintenance of heterosexual-social anxiety. Paper presented at the Midwestern Psychological Association, Chicago, May 1977.
Diener, C., & Dweck, C. An analysis of learned helplessness: Continuous changes in performance, strategy, and achievement cognitions following failure. *Journal of Personality and Social Psychology*, 1978, *36*, 461–462.
Ellis, A. *Reason and emotion in psychotherapy.* New York: Lyle Stuart, 1962.
Epstein, S. The ecological study of emotions in humans. In P. Pliner, K. Blankstein, & I. Spegel (Eds.), *Advances in the study of communication and affect: Perception of emotion in self and others.* vol. 5. New York: Plenum, 1979.
Ericcson, K., & Simon, H. *Protocols as data: Effects of verbalizations.* Unpublished manuscript, Carnegie-Mellon University, 1978.
Fiedler, D., & Beach, L. R. On the decision to be assertive. *Journal of Consulting and Clinical Psychology.* 1978, *46*, 537–546.
Genest, M., Turk, D., & Meichenbaum, D. A cognitive behavioral approach to the management of of pain. Paper presented at the meeting of the Association for the Advancement of Behavior Therapy, Atlanta, April, 1977.
Glass, C., Gottman, J., & Schmurak, S. Response acquisition and cognitive self-statement modification approaches to dating skills training. *Journal of Counseling Psychology*, 1976, *23*, 520–526.
Goodman, S. *The integration of verbal and motor behavior in preschool children.* Unpublished doctoral dissertation, University of Waterloo, 1978.
Goor, A., & Sommerfeld, R. A comparison of problem-solving processes of creative students and non-creative students. *Journal of Educational Psychology*, 1975, *67*, 495–505.
Greenburg, D., & Jacobs, M. *How to make yourself miserable.* New York: Random House, 1966.
Halford, K. *Cognitive and social skill variables in social anxiety.* Unpublished doctoral thesis, La Trobe University, Australia, 1979.
Henshaw, D. *A cognitive analysis of creative problem-solving.* Unpublished doctoral dissertation, University of Waterloo, 1978.
Hollandsworth, J., Glazeski, R., Kirkland, K., Jones, G., & van Norman, L. *An analysis of the nature and effects of test anxiety: Cognitive, behavioral and physiological components.* Unpublished manuscript, University of Southern Mississippi, 1978.
Hurlburt, R. *Self-observation and self-control.* Unpublished doctoral dissertation, University of North Dakota, 1976.
Izard, C. *The face of emotion.* New York: Appleton-Century-Crofts, 1971.
Keiser, L. *The Vice Lords: Warriors of the streets.* New York: Holt, Rinehart, & Winston, 1969.
Kendall, P., & Korgeski, G. Assessment and cognitive-behavioral interventions. *Cognitive Therapy and Research*, in press.

Kendall, P., Williams, L., Pechacek, T., Graham, L., Shisslak, C., & Herzoff, N. Cognitive-behavioral and patient education in catheterization procedures. *Journal of Consulting and Clinical Psychology*, in press.

Langer, E. Rethinking the role of thought in social interaction. In J. Harvey, W. Ickes, & R. Kidd (Eds.), *New directions in attribution research*, vol. 2. Hillsdale, N.J.: Erlbaum, 1978.

Lazarus, R., Kanner, A., & Folkman, S. Emotions: A cognitive phenomenological analysis. In R. Plutchik and H. Kellerman (Eds.), *Theories of emotion.* New York: Academic, in press.

Loftus, E. Leading questions and eyewitness report. *Cognitive Psychology*, 1975, *7*, 560–572.

Mahoney, M., & Avener, M. Psychology of the elite athlete: An explanatory study. *Cognitive Therapy and Research*, 1977, *1*, 135–142.

Meichenbaum, D. Enhancing creativity by modifying what subjects say to themselves. *American Educational Research Journal*, 1975, *12*, 129–145.

Meichenbaum, D. *Cognitive behavior modification: An integrative approach.* New York: Plenum, 1977.

Meichenbaum, D., & Butler, L. Toward a conceptual the treatment of test anxiety: Implications for research and treatment. In I. Sarason (Ed.), *Test anxiety: Theory, research and applications.* Hillsdale, N.J.: Erlbaum, in press.

Meichenbaum, D., Butler, L., & Joseph, C. Toward a conceptual model of social competence. In J. Wine and M. Smye (Eds.), *The identification and enhancement of social competence.* Washington, D.C.: Hemisphere, in press.

Meichenbaum, D., & Goodman, S. Critical questions and methodological problems in studying children's private speech. In G. Zivin (Ed.), *Development of self-regulation through speech.* New York: Wiley, 1979.

Meichenbaum, D., Henshaw, D., & Himel, N. Coping with stress as a problem-solving process. In W. Krohne and L. Laux (Eds.), *Achievement stress and anxiety.* Washington, D.C., Hemisphere, in press.

Nisbett, R., & Wilson, T. Telling more than we can know: Verbal reports on mental processes. *Journal of Personality and Social Psychology*, 1976, *34*, 641–653.

Nisbett, R., & Bellows, N. Verbal reports about causal inferences on social judgments: Private access versus public theories. *Journal of Personality and Social Psychology*, 1977, *35*, 613–624.

Plutchik, R. *Cognitions in the service of emotions: An evolutionary perspective.* Unpublished manuscript, New York, 1978.

Pope, K., & Singer, J. *The stream of consciousness.* New York: Plenum, 1978.

Saarni, C. "Body Language:" A key to understanding cognitive-affective processes. Paper presented at the meeting of the Conference on Cognitive Behavior Therapy, New York, April 1978.

Schwartz, R., & Gottman, J. Toward a task analysis of assertive behavior. *Journal of Consulting and Clinical Psychology*, 1976, *44*, 910–920.

Shapiro, D. *Neurotic styles.* New York: Basic Books, 1965.

Smith, E., & Miller, F. Limits on perception of cognitive processes: A reply to Nisbett and Wilson. *Psychological Review*, 1978, *85*, 355–362.

Smye, M. *Verbal, cognitive and behavioral correlates of social anxiety.* Unpublished doctoral dissertation, University of Toronto, 1977.

Stewart, A. A longitudinal study of coping styles in self-defining and socially defined women. *Journal of Consulting and Clinical Psychology*, 1978, *46*, 1079–1084.

Strickland, B., Hale, W., & Anderson, L. Effect of induced mood states on activity and self-reported affect. *Journal of Consulting and Clinical Psychology*, 1975, *43*, 587.

Thorngate, W. Must we always think before we act? *Personality and Social Psychology Bulletin*, 1976, *2*, 31–35.

Thorngate, W. *Memory, cognition and social performance*. Unpublished manuscript, University of Alberta, 1977.

Tversky, A., & Kahneman, D. Availability: A heuristic for judging frequency and probability. *Cognitive Psychology*, 1973, *5*, 207–232.

Velten, E. A laboratory task for induction of mood states. *Behaviour Research and Therapy*, 1968, *6*, 473–482.

Watson, D., & Friend, R. Measurement of social-evaluative anxiety. *Journal of Consulting and Clinical Psychology*, 1969, *33*, 448–457.

Wine, J. Cognitive-attentional theory of test anxiety. In I. Sarason (Ed.), *Test Anxiety: Theory, research and application*. Hillsdale, N.J.: Erlbaum, in press.

Zivin, G. (Ed.). *The development of self-regulation through private speech*. New York: Wiley, in press.

CHAPTER 8

Personality Differences in Decision Making under Stress

Irving Janis

Department of Psychology
Yale University
New Haven, Connecticut

When we examine the personal decision making of large numbers of people, we can discern two major types of dilemma that they frequently encounter, both of which generate anxiety, shame, and guilt. One major type of stressful dilemma occurs when people have already decided what is the best thing to do but feel too weak to exercise the self-control necessary to carry out their intentions. This type of dilemma impells many people to go to clinics that offer help for those who want to quit smoking or to lose weight, where they sometimes benefit from supportive guidance for executing and sticking with a difficult decision. Another type of personal dilemma arises when a man or woman is facing a vital choice concerning marriage, career, health, or life style and is in so much conflict that he or she cannot decide what to do. People wanting help in such a crisis have much more difficulty finding an appropriate professional to consult. There is, however, an emerging development of decision counseling to help people make the fullest use of their own resources to resolve the realistic conflicts that arise from a choice dilemma by becoming aware of neglected alternatives and making the best decision in terms of their own value systems (see Janis & Mann, 1978).

Recently I have been working on and testing two theoretical models, one pertaining to the first type of dilemma (Janis, in press) and the other to the second type (Janis & Mann, 1977). In this paper I shall briefly summarize the two models and examine their implications for individual differences in responsiveness to counseling interventions that are intended to help people cope effectively with the stresses of one or the other type of decisional dilemma. I shall also examine briefly what little evidence is available from systematic research bearing on those implications.

Social Power of Supportive Helpers

One theoretical analysis takes as its point of departure some well-known assumptions about a primary basis of social power, as described by social psychologists—becoming a significant other, a reference person whose signs of approval and acceptance are highly rewarding. The widely-used typology by French and Raven (1959, pp. 150–167) designates *referent power* as a major determinant of social influence. A person has referent power for those who perceive him or her as likeable, benevolent, admirable, and accepting. Any such reference person is able to induce genuine changes in attitudes, decisions, and actions. French and Raven also describe four other bases of social influence which are effective in inducing acquiescence, but are much less likely to create sustained change or internalization: coercive power, reward power, legitimate power, and expert power.

In a recent review of systematic research bearing on the bases of social influence, Tedeschi and Lindskold (1976) conclude that the evidence supports a number of relatively independent dimensions pertaining to one person's influence on another, five of which correspond roughly to the French and Raven typology. Two additional components suggested by the empirical evidence are trustworthiness and credibility, which can be regarded as supplementary to the knowledge and skill components of expert power.

According to social psychological research on interpersonal attraction, there are several different ways that a counselor, or anyone else, can build the type of relationship that results in his becoming a significant reference person for the people he deals with (Bennis, Schein, Berlew, & Steele, 1973; Berscheid & Walster, 1969; Byrne, 1971; Levinger & Breedlove, 1966; Tedeschi & Lindskold, 1976). One way is to make salient the *similarities* between himself and his clients, particularly with regard to beliefs, attitudes, and values. Another way is to give *contingent praises* for specific accomplishments, actions, or intentions that are in line with the goals of the counseling sessions. A third way is to talk and act in a manner than conveys a *benevolent attitude* toward a client, an unselfish willingness to provide help out of a genuine sense of caring about the client's welfare. Still another, which may overlap somewhat the third way, is to give *noncontingent accep-*

tance statements, which convey to the clients that they are held in high regard as worthwhile persons despite whatever weaknesses and shortcomings might be apparent.

Some counselors fail to do anything at all to build up their power as a reference person. These counselors are to be found among psychologists who overvigorously apply the rules of one or another form of behavioral modification and also among those attorneys, physicians, nurses, and social workers who conscientiously concentrate on their professional tasks and tell their clients exactly what they ought to do without paying much attention to clients' psychological resistances. Some are so businesslike that they do not openly show any concern about the client's plight and never say anything to indicate that they care about their client's welfare. Such counselors, in effect, rely heavily on coercive, reward, legitimate, and expert power but neglect the potential increase in their ability to influence clients that could come from acquiring referent power as well. Even if businesslike counselors are using the other four sources of power to the very limit, their effectiveness would be expected to increase if they were to adopt one or another of the means for acquiring social power as a significant reference person in the life of each of their clients. By adding referent power to the other bases of social power, according to the foregoing theoretical assumptions, a helper would become a model with whom his or her clients identify. Then recommendations would meet with less initial psychological resistance and would also be more conscientiously adhered to long after the counseling sessions have come to an end. Contact with an authority figure who is exercising referent power is also likely to be anxiety reducing. By giving reassurance and satisfying the patients' stress-induced motivation for affiliation, a practitioner can alleviate fear and related emotional states (Janis, 1971; Schachter, 1959). Further, a reassuring counselor can have a major impact on whether or not warnings that require new courses of action are attended to and carried out (Janis, 1967; Rogers & Thistlethwaite, 1970; Rogers & Mewborn, 1976).

The theoretical analysis of critical phases in helping relationships, to which we now turn, is intended to add something to our understanding of how a professional counselor or any other kind of helper can influence clients to attain their own goals, such as exercising sufficient self-control to stick to a diet. It attempts to answer the following question: What else does it take, besides the factors already discussed, for a helper to build up and use effectively his or her power as a significant reference person?

Crises in a Helping Relationship

Where do the theoretical ideas come from? Mainly from my own clinical observations (in a variety of different counseling settings) of clients who sought help in deciding what to do about marital problems, choosing a career, changing jobs, giving up smoking, going on a diet, or undergoing a disagreeable course of medical treatments recommended by a physician (Janis, 1975). I met with each client once or twice a week for several weeks, the usual range being from three to twelve sessions. Sometimes, as in the case of the dieting clinics, the goal of counseling was to help the clients carry out a difficult course of action in the face of temptations to backslide; in other settings, the goal was to help the clients arrive at their own decisions concerning marriage or career by encouraging them to go through the necessary steps of exploring alternatives, seeking pertinent information, and making unbiased appraisals.

Impressionistic comparisons were made of what was going on in the most successful cases with what was happening in the unsuccessful cases. I have tried to evaluate the plausibility of my inferences from these impressionistic clinical observations in light of the clinical and social psychological literature on helping relationships. For example, the main hypotheses are consistent with findings from systematic studies indicating that social support from a significant person or group can have markedly positive effects when two main conditions are met: (1) the relationship is characterized by a high degree of *cohesiveness*, which is determined by the participants' anticipations of socioemotional gains (such as friendship and esteem), as well as utilitarian gains (such as improved health or better career opportunities), resulting from the relationship with the significant person or group; and (2) the relationship entails being exposed to *norm-setting* communications which convey the behavioral standards that the significant person or group expects one to live up to (Cartwright & Zander, 1968; Hare, 1976; Shaw, 1971).

All the hypotheses pertain to crises that typically arise in helping relationships. These hypotheses specify a number of new variables in addition to the more familiar ones pertaining to social power and positive social reinforcements that I have just discussed—variables that are likely to be overlooked by many counselors, but that nevertheless can affect the degree to which a person will be favorably influenced by a would-be helper.

From my observations, there appear to be three critical phases in almost every helping relationship, which are surmounted successfully when a person benefits from the attempts of a professional counselor or anyone else who tries to help that person adhere to a decision that is difficult to carry out.

1. In the first critical phase, the practitioner dissipates the patient's wariness and acquires motivating power as a significant "reference person." The client develops an attitude of reliance upon the practitioner for enhancing and maintaining his or her self-esteem if the practitioner encourages the

person to disclose personal feelings, troubles, or weaknesses and responds to the self-disclosures with noncontingent acceptance statements. The client's image of the practitioner then becomes that of a warm, understanding parental figure who can be counted on to accept personal weaknesses and defects. One of the advantages of encouraging a moderate degree of self-disclosure about personal problems, such as an overweight client's craving for rich desserts, is that the professional can use those disclosures to help the client reappraise his or her difficulties, and to develop a more facilitating set of cognitions that are incompatible with self-defeating thoughts (Rodin, 1978). When the individual must learn to take personal responsibility for his or her actions, some elementary insights are required, which a practitioner can provide, about when, where, and how to do so. (Janis & Rodin, 1979). Self-blame is less likely to generate low self-esteem and more likely to have positive behavioral outcomes when the causes are seen by the patient as situational and not dispositional (Janoff-Bulman, 1978; Rodin, 1978).

2. In the second critical phase, the practitioner begins to use his or her motivating power. However, the relationship built up during the first phase is impaired as the practitioner begins to function as a norm-sending communicator by encouraging or urging the client to carry out a necessary but stressful course of action. If the practitioner makes no such demands, either explicitly or implicitly, the relationship will continue in a warm, friendly way but will be totally ineffective in achieving the objectives of helping the person carry out a difficult decision. The crisis arising when the practitioner recommends a new course of action probably can be successfully surmounted if he or she makes it clear that the demands being made are very limited in scope, and that occasional failures to live up to those demands following a sincere attempt to do so will not change his or her basic attitude of acceptance toward the patient. A norm-sending practitioner is most likely to retain motivating power if he or she uses a *selective pattern of social reinforcement* whereby criticism is given in a nonthreatening way for counternorm assertions by the patient and positive regard is expressed the rest of the time, including when the patient admits to personal weaknesses or shortcomings that are irrelevant to the task at hand. By expressing noncontingent acceptance most of the time, and restricting contingent acceptance to the agreed-upon task, a practitioner can build an authentic image of himself or herself in the patient's mind as a quasi-dependable source of self-esteem enhancement, which greatly facilitates the practitioner's effectiveness. It may also be helpful for the practitioner to attribute the norms that are being endorsed to a respected secondary group and to negotiate an agreement with the patient so that he or she becomes committed to those norms.

3. In the third critical phase, the influence of the supportive norm-

sending practitioner is threatened by the patient's disappointment and resentment about the termination of direct contact. The practitioner's goal is to promote internalization of his or her recommended changes. However, once the sessions with the practitioner have ended, the client may fail to internalize the norms the practitioner has been advocating if he or she interprets the termination of contact as a sign of rejection or indifference. Patients whose chronic diabetes has been stabilized, for example, may stop following the prescribed medical regimen after a period of several months when they no longer have any appointments to see the physician. Adverse reactions to separation may be minimized if the practitioner gives *assurances of continuing positive regard* and arranges for *gradual*, rather than abrupt, termination of contact. In order to prevent backsliding and other adverse effects when contact with the practitioner is terminated, the client must internalize the norms sponsored by the practitioner by somehow converting other-directed approval motivation into self-directed approval motivation. Little is known as yet about the determinants of this process, but it seems plausible to expect that internalization might be facilitated by communications and training procedures that build up a sense of personal responsibility. The counselor can attempt to give communications that continue to build up self-control attributions and a sense of personal responsibility. This attempt may have begun in phase 2, but clients must now feel fully confident that they are able to go forward on their own. In diet programs, for example, the health counselor can emphasize that the clients' initial weight loss and changes in eating habits demonstrate their capabilities for successful self-control.

Evidence on the Effects of Building Referent Power

Part of the art of effective counseling may require dealing with each of the three phases in a way that minimizes adverse reactions. Perhaps only a small proportion of practitioners have the interpersonal skills that enable them to function with greater artistry when treating the majority of their clients. Nevertheless, practitioners with modest amounts of skill in dealing with people in trouble may be able to improve their percentage of successful cases by taking account of the main prescriptive hypotheses that follow from the above analysis.

The hypotheses are presented in Table 1. The variables specified for each critical phase can be subjected to experimental investigation in clinical settings where counselors interact with clients. Evidence from controlled

Table 1. Critical Phases and Eleven Key Variables that Determine the Degree of Referent Power of Professional Practitioners as Change Agents[a]

Phase 1 (In order for practitioners to *build up* motivating power)	(1) Encouraging a moderate amount of self-disclosure by the clients versus encouraging little or no self-disclosure. (2) Giving positive feedback (acceptance and understanding) versus giving neutral or negative feedback in response to self-disclosure. (3) Using self-disclosures to give insight and cognitive restructuring versus giving little insight or cognitive restructuring.
Phase 2 (In order for practitioners to *use* their motivating power)	(4) Making directive statements or endorsing specific recommendations regarding actions the patient should carry out versus abstaining from any directive statements or endorsements. (5) Eliciting commitment to the recommended course of action versus not eliciting commitment. (6) Attributing the norms being endorsed to a respected secondary group versus not doing so. (7) Giving selective positive feedback versus giving noncontingent acceptance or predominantly neutral or negative feedback. (By selective feedback is meant negative feedback in response to any of the patient's comments about wanting to avoid acting in accordance with the recommendations combined with positive feedback in response to all other comments, whether relevant to the decision or not). (8) Giving communications and training procedures that build up self-control attributions and a sense of personal responsibility versus giving no such communications or training.
Phase 3 (In order for practitioners to *retain* their motivating power and to *promote internalization* after contact ends)	(9) Giving reassurances that the practitioner will continue to maintain an attitude of positive regard versus giving no such reassurances. (10) Making arrangements for phone calls, exchange of letters, or other forms of communication that foster hope for future contact, real or symbolic, at the time of terminating face-to-face meetings versus making no such arrangements. (11) Giving reminders that continue to foster self-control attributions and a sense of personal responsibility versus giving no such reminders.

[a] Based on Janis (in press).

field experiments that I and my co-workers carried out in antismoking clinics, weight-reduction clinics, and other health-related settings indicates that most of the key variables listed in Table 1 markedly affect the degree to which a professional helper is perceived as a source of self-esteem enhancement and facilitates adherence to a recommended regimen (Janis, 1975; in press).

Level of Self-Esteem

Do clients with different personality characteristics or other predispositional attributes react differently to a helping relationship that is intended to bolster their self-control in carrying out a difficult course of action? Empirical results bearing on this question come from the series of field experiments that were designed to investigate the key variables derived from the theoretical analysis of the critical phases. These studies included personality measures along with measures of the behavioral effects of experimental variations in counseling procedures (Janis, in press).

Obviously, it is always difficult to draw definitive conclusions from studies of relationships between predispositional attributes and behavior changes because such studies are correlational, and therefore, alternative interpretations in terms of hidden third factors cannot be precluded. Nevertheless, if observed correlations or interactions between predispositional measures and treatments prove to be well replicated in a series of studies, they can provide dependable information about who is likely to respond in what way.

The theoretical analysis of critical phases in helping relationships alerts us to the potential importance of the clients' initial level of self-esteem as a determinant of responsiveness to supportive counseling. The theory postulates that when people have the intention of changing to a difficult course of action, such as dieting, the incentive value of gaining the approval of a counselor or advisor can help to get them started and to continue. A supportive norm-sending advisor can build up and use potential motivating power, according to the theory, if he or she meets the main conditions specified for the three critical phases (see Table 1). When those conditions are met, the client builds up an image of the counselor as a quasi-dependable source of self-esteem enhancement: the person who seeks help comes to realize that he or she will mostly receive spontaneous acceptance, even when revealing weaknesses and shortcomings, *except* when he or she fails to make a sincere effort to live up to a *limited* set of norms. This modified expectation of partly contingent acceptance from the helper allows the client to look forward to receiving genuine acceptance and approval from the helper much of the time, practically all the time, provided he or she makes a sincere effort to follow just a few rules recommended by the helper pertaining to only a specific sphere of personal behavior.

This theoretical analysis leads us to expect that it is worthwhile to investigate individual differences in initial level of self-esteem because such differences might be related to the outcome of supportive counseling. But the theory does not state exactly what the relationship will be. One plausible hypothesis is that clients initially low in self-esteem are most demoralized and therefore most in need of self-esteem bolstering to counteract their lack of confidence about succeeding on a difficult new course of action. According to this hypothesis, the initially low self-esteem clients will show relatively little adherence to the counselor's recommendations if the counselor gives neutral feedback or shows signs of being critical or detached, but will show a marked increase in adherence if the counselor consistently meets the optimal conditions for functioning as a quasi-dependable source of self-esteem enhancement. The clients with initially high self-esteem, on the other hand, will be relatively self-confident about succeeding to start with, and therefore, will show a relatively high degree of adherence irrespective of variations in the counselor's acceptance behavior.

An alternative hypothesis, which also seems quite plausible in light of clinical observations, is that clients with low self-esteem are not initially more demoralized or less self-confident than others but are more dissatisfied with themselves as they now are. Therefore, they are more strongly motivated to obtain whatever self-esteem enhancement they can from living up to the counselor's norms and from their own achievement of success on a difficult task, such as dieting. Clients with an initially high level of self-esteem, on the other hand, being less discontented with themselves, are less motivated to work hard to make use of the opportunity for self-esteem enhancement offered by the relationship with the counselor or by succeeding on the difficult task at hand. The predictions that follow from the second hypothesis are different from those that follow from the first one. The second hypothesis leads us to expect that clients initially low in self-esteem will show more adherence to the counselor's recommendations than clients with initially high self-esteem for all forms of counseling (including when the counselor gives mainly neutral feedback), and will do even better when the counselor is explicitly accepting.

Turning now to the available evidence from eight field experiments that included personality measures, we find more support for the second hypothesis than for the first. In our initial field experiment in a weight-loss clinic (Dowds, Janis, & Conolley, in press). The client's scores on the Janis and Field (1959, pp. 55–68) self-esteem scale were found to be related to successful adherence to the counselor's recommendations, irrespective of whether the counselor gave positive or neutral feedback in response to self-disclosures. During the two-month follow-up period, clients with relatively low self-esteem scores (below the median) mailed back significantly more weekly reports and reported following the diet to a significantly greater extent than clients with relatively high self-esteem scores. There was a difference in the same direction for weight loss over the two-month period, but the difference was not large enough to be statistically significant.

The differences between low and high self-esteem clients were replicated and emerged even more strongly in a pair of field experiments that followed by Conolley, Janis, and Dowds (in press). The low self-esteem clients again showed significantly more weight loss than the high self-esteem clients; this time the difference was significant. And again the clients with low self-esteem scores returned a significantly larger number of weekly reports, on the average, over the two-month follow-up period and reported following the diet for a significantly larger number of days.

Thus, the results from both studies indicate that the clients who benefit most from the type of short-term counseling provided in the dieting clinic are those who initially have a relatively low level of self-esteem, as manifested by their answers to questions about feelings of personal inadequacy, self-blame, and lack of confidence in dealing with people. These differences were observed irrespective of the type of feedback given by the counselor.

In a completely different setting, involving brief counseling sessions for elementary school teachers who were attending a workshop on new methods of arithmetic instruction, Smith (in press) again found that low initial self-esteem was related to adherence to recommendations. In Smith's study the counseling treatment consisted of enhancing the teachers' self esteem by making encouraging comments about their progress and their potentialities for mastering the new instructional methods despite whatever problems they were having. The teachers who were most responsive to the self-esteem enhancement counseling, as manifested by behavioral measures of subsequent adherence to the workshop recommendations in their own classrooms, were those who initially obtained low self-esteem scores on the California Personality Inventory. (For the control group, which was given a tutoring treatment that did not involve any discussions of personal problems, no relationship was found between initial level of self-esteem and subsequent adherence to the recommendations.) Smith points out that the initial low self-esteem scores of those who responded best to the counseling treatment do not necessarily imply a chronically low level of self-esteem. All of them were working at inner-city schools under adverse conditions that make for disillusionment and loss of self-esteem. Their low self-esteem scores could reflect, therefore, a situationally-induced state, resulting from the stresses of their work, which might make them especially responsive to a brief counseling treatment involving self-esteem enhancement. Nevertheless, the fact that clients with low self-esteem in the two studies conducted in the dieting clinic were also found to be more responsive to the recommendations, just as in the teachers workshop, suggests that Smith's findings are not just limited to teachers working in inner-city schools.

Among those overweight clients who came to the dieting clinic, low self esteem might also have been situationally induced, as a result of distressing circumstances quite different from those besetting the teachers. Nevertheless, we should be open-minded about the possibility that in the dieting clinic, as well as in the teachers' workshop, the relatively low self-esteem scores of those who proved to be most responsive to the counseling procedures may indicate a *chronic* personality characteristic. If so, one would predict that subsequent research will reveal repeated confirmation of the self-esteem findings from the three studies, showing that, in a wide variety of counseling settings, those clients who initially manifest low self esteem are generally the ones who respond best, irrespective of whether there are specific situational circumstances that could account for their low self-esteem. This hypothesis does not appear to be very plausible, however, in light of evidence from a large number of attitude-change studies that have investigated the relationship between level of self-esteem and responsiveness to persuasive communications. Although some of the attitude change studies show the predicted relationship between low self-esteem and high responsiveness to social influence, just as was observed in the three field experiments on counseling, other attitude change studies show no relationship at all, and still others show the opposite relationship (see McGuire, 1969). One possible explanation for the inconsistent findings is that situational factors interact with level of self-esteem as determinants of responsiveness to social influence. Such interacting effects are to be expected in counseling clinics, as well as other settings where people are given recommendations that attempt to influence their decisions.

An instructive example of an interaction effect, of the kind I am referring to, was found in a counseling study in the Yale weight-reduction clinic by Riskind (in press). Using the self-acceptance scale from the California Personality Inventory to assess level of self-esteem, Riskind found that when the clients were given a long-term perspective that emphasized difficulties to be expected in the future, those clients with initially low self-esteem scores showed more adherence, including more weight loss. Essentially the same finding was obtained in the two prior studies in the weight-reduction clinic that showed low self-esteem to be related to high adherence. But Riskind found that the relationship was reversed when clients were encouraged to adopt a short-term (day-by-day) approach to dieting, which fostered a sense of personal control. Under this situational condition, clients who obtained high self-esteem scores showed more adherence.

I suspect that many other situational variables will also be found to affect the relationship between level of self-esteem and responsiveness to a counselor's recommendations. Perhaps, if subsequent research focuses on counseling variables that give rise to interaction effects, it will become possible to formulate some dependable generalizations.

Another type of interaction effect that needs to be looked into involves the different components that go into the self-esteem scales currently in use. For example, one scale may primarily tap the subjects' chronic level of self-esteem while another may tap the subjects' temporary state during recent days or weeks, induced by the current life situation, and a third may tap the subjects' mood of the moment. These diverse components of a hetrogeneous personality scale that purports to measure self-esteem might not be related to adherence in the same way. Later on, we shall see that there are theoretical grounds for expecting that chronically low self-esteem makes for a coping pattern of defensive avoidance, which leads to low adherence, whereas, a temporary state of current dissatisfaction with oneself could function as a positive incentive that leads to vigilance and high adherence.

The need for a similar type of differentiation is indicated by seemingly contradictory findings from two other studies carried out in our weight-reduction clinic. Quinlan, Janis, and Bales (in press) noted that those groups of overweight women who reported on a questionnaire that they felt guilty about their lack of control over their eating behavior showed more successful adherence to the diet after two months than those groups who reported less guilt. This finding appears to be in line with the previous findings on the relationship between low self-esteem and adherence. But a study by Janis and Quinlan (in press), which used a comparable interview procedure with a small sample of overweight women, indicates that those who initially expressed low self-confidence about succeeding at the task of dieting were *less* likely to lose weight. Lack of self-confidence is, of course, generally regarded as a component of low self-esteem, If we were to regard it that way, we would be obliged to say that these findings on level of self-confidence contradict the other findings on level of self-esteem because they show exactly the reverse relationship. But there may not be any contradiction here because the two measures may not be measuring the same thing. In subsequent work with predispositional measures, it would appear to be worthwhile to separate the two components into independent scales, one dealing with demoralization as manifested by lack of self-confidence about future success at solving the overweight problem, and the other dealing with shame or guilt about failure to exercise sufficient self-control to solve the problem. As was mentioned earlier, the latter component of self-esteem might function as a positive incentive to adopt a new course of action whereas the former component implies a lack of hope, which according to the conflict theory of coping with decisional stress, makes for defensive avoidance in the form of procrastinating, shifting responsibility to others, or bolstering the current course of inaction (see page 179).

Field Dependence

Field dependence is a related personality variable that has been extensively investigated and, again, the results have been somewhat inconsistent (see Horn, 1976, pp. 437–485). In a field study in the Yale dieting clinic by Greene (in press), this variable was found to be predictive of clients' acquiescent behavior during the initial interview but not of subsequent compliance with the recommended diet. As expected, the clients who obtained the highest scores on field dependence (based on Witkins' embedded figures test) displayed fewer signs of withdrawal during the interview, expressed more positive feelings toward the counselor, and also expressed greater willingness to accept the recommended diet than those who obtained lower scores. These reactions can be regarded as manifestations of a strong need for approval from the counselor. But what happens afterwards, when these dependent clients have to carry out their good intentions without being in contact with the counselor? During the five weeks following the initial interview, the clients who scored high on field dependence showed *less* adherence than the others—they mailed back fewer weekly reports and were less successful in losing weight. In terms of the theoretical analysis of phases in the development of an effective supportive relationship with a counselor, the high-scoring clients on field dependence might be more responsive than others to cues indicating interest and acceptance on the part of the counselor in Phase 1, and perhaps also in Phase 2, when the counselor gives specific recommendations, but less tolerant of separation from the counselor in Phase 3. Thus, despite getting off to a very good start in the initial session at the clinic, the field dependent clients appear to do relatively poorly at home when it comes to adhering to a difficult course of action without having contact with a supportive counselor.

Theoretical Analysis of Coping Predispositions

Having examined the meager findings bearing on relationships between predispositional measures and adherence from our short-term counseling studies, we turn next to predispositional variables that are suggested by the theoretical analysis of coping patterns as being predictive of effective versus defective reactions to the stresses of intense decisional conflict when a vital choice is being made. The conflict-theory model developed by Janis and Mann (1977) starts with the assumption that stress, engendered by decisional conflict, is frequently a major determinant of failure to achieve high-quality decision making. "Decisional conflict" refers to simultaneous opposing tendencies within the individual to accept, and at the same time, to reject a given course of action. The most prominent symptoms of such conflicts are hesitation, vacillation, feelings of uncertainty, and signs of acute psychological stress (anxiety, shame, guilt, or other unpleasant affect) whenever the decision comes to the focus of attention.

Psychological stress arising from decisional conflict stems from at least two sources. First, the decision maker is concerned about the material and social losses he or she might suffer from whichever course of action is chosen, including the costs of failing to live up to prior commitments. Second, the person recognizes that his or her reputation and self-esteem as a competent decision-maker are at stake. The more severe the anticipated losses, the greater the stress. In assuming that the stress itself is frequently a major cause of errors in decision making, we do not deny the influence of other common causes, such as information overload and the limitations of human information processing, group pressures, blinding prejudice, and ignorance. We maintain, however, that a major reason for many ill-conceived and poorly implemented decisions has to do with the motivational consequences of decisional conflict, particularly attempts to ward off the stresses generated by agonizingly difficult choices. Over and above the effects of the individual's cognitive limitations in judging evidence and other sources of error, a harassed decision-maker is likely to suffer a further decline in cognitive functioning as result of the anxiety generated by the stress of being confronted with a task too complicated to manage, especially when it can entail serious losses. Janis and Mann's (1977) analysis of the ways that people cope with the stresses of making vital decisions emphasizes the tendency of people to short-circuit the essential stages of search and appraisal when they become aware of undesirable consequences to be expected from whichever choice they make. Decision-makers are often inclined to deceive themselves into thinking they have conducted a complete information search after brief contact with a so-called expert and perhaps a few informal discussions with friends and acquaintances. This deception sometimes happens even when the decision is a vital one, such as quitting college, choosing a career, changing to a different job, getting married, obtaining a divorce, or moving to a different city. In such instances—whenever the decision could entail serious, lifelong consequences—a decision counselor can serve a valuable function. Even highly experienced decision-makers might benefit from professional guidance designed to help them to carry out a more effective information search, to correct some of their biased judgments, and to become more aware of the consequences of inadequate courses of action that they might be tempted to choose.

In line with their initial assumptions, Janis and Mann (1977) postulate that there are five basic patterns of coping with the stresses generated by any realistic challenge that confronts a person with a vital choice. Each pattern is associated with a specific set of antecedent conditions and a characteristic level of stress. These patterns were derived from an analysis of the research literature on psychological stress bearing on how people react to warnings that urge protective action to avert health hazards or other serious threats.

The five coping patterns are:

1. *Unconflicted adherence:* The decision-maker complacently decides to continue whatever he has been doing, ignoring information about the risk of losses.

2. *Unconflicted change* to a new course of action: The decision-maker uncritically adopts whichever new course of action is most salient or most strongly recommended to him.

3. *Defensive avoidance.* The decision-maker escapes the conflict by procrastinating, shifting responsibility to someone else, or constructing wishful rationalizations to bolster the least objectionable alternative, remaining selectively inattentive to corrective information.

4. *Hypervigilance.* The decision-maker searches frantically for a way out of the dilemma and impulsively siezes upon a hastily contrived solution that seems to promise immediate relief, overlooking the full range of consequences of his choice as a result of emotional excitement, perserveration, and cognitive constriction (manifested by reduction in immediate memory span and simplistic thinking). In its most extreme form, hypervigilance is referred to as "panic."

5. *Vigilance.* The decision-maker searches painstakingly for relevant information, assimilates information in an unbiased manner, and appraises alternatives carefully before making a choice.

While the first two patterns are occasionally adaptive in saving time, effort, and emotional wear-and-tear, especially for routine or minor decisions, they often lead to defective decisions if the person must make a choice that has serious consequences for himself, for his family, or for the organization he or she represents. Similarly, defensive avoidance and hypervigilance may occasionally be adaptive, but generally reduce the decision-maker's chances of averting serious losses. Consequently, all four are regarded as defective patterns of decision making. The fifth pattern, vigilance, although occasionally maladaptive if danger is imminent and a split-second response is required, generally leads to decisions that meet the main criteria for high-quality decision making, which we shall discuss shortly.

The five coping patterns are represented in Figure 1, which is a schematic summary of Janis and Mann's conflict-theory of decision making. This conflict model specifies the psychological conditions responsible for the five coping patterns and the level of stress that accompanies them.

Later on I shall discuss the sources of individual differences in readiness to acknowledge serious risks, to maintain hope or optimism about finding a better alternative, and to believe that there is adequate time in which to search and deliberate. Janis and Mann assume that despite those predispostional differences, the same five coping patterns are in the repertoire of every person when he or she functions as a decision-maker, that the use of one pattern rather than another is determined by the mediating psychological conditions shown in Figure 1, and that the five patterns lead to distinctive behavioral consequences, which are summarized in Table 2.

The columns of the table represent the major criteria that can be used to judge whether a decision made by a person or a group is of high quality with regard to the problem-solving procedures that lead up to the act of commitment. These criteria were extracted from the extensive literature on effective decision making. (See Janis & Mann, 1977, Chapters 1 and 2.) The seven procedural criteria, named at the head of the columns in Table 1, are as follows: (1) the decision-maker thoroughly canvasses a wide range of alternative courses of action; (2) the decision-maker takes account of the full range of objectives to be fulfilled and the values implicated by the choice; (3) the decision-maker carefully weighs whatever he or she knows about the costs or drawbacks and the uncertain risks of negative consequences, as well as the positive consequences, that could flow from each alternative; (4) the decision-maker intensively searches for new information relevant for further evaluation of the alternatives; (5) the decision-maker conscientiously takes account of any new information or expert judgment to which he or she is exposed, even when the information or judgment does not support the course of action he or she initially prefers; (6) the decision-maker reexamines the positive and negative consequences of all known alternatives, including those originally regarded as unacceptable, before making a final choice; and (7) the decision maker makes detailed provisions for implementing or executing the chosen course of action, with special attention to

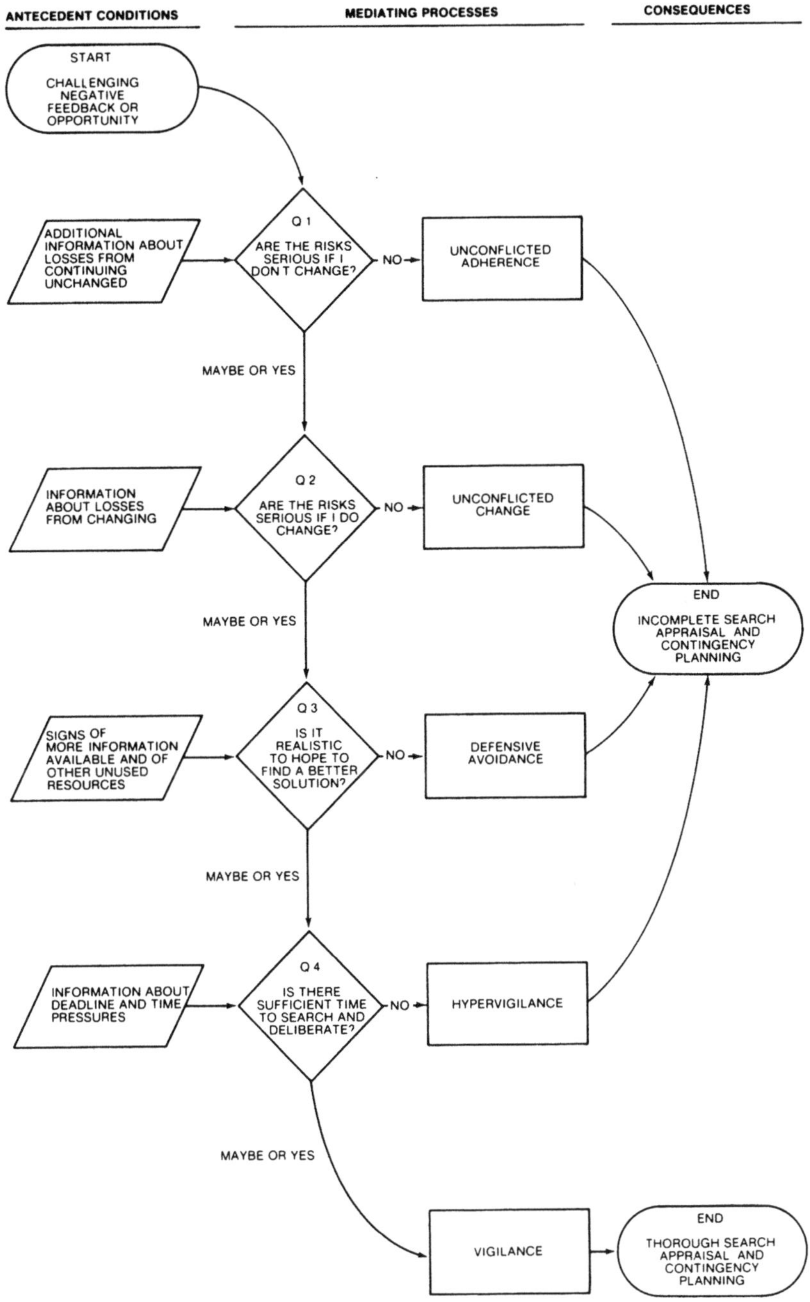

Fig. 1. The conflict–theory model of decision making (from Janis and Mann, 1977).

Table 2. Predecisional Behavior Characteristics of the Five Basic Patterns of Decision Making[a]

Pattern of coping with challenge	Thorough canvassing of alternatives	Thorough canvassing of objectives	Careful evaluation of consequences of		Thorough search for information	Unbiased assimilation of new information	Careful reevaluation of consequences	Thorough planning for implementation and contingencies
			(1) current policy	(2) new policies				
Unconflicted adherence	−	−	−	−	−	+	−	−
Unconflicted change	−	−	+	−	−	+	−	−
Defensive avoidance	−	−	−	−	−	−	−	−
Hypervigilance	−	−	±	±	±	±	−	−
Vigilance	+	+	+	+	+	+	+	+

[a] From Janis and Mann (1977). Note: + = the decision maker meets the criterion to the best of his ability; − = the decision maker fails to meet the criterion; ± = the decision maker's performance fluctuates, sometimes meeting the criterion to the best of his ability and sometimes not. All evaluative terms such as *thorough* and *unbiased* are to be understood as intrapersonal comparative assessments, relative to the person's performances under the most favorable conditions that enable him to display his cognitive capabilities to the best of his ability.

contingency plans that might be required if various known risks were to materialize.

Janis and Mann assume that failure to meet any of these seven criteria is a defect in the decision-making process. The more such defects are present before the decision-maker becomes committed, the greater the chances that he or she will undergo unanticipated setbacks and postdecisional regret, which make for reversal of the decision. Although systematic data are not yet available on this point, it seems plausible to assume that "high-quality" decisions—in the sense of satisfying these procedural criteria—have a better chance than others of attaining the decision-maker's objectives and of being adhered to in the long run.

What is unique about the model is the specification of conditions relating to conflict, hope, and time pressure, which mediate the distinctive coping patterns. We do not claim that the five patterns occur *only* as a result of the specified conditions. A habitual procrastinator, for example, may almost invariably approach any decision, large or small, in a defensive manner; a flexible person may display vigilance in response to most threats but become hypervigilant each time he reencounters a situation in which he had once been traumatized. Our claim is that the patterns are linked dependably with the conditions specified in Figure 1–a claim that has testable implications about environmental circumstances that generate vigilance and about deliberate interventions which could counteract the beliefs and perceptions responsible for defective coping patterns. It follows from this theoretical analysis that information inputs and special intervention procedures used by a counselor when consulted by clients about making a vital choice can modify the way the clients cope with the stresses of decisional conflict in the direction of improving the quality of their decision-making activity. A number of testable implications of the model have been investigated, and at least partially confirmed, concerning the conditions that determine whether the decision-makers' information search will be cursory or thorough, whether their deliberations will be biased or unbiased, and whether their adherence to their decisions will be short-lived or persistent. (The pertinent studies are reviewed in Janis & Mann, 1977, Chapters 4–12.)

Three conditions are essential for vigilant search and appraisal, according to the conflict-theory analysis of coping patterns, in response to threats or opportunities that induce changes in behavior: (1) belief that there are serious risks for whichever alternative course of action is chosen; (2) belief that it is realistic to be optimistic about finding a better alternative solution than the objectionable ones that are being contemplated; (3) belief that there is adequate time in which to search and deliberate before a decision is required. A person who is generally unresponsive to authentic information that promotes one or another of these beliefs would be expected to show a consistently defective coping pattern that generally would lead either to no change at all or to a poorly worked out decision without adequate contingency planning, which would soon be followed by reversal of the decision in response to acute postdecisional regret.

There are various bits and pieces of evidence from prior research on personality differences that appear to be in line with these assumptions. For example, a number of studies employing Byrne's (1964) repression-sensitization scale and Goldstein's (1959) closely related "coper versus avoider" test suggest that persons diagnosed as chronic repressors or avoiders tend to minimize, deny, or ignore any warning that presents disturbing information about impending threats. Such persons appear to be predisposed to display the characteristic features of defensive avoidance, and, unlike those who are predisposed to be vigilant, do not respond adaptively to preparatory information that provides realistic forecasts about stressful experiences to be expected along with reassurances. Some confirmatory findings are to be found in the reports on two field experiments conducted on surgery wards by Andrew (1970) and De Long (1971). In both studies, patients awaiting surgery were given Goldstein's test in order to assess their preferred mode of coping with stress and then were given preparatory information. The reactions of the following three groups were compared: (1) copers who tended to display vigilance or sensitizing defenses; (2) avoiders, who displayed avoidant or denial defenses; and (3) nonspecific defenders who showed no clear preference. In Andrew's (1970) study, preparatory information describing what the experience of the operation and the postoperative convalescence will be like, had an unfavorable effect on the rate of physical recovery of avoiders, but a positive effect on nonspecific defenders. Copers recovered well irrespective of whether they were given the preoperative information. In De Long's (1971) study, avoiders were found to have poorest recovery regardless of whether they were given the preparatory information; copers showed the greatest benefit from the preparatory information.

Although not completely consistent with each other, the findings from the two studies appear to agree in indicating that persons who display defensive avoidance tendencies do not respond well to preoperative counseling that presents preparatory information. This conclusion seems to be in line with evidence on stress tolerance obtained in some (though not all) of the laboratory stress experiments in which differences between repressors (or avoiders) versus sensitizers have been studied. For example, Davidson and Bobey (1970) found that repressors showed a decrease in tolerance for experimentally-induced pain following an initial exposure to the painful stimulus whereas sensitizers showed a trend in the opposite direction. In a laboratory experiment by Olson and Zanna (1979), which required subjects to make a minor decision, repressors displayed selective exposure in the form of avoiding exposing themselves to dissonance-producing perceptions whereas sensitizers did not.[1]

The evidence from the various studies I have just cited is suggestive but bears only indirectly on the main implications of the conflict-theory analysis of coping patterns with respect to personality predispositions. The following propositions specify how, according to the theory, personality predispositions are expected to be conducive to faulty decision making in response to challenging communications or events that call attention to serious risks from continuing defective courses of action or inaction:

1. If a person has a consistently high threshold for assimilating information about risks—such as low intellectual ability, which prevents comprehension of warnings about impending threats or lack of vivid imagery, which dampens the emotional impact and the subsequent salience of the warnings—he or she will show: (a) *unconflicted adherence* to his or her old course of action in response to challenging events or communications that induce most other people to change their behavior; or (b) *unconflicted change* to a new course of action, without adequate preparation for avoiding acute postdecisional regret (when the challenge is so powerful that

[1] Evidence from a correlational study of surgical patients appears to contradict the implications of all the predispositional studies just discussed bearing on vigilance versus defensive avoidance. Cohen and Lazarus (1973) report that patients who were rated as "vigilant" before the operation showed more negative postoperative reactions than those rated as "avoidant." This finding seems not only to contradict the earlier surgery findings, but also to go against the expectation from the conflict-theory model that people who are vigilant will cope better with unfavorable consequences of their decisions than will those whose dominant coping patterns is defensive avoidance or hypervigilance. But a careful examination of Cohen and Lazarus's procedures reveals that these investigators did not differentiate between hypervigilance and vigilance. The investigators state that they classified as vigilant any patient who sought out information about their operation (which hypervigilant people do even more than vigilant ones), or who were sensitized in terms of remembering the information and displaying readiness to discuss their thoughts about the operation. (Again, the hypervigilant people tend to be much more preoccupied with information about threatening consequences than those who are vigilant.) The one example Cohen and Lazarus give of a so-called vigilant reaction would be classified as "hypervigilant" according to the criteria given in Janis and Mann (1977, pp. 74, 205–206): "I have all the facts, my will is all prepared [in the event of death] . . . you're put out, you could be put out too deep, your heart could quit, you can have shock . . . I go not in lightly." Consequently, the correlation observed by these investigators might be attributable to the relationship between preoperative hypervigilance and low tolerance for postoperative stress, which has been observed by other investigators (Janis, 1958; Leventhal, 1965; Leventhal & Sharpe, 1965).

Sime (1976) attempted to replicate Cohen and Lazarus's (1973) finding using the same categories but was unable to do so. When there are disagreements like this, one suspects that either there are unrecognized differences in procedures or the relationship between the two variables is determined by an uninvestigated third variable, such as severity of the patient's illness.

it is above the person's high threshold for assimilating the information about the risks of continuing the same old course of action, and information about the risks entailed by the new course of action is not sufficiently impressive to be above the person's high threshold).

2. If a person has a consistently high threshold for assimilating information that for most people promotes optimism about available opportunities and resources for finding an acceptable solution to the challenging event or communication—for example, because of pessimistic expectations resulting from a chronic mood of depressive self-disparagement—he or she will generally display a *defensive avoidance* pattern (in the form of chronic procrastination, shifting responsibility to someone else, or bolstering the least objectionable alternative with rationalizations), which involves denying or minimizing the risks and interferes with developing plans that lead to stable changes in behavior.

3. If a person has a consistently high threshold for assimilating information that leads most people to expect to have sufficient time for search and appraisal before being required to make a choice among alternative courses of action—for example, because of a chronic sense of time urgency, as has been found among "type A personalities" who are at high risk with regard to coronary heart disease (Glass, 1977)—*hypervigilance* will frequently be displayed in response to challenging events or communications, which leads to impulsive, ill-considered, and unstable decisions.

The examples of predispositonal variables given in the above three propositions refer to personality traits that are so broad in scope that they would affect all types of decision, pertaining to health, career, marriage, social affiliations, or even policy making in an executive role. But most psychologists have learned to be skeptical about being able to make significant predictions on the basis of such broad predispositional attributes because so much prior research shows that personality traits, as measured by the most widely used tests and rating scales, do not show high consistency across different situations and do not account for very much of the variance in observable behavior change (see Mischel, 1968). Some recent studies, however, indicate that general personality traits are not quite in such bad shape as they seemed in 1968 (see Sechrest, 1976). In any case, the above three propositions do not necessarily need to be so imperialistic in scope; they can be reformulated in terms of less sweepingly broad predispositions that pertain to a more limited domain of decision making. In a less imperialistic version, the propositions could be confined to the home territory of just one type or subtype of decision, such as those pertaining to health risks.

There is no reason, in my opinion, to be pessimistic about the prospects of finding consistent individual differences in the three thresholds specified in the above propositions. I expect that in some persons such thresholds may be consistently high and in others consistently low due to a variety of causes, including both chronic personality characteristics and current social circumstances, such as recent exposure to demoralizing or sensitizing events that could affect a person's responsiveness to information bearing on more than one type of decision.

A number of recent studies show that some patients who have recently had heart attacks become temporarily depressed, worry about the possiblity of having another attack, and continue to preoccupied with the losses entailed by their illness and the poor prospects for recovering fully. There is some evidence suggesting that these patients are more likely to fail to adopt the recommended course of action necessary for rehabilitation than the equally ill patients who show less depression and less anxiety (Gentry, Foster, & Haney, 1972; Hackett, Cassem, & Wishnie, 1968; McGill, 1975). This observation has been interpreted as suggesting that those heart patients who deny their illness do better in rehabilitation programs than those who do not engage in denial. This formulation creates a paradox because other observations indicate that denial of illness generally has adverse effects on patients' behavior. But we suspect that "denial" versus "non-denial" may not be the appropriate terms to describe the patients' reactions. Rather, the crucial difference may be between developing and maintaining some degree of *hope* about solving the health problem despite current suffering versus remaining *hopeless* about the value of doing anything. That is to say, the defensive avoidance pattern described above might provide an explanation: Those coronary heart disease patients who become pessimistic about finding a satisfactory solution to their current health problem—whether their pessimism is attributable to a life-long personality predisposition, recent untoward events, pessimistic communications from a physician, or current suffering and lack of social support—would tend to be relatively unresponsive to information that encourages most others to have a hopeful outlook about finding a satisfactory solution to the health problems posed by suffering from heart disease. As a result, they may shift responsibility and pin all their hopes on the physicians' protective powers, displaying a pattern of defensive avoidance. This denial of personal responsibility is antithetical to adopting and adhering to the recommended course of action required for rehabilitation. Alternatively, defensive avoidance may take the form of bolstering a business-as-usual stance, which consists of doing nothing about the hazards.

Some of the evidence on level of self-esteem reviewed earlier in this chapter is also pertinent to Proposition #2 (concerning pessimism and defensive avoidance). Among overweight persons who come to our weight-reduction clinic, the majority of cases who obtain low self-esteem scores on personality scales may not be asserting a lack of confidence about succeeding on the diet but, rather, expressing feelings of guilt of shame about their past failures to control overeating, which is a different component of low self-esteem. Nevertheless, in a minority of clients who obtain low self-esteem scores, we have observed what appears to be a similar syndrome of pessimism combined with manifestations of defensive avoidance, which usually takes the form of procrastination or shifting responsibility to others. In some of these cases, pessimism about finding a successful solution to their overweight problem seems to be the result of a series of past failures at dieting, but in other cases, the causes seem to be quite different. Whatever the causes, however, the relatively hopeless cases, those who express very low confidence about attaining their goal of bringing their weight down to a normal level and keeping it down, were found to be more likely to fail to adhere to the recommended diet than those who are more hopeful (Janis & Quinlan, in press; Quinlan & Janis, in press). This observed phenomenon might again be explained by the second proposition, which is compatible with the recent reemphasis on *self-efficacy* as a key determinant of successful behavior change by Bandura (1977) and other behavior theorists.

In future research, investigations of individual differences in self-confidence, and in feelings of hope, should provide the type of data needed for more rigorous testing of the second proposition. By using appropriate questions in pretreatment interviews and questionnaires, it should be possible to determine whether such individual differences are related to manifestations of the defensive avoidance pattern and whether those manifestations, in turn, are predictive of failure to adhere to a counselor's recommendations.

Appropriate questions could also be devised for use in pretreatment interviews and questionnaires in order to assess individual differences in the predispositional variables specified by the first and third propositions. Obviously, it should be worthwhile to start off using seemingly pertinent measures that are already in the literature, such as the measures of time urgency developed by Glass (1977), which we suggested in the formulation of Proposition #3 on hypervigilance. If such measures fail to discriminate very well, the next step should be to develop new measures designed to tap more directly the predispositional factors specified in the three propositions. Some of those theoretically-based measures might prove to be more predictive of behavior change than the predispositional measures currently being used in research on counseling, therapy, and attitude change.

Acknowledgment

This paper is based primarily on my chapter on "Personality differences in responsiveness to counseling procedures" in a forthcoming book: I. Janis (Ed.), *Counseling on personal decisions: Theory and research on short-term helping relationships*. New Haven, Conn.: Yale University Press, in press. It also contains some material from my chapter on "Helping relationships" and from my chapter in collaboration with Leon Mann on "A theoretical framework for decision counseling" in the same forthcoming book.

References

Andrew, J. M. Recovery from surgery, with and without preparatory instructions, for three coping styles. *Journal of Personality and Social Psychology*, 1970, *15*, 223–226.

Bandura, A. Self-efficacy: Toward a unifying theory of behavioral change. *Psychological Review*, 1977, *84*, 191–215.

Bennis, W. G., Schein, E. H., Berlew, D. E., & Steele, F. I. Introductory Essay: Some interpersonal aspects of self-confirmation. In W. G. Bennis *et al.* (Eds.), *Interpersonal dynamics: Essays and readings on human interaction*. Homewood, Ill.: Dorsey, 1973.

Berscheid, E., & Walster, E. H. *Interpersonal attraction*. Reading, Mass.: Addison-Wesley, 1969.

Byrne, D. Repression-sensitization as a dimension of personality. In B. A. Maher (Ed.), *Progress in experimental personality research*, Vol. 1 New York: Academic, 1964.

Byrne, D. *The attraction paradigm*. New York: Academic, 1971.

Cartwright, D., & Zander, A. (Eds.). *Group dynamics: Research and theory*. 3rd ed. New York: Harper and Row, 1968.

Cohen, F. C., & Lazarus, R. S. Active coping processes, coping dispositions, and recovery from surgery. *Psychosomatic Medicine*, 1973, *35*, 375–389.

Conolley, E., Janis, I., & Dowds, M. Effects of variations in the type of feedback given by the counselor. In I. Janis (Ed.), *Counseling on personal decisions: Theory and research on short-term helping relationships*. New Haven: Yale University Press, in press.

Davidson, P. O., & Bobey, M. J. Repressor-sensitizer differences on repeated exposure to pain. *Perceptual and Motor Skills*, 1970, *31*, 711–714.

Delong, D. R. Individual differences in patterns of anxiety arousal, stress-relevant information and recovery from surgery. Unpublished doctoral dissertation, University of California, Los Angeles, 1971.

Dowds, M., Janis, I., & Conolley, E. Effects of acceptance by the counselor. In I. Janis, (Ed.), *Counseling on personal decisions: Theory and research on short-term helping relationships*. New Haven: Yale University Press, in press.

French, J. R., & Raven, B. The bases of social power. In D. Cartwright (Ed.), *Studies in social power*. Ann Arbor: University of Michigan, 1959.

Gentry, D., Foster, S., & Haney, T. Denial as a determinant of anxiety and perceived health in the coronary care unit. *Psychosomatic Medicine*, 1972, *34*, 39.

Glass, D. *Behavioral antecedents of coronary heart disease*. Hillsdale, N.J.: Erlbaum, 1977.

Goldstein, M. J. The relationship between coping and avoiding behavior and response to fear-arousing propoganda. *Journal of Abnormal and Social Psychology*, 1959, *58*, 247–252.

Greene, L. Effects of the counselor's verbal feedback, interpersonal distance and client's field dependence. In I. Janis (Ed.), *Counseling on personal decisions: Theory and research on short-term helping relationships*. New Haven: Yale University Press, in press.

Hackett, T. P., Cassem, N. H., & Wishnie, H. A. The coronary care unit: An appraisal of its psychological hazards. *New England Journal of Medicine*, 1968, *279*, 1365.

Hare, A. P. *Handbook of small group research*. 2nd ed. New York: The Free Press, 1976.

Horn, J. L. Human abilities: A review of research and theory in the early 1970's. In M. Rosenzweig & L. W. Porter. (Eds.), *Annual Review of Psychology* Vol. 27. Palo Alto: Annual Reviews Inc., 1976.

Janis, I. *Psychological stress: Psychoanalytic and behavioral studies of surgical patients.* New York: Wiley, 1958.

Janis, I. Effects of fear arousal on attitude change: Recent developments in theory and experimental research. In L. Berkowitz (Ed.), *Advances in experimental social psychology*, Vol. 3. New York: Academic, 1967.

Janis, I. *Stress and frustration.* New York: Harcourt Brace Javanovich, 1971.

Janis, I. Effectiveness of social support for stressful decisions. In M. Deutsch & H. Hornstein (Eds.), *Applying social psychology: Implications for research, practice, and training.* Hilldale, N.J.: Erlbaum, 1975.

Janis, I. Helping relationships: A preliminary theoretical analysis. In I. Janis (Ed.), *Counseling on personal decisions: Theory and research on short-term helping relationships.* New Haven: Yale University Press, in press.

Janis, I., & Field, P. B. Sex differences and personality factors related to persuasibility. In C. I. Hovland & I. Janis (Eds.), *Personality and Persuasibility.* New Haven: Yale University Press, 1959.

Janis, I., & Mann, L. *Decision making: A psychological analysis of conflict, choice, and commitment.* New York: The Free Press, 1977.

Janis, I. and Mann, L. Decision counseling: Theory, research, and perspectives for a new professional role. In H. L. Pick Jr., H. W. Leibowitz, J. E. Singer, A. Steinschneider, & H. W. Stevenson (Eds.), *Psychology: From research to practice.* New York: Plenum, 1978.

Janis, I. & Quinlan, D. What disclosing means to the client: Comparative case studies. In I. Janis (Ed.), *Counseling on personal decisions: Theory and research on short-term helping relationships.* New Haven: Yale University Press, in press.

Janis, I., & Rodin, J. Attribution, control and decision-making: Social psychology in health care. In G. C. Stone, F. Cohen, & N. E. Adler (Eds.), *Health psychology.* San Francisco: Jossey-Bass, 1979.

Janoff-Bulman, R. Self-blame in rape victims: A control-maintenance strategy. Paper presented at the meeting of the American Psychological Association, Toronto, August 1978.

Leventhal, H. Fear communications in the acceptance of preventive health practices. *Bulletin of the New York Academy of Medicine*, 1965, *41*, 1144–1168.

Leventhal, H., & Sharpe, E. Facial expressions as indicators of stress. In C. Izard and S. Tompkins (Eds.), *Studies of Emotion.* New York: Springer, 1965.

Levenger, G., & Breedlove, J. Interpersonal attraction and agreement: A study of marriage partners. *Journal of Personality and Social Psychology*, 1966, *3*, 367–372.

McGill, A. M. Review of literature on cardiovascular rehabilitation. In S. M. Weiss, (Ed.), *Proceedings of the National Heart and Lung Institute Working Conference on Health Behavior.* DHEW (Publication No. [NIH] 76–868), Washington, D.C.: U.S. Government Printing office, 1975.

McGuire, W. J. The nature of attitudes and attitude change. In G. Lindzey & E. Aronson (Eds.), *The Handbook of social psychology.* Vol. 3. Reading, Mass.: Addison-Wesley, 1969.

Mischel, W. *Personality and assessment.* New York: Wiley, 1968.

Olson, J. M., & Zanna, M. P. A new look at selective exposure. *Journal of Experimental Social Psychology.* 1979, *15*, 1–15.

Quinlan, D. & Janis, I. Unfavorable effects of high levels of self-disclosure. In I. Janis (Ed.), *Counseling on personal decisions: Theory and research on short-term helping relationships.* New Haven: Yale University Press, in press.

Quinlan, D. M., Janis, I., & Bales, V. Effects of moderate self-disclosure and frequency of contact. In I. Janis (Ed.), *Counseling on personal decisions: Theory and research on short-term helping relationships*. New Haven: Yale University Press, in press.

Riskind, J. The clients' sense of personal control: Effects of time perspective. In I. Janis (Ed.), *Counseling on personal decisions: Theory and research on short-term helping relationships*. New Haven: Yale University Press, in press.

Rodin, J. Cognitive-behavioral strategies for the control of obesity. Paper presented at the Conference on Cognitive-behavior Therapy: Applications and Issues, Los Angeles, September 1978.

Rogers, R. W., & Mewborn, C. R. Fear appeals and attitude change: Effects of a threat's noxiousness, probability of occurrence, and the efficacy of coping responses. *Journal of Personality and Social Psychology*, 1976, *34*, 54–61.

Rogers, R. W., & Thistlethwaite, D. L. Effects of fear arousal and reassurance upon attitude change. *Journal of Personality and Social Psychology*, 1970, *15*, 227–233.

Schachter, S. *The psychology of affiliation*. Stanford: Stanford University Press, 1959.

Sechrest, L. Personality. In M. R. Rosenzweig, & L. W. Porter (Eds.), *Annual review of psychology*. Vol. 27. Palo Alto, Calif.: Annual Reviews, Inc., 1976.

Shaw, M. *Group dynamics*. New York: McGraw-Hill, 1971.

Sime, A. M. Relationship of preoperative fear, type of coping, and information received about surgery to recovery from surgery. *Journal of Personality and Social Psychology*, 1976, *34*, 716–724.

Smith, A. D. Effects of self-esteem enhancement on teachers' acceptance of innovation in a classroom setting. In I. Janis (Ed.), *Counseling on personal decisions: Theory and research on short-term helping relationships*. New Haven: Yale University Press, in press.

Tedeschi, J. T., & Lindskold, S. *Social psychology: Interdependence, interaction, and influence*. New York: Wiley, 1976.

CHAPTER 9

Stress, Behavior Patterns, and Coronary Disease[1]

David C. Glass

Department of Psychology
Graduate School and University Center
City University of New York
33 West 42 Street
New York, New York

Coronary heart disease is a clinical disorder that results from damage to the coronary arteries, the latter being called coronary artery disease or atherosclerosis (Friedberg, 1966); a nontechnical term for it is hardening of the arteries. Myocardial infarction is one of the most common forms of clinical coronary disease.

Epidemiologists trace the beginnings of the heart disease problem in the United States to the early part of this century. Since the 1920s, in particular, mortality rates have increased dramatically. Between 1940 and 1950, for example, the rate for white males aged 35 to 64 increased by 23% (Borhani, 1966). While recent research suggests a decline in mortality due to coronary disease in American men during the five years from 1968 to 1972, it still remains the major cause of death in this country. In 1975, the National Heart, Lung, and Blood Institute estimated that 1.3 million Americans would experience coronary disease; approximately 675,000 of them would die, and 175,000 would be premature deaths under the age of 65.

[1] Reprinted from *American Scientist*, 1977, *65*(2), pp. 177–187. Copyright © 1977 by Sigma Xi, the Scientific Research Society of North America, Incorporated. Reprinted by permission of author and publisher.

Data collected in various epidemiologic studies (e.g., Dawber & Kannel 1961; Brand, Rosemann, Sholtz, & Friedman, 1976) indicate that the following factors are associated with high risk of coronary heart disease: (1) aging; (2) sex (i.e., being male rather than female); (3) elevated levels of cholesterol and related fats in the blood; (4) hypertension; (5) heavy cigarette smoking (i.e., 20 or more per day); (6) diabetes mellitus; (7) parental history of heart disease; (8) obesity; and (9) physical inactivity. While the likelihood of heart disease is greater when more of the risk factors are present, nevertheless the best combination of these factors still fails to identify most new cases of the disease (Jenkins, 1971). The majority of cardiac patients do not have excessive levels of serum cholesterol; only a small number are hypertensive; and even fewer are diabetic. Moreover, there is considerable controversy surrounding some of the risk factors themselves (Friedman, 1969). It is by no means clear, for example, that obesity and/or lack of exercise increases the risk of heart disease.

Psychological Risk Factors

The limitations in current knowledge argue for broadening the search for contributing causes of cardiovascular disease. Indeed, there is a sizable body of research designed to elucidate psychological factors that enhance the risk of developing cardiac disorders (Jenkins, 1971; Jenkins, Zyzanski, & Rosenman, 1976). Two promising variables have been identified in recent years—psychological stress and the Type A coronary-prone behavior pattern. Consider the notion of stress, which may be defined as an internal state of the individual when he is faced with threats to his physical and/or psychic well-being (cf. Lazarus, 1966). Implicit in the definition is the assumption that this internal state can be inferred by physiological, self-report, and over behavioral measurements—for example, increased or decreased heart rate, inability to concentrate, or impaired interpersonal relations.

Stressful life events, including job dissatisfactions, economic frustration, and excessive work and responsibility, all appear related to the risk of coronary disease (Jenkins, 1971; House, 1975). The jobs of high-risk people generally entail a high degree of responsibility for others, work overloads, and role conflicts, among other stresses. Unhappiness in nonoccupational areas such as marital and family relations has also been implicated in the occurrence of coronary disease, and acute stressors over which the individual has little control—for example, the sudden death of a spouse—have been correlated with the subsequent onset of cardiac disorders (e.g., Parkes, Benjamin, & Fitzgerald, 1969).

Recent research suggests some of the physiological mechanisms by which stress may enhance the production of coronary disease (see Friedman, 1969; Eliot, 1974; Rosenman & Friedman, 1974). They include increases in such traditional risk factors as serum cholesterol and blood pressure; acceleration of the rate of development of damage to the intima (inner layer) of the coronary arteries over time; and facilitation of the aggregation of blood platelets (i.e., substances found in the blood that are important in coagulation), which are then incorporated into arterial plaques and contribute to narrowing of the coronary vessels and atherosclerosis.

Consider, for example, several studies that document an association between cholesterol level in the blood and stressful life events. During the first two weeks in April (prior to the April 15 tax deadline), serum cholesterol levels among tax accountants were noted to be significantly higher than during the months of February and March (Friedman, Rosenman, & Carroll, 1958), and their average cholesterol level fell sharply after April 15. These findings have been replicated several times using a variety of procedures for inducing stress (see Rosenman & Friedman, 1974 for a summary of these studies).

Stress can also contribute to coronary disease through the body's general reactions to aversive stimulation. It is widely agreed that such stimulation leads to the discharge of the sympathetic nervous system and related hormones such as adrenalin and noradrenalin (see, for example, Mason, 1972). These hormonal substances, called catecholamines, are secreted from the adrenal medulla and, in the case of noradrenalin, from sympathetic nerve endings as well. Adrenalin and noradrenalin can accelerate the rate of arterial damage and, indeed, induce myocardial lesions (e.g., Raab, Stark, MacMillan, & Gigee, 1961; Raab, Chaplin, & Bajusz, 1964). These hormones also potentiate the aggregation of blood platelets, and the release of platelet contents is considered to be an important factor in atherogenesis as well as in the genesis of thrombosis (Duguid, 1946; Ardlie, Glew, & Schwartz, 1966; Theorell, 1974).

It appears, then, that catecholamines may have a special significance in the development of coronary disease. It follows that any psychological agent that increases catecholamines in the blood may be a potential pathogen for cardiovascular function. Since psychological stressors enhance the release of adrenalin and noradrenalin, stress may, in part, be related to coronary disease because of its generalized effects on the sympathetic nervous system and adrenal medulla.

Type A Behavior Pattern

The Type A coronary-prone behavior pattern consists of such predispositions as competitive achievement striving, a sense of time urgency, and hostility, all of which can be elicited and observed primarily in the presence of appropriate environmental circumstances (Friedman & Rosenman, 1974). Although the assumption of an interrelated pattern of responses has yet to be demonstrated conclusively, Pattern A does appear to be linked to the occurrence of coronary disease. For example, one study shows that Pattern A men have more than twice the rate of heart disease during 8½ years of follow-up as men originally judged to be Pattern B (Rosenman, Rahe, Borhani, & Feinlieb, 1975). A higher incidence in Type As still prevails when adjustments are made for traditional risk factors like cigarette smoking, serum cholesterol, and hypertension. Thus the predictive relationship of Pattern A to coronary disease cannot be totally explained away by other risk factors; Pattern A independently exerts a pathogenic influence. Other research has found that an objective measure of the behavior pattern is the strongest single predictor of recurring heart attacks from an available set of variables, including cigarette smoking and serum cholesterol (Jenkins, Zyzanski, & Rosenman, 1976). There is also evidence indicating an association between atherosclerosis and the behavior pattern, with Type A patients showing a greater degree of occlusion than Type Bs (e.g. Blumenthal, Williams, Kong, Thompson, Jenkins, & Rosenman, 1975; Zyzanski, Jenkins, Ryan, Flessas, & Everist, 1976).

Despite the independent contribution of Pattern A to the occurrence of coronary disease, it may still exert its influence, at least in part, through certain of the traditional risk factors. For example, some studies indicate that fully developed Pattern A individuals over 35 years of age have significantly higher serum cholesterol levels than their Pattern B counterparts (Friedman & Rosenman, 1959), and similar differences have been reported for other fats and related substances in the blood (e.g., Rosenman & Friedman, 1974). In my own laboratory, greater serum cholesterol concentrations were observed in extreme Type A compared to extreme Type B subjects as young as 19 years of age (Glass, 1977).

There is little evidence of a relationship between prevalence of hypertension and Pattern A (e.g., Shekelle, Schoenberger, & Stamler, 1976), although one study indicates that elevated diastolic blood pressure enhances the risk of coronary disease only when this factor occurs in Pattern A men (Rosenman, Friedman, Strans, Wurm, Jenkins, & Messinger, 1966). Laboratory experiments, however, find that Pattern A traits such as hostility—at least when induced by acute frustration manipulations—

produce episodic rises in both systolic and diastolic blood pressure (see McGinn, Harburg, Julius, & McLeod, 1964). In addition, a very recent paper reports that Type As more often responded to a stress interview with increased diastolic blood pressure, whereas Type Bs showed decreased pressure (Scherwitz, Berton, & Leventhal, unpublished manuscript). These findings suggest the possibility that future research may yet uncover associations between the behavior pattern and increased blood pressure.

As in the case of stress, the relation of Pattern A to coronary disease may be mediated by the sympathetic-adrenal medullary system. Support for this hypothesis comes from a number of sources, including research which indicates that, compared to Type Bs, Type A men show less decrease in platelet aggregation in response to noradrenalin after stressful treadmill exercises (Simpson, Olewine, Jenkins, Ramsey, Zyzanski, Thomas, & Hames, 1974). Other studies indicate that the average blood-clotting time of Type As is hastened during periods of stress compared to that of Type Bs (Rosenman & Friedman, 1974). Of greater significance, perhaps, is the finding that, relative to Pattern B individuals, Pattern A individuals exhibit elevated plasma levels of noradrenalin immediately before, during, and after a stressful competitive situation (Friedman, Byers, Diamant, & Rosenman, 1975). Simpson *et al.* (1974) also showed that physically fit Type As have the largest increase in noradrenalin immediately after a treadmill test, whereas the less fit among the Bs exhibited the lowest increase in noradrenalin. In addition, there is evidence that extreme Type As excrete considerably more noradrenalin in their urine during active working hours than do Type Bs (e.g., Friedman, St. George, Byers, & Rosenman, 1960).

Measuring the A and B Behavior Patterns

Classification of subjects as Type A or Type B is customarily based on a standardized stress interview (Friedman, 1969; Jenkins, Rosenman, & Friedman, 1968). The subject is asked questions dealing with the intensity of his ambitions, competitiveness, time urgency, and hostile feelings. While the manner and tone in which the subject responds are given somewhat more weight than the content of his answers (e.g., the Type A individual uses explosive vocal intonations), nevertheless the content is certainly an important determinant of an individual's behavior pattern classification. Descriptions of Type A and Type B individuals represent extremes of a bipolar continuum that is probably normally distributed in the United States. Indeed, diagnoses based on the interview are typically made on a 4-point scale: fully developed As, incompetely developed As, incompletely developed Bs, and fully developed Bs.

Another approach to Pattern A classification is based on a self-administered questionnaire called the JAS, or the Jenkins Activity Survey for Health Prediction (Jenkins, Rosenman, & Zyzanski, 1972). It consists of a series of items such as the following: (1) "How would your wife (or closest friend) rate you?" where "Definitely hard-driving and competitive" is an extreme Pattern A response and "Definitely relaxed and easy going" is a Pattern B response. (2) "Do you ever set deadlines or quotas for yourself at work or at home?" where "Yes, once per week or more often" is a Pattern A response and "No" and "Yes, but only occasionally" are Pattern B responses. The JAS provides a continuous distribution of A–B scale scores.

My own laboratory has recently modified the JAS for use with college students, and most of the research described in this paper used this student version. The typical procedure classified subjects into As and Bs by adopting as cut-off criterion the median of a large distribution of JAS scores obtained from male college students over a 3-year period. In some experiments, however, subjects were deliberately selected from the extremes (e.g., upper and lower thirds) of the JAS distribution. The two approaches to classification produced similar patterns of results, although, not surprisingly, the effects were somewhat stronger with extreme As and Bs.

Pattern A, as I have already discussed, can be defined and measured reliably. It has good validity for predicting coronary disease. There is even evidence regarding some of the mechanisms by which Pattern A contributes to cardiovascular pathology. Despite these data, there is virtually no systematic evidence indicating that individuals classified as Pattern A do, indeed, exhibit excessive achievement striving, time urgency, and hostility. About five years ago. I began a research project designed to elucidate the interplay of Pattern A and psychological stress in the production of coronary disease. Empirical documentation of the alleged characteristics of Pattern A was taken as the first order of business. (See Glass, 1977 for a complete report of the research.) My intention was to try to understand the behavior pattern in terms of controlled procedures that are familiar to experimental psychology.

In both laboratory and field settings, Type As tend to be achievement-oriented people who work at near maximum capacity relative to Type Bs. For example, college-age As attempted reliably more complex arithmetic problems than Bs on a test in which all subjects were told that there was no time limit for completion (Burnam, Pennebaker, & Glass, 1973). There were essentially no differences between As and Bs when the arithmetic test was administered with an explicit 5-minute deadline, but this null difference was due largely to the increased performance of the Bs. Type A subjects worked at about the same elevated level, irrespective of the presence or absence of a deadline.

A later study revealed that success-oriented Type As remembered more verbal and pictorial items than Type Bs on a test of immediate recall ($p <$ .02). Superior memory in this study was interpreted in terms of greater achievement motivation in As because instructions emphasized the importance of trying to remember as many items as possible. Standard measures of IQ were, incidentally, unrelated to behavior Pattern A (correlations were less than .10). It should also be noted that correlations between Pattern A and indices of social class, while statistically significant, are uniformly low—in the area of .23 (e.g., Shekelle *et al.*, 1976).

Other research indicates that achievement striving is evident in the day-to-day activities of Type As. For example, college student As earned reliably more academic honors than their Type B counterparts, and when asked about their "plans after college," approximately 60% of the As said they would "go on to graduate or professional school," whereas 70 percent of the Bs said, "go to work, get a job." Still other studies indicate that while Pattern A itself does not show a significant heritability estimate (Rosenman *et al.*, 1975), the behavior pattern correlates about .50 with activity level, as measured by standard temperament scales. Since activity level does have a reliable heritability coefficient (Rosenman *et al.*, 1975; Matthews & Krantz, 1976), it may be that the hard-driving and achievement-oriented behavior of the Type A reflects a more basic genetic predisposition. Another, perhaps more likely, possibility is that Pattern A is learned by individuals whose genetic make-up renders them susceptible to shaping processes that lead to emergence of the behavior pattern (see Glass, 1977; Butensky, Faralli, Heebner, & Waldron, 1976).

The preceding set of findings, while not surprising in themselves, call to mind descriptions of Pattern A individuals who believe that with sufficient effort they can overcome any obstacle (e.g., Friedman, 1969). This thought led to the speculation that As might suppress feelings of fatigue to a greater extent than their Pattern B counterparts in order to persist at a tiring but challenging task and thus achieve success in its mastery (Carver, Coleman, & Glass, 1976). The task chosen to test this hypothesis was designed to produce feelings of fatigue; that is, subjects were required to walk continuously on a motorized treadmill at increasingly sharp angles of incline (see Balke, 1954; Balke, Grillo, Konecci, & Luft, 1954).

Type A and Type B subjects completed this treadmill test while rating their fatigue on an 11-point scale at 2-minute intervals. Each subject also completed another treadmill test that was designed to assess maximum aerobic capacity—that is, his maximum rate of oxygen consumption. Each subject's walking performance was scored as a proportion of his maximum capacity.

While physical characteristics (e.g., percentage of body fat) of Type A and Type B subjects were essentially the same, Pattern A subjects reached an oxygen absorption rate on the walking treadmill test equal to 91.4% of their maximum capacities, whereas Pattern B subjects reached an average rate equal to only 82.8% of their capacities.

It would appear that compared to Bs, As worked at a level closer to the limits of their endurance. Even as they did so, As expressed less overall fatigue than did Bs. Type As rated their fatigue as significantly lower than Type Bs on each of the last four ratings made prior to termination of the walking treadmill test. They also expressed less overall fatigue than Bs for the entire treadmill session (means = 6.2 and 5.2, $p < .04$).

This tendency toward fatigue suppression—or at least public denial of fatigue—may be understood in terms of the achievement-oriented character of the Type A. Denial or suppression of fatigue has instrumental value for As because it aids in their struggle for attainment of desired goals—in this case superior treadmill performance. The acknowledgment of fatigue, on the other hand, might interfere with successful task mastery—a situation that As could not easily tolerate.

Another area where differences show up between Type As and Bs is a sense of time urgency. Experimentation indicates that As become impatient with delay and report that a time interval of one minute elapses reliably sooner than Type Bs (Burnam, Pennebaker, & Glass, 1973). The arousal of impatience has behavioral consequences as well (see, for example, Glass, Snyder, & Hollis, 1974). Thus Type As did more poorly than Type Bs on a timing task that required a delayed response—that is, a task involving differential reinforcement of low rates of responding (DRL). On a DRL task, the subject must wait during fixed time intervals before responding; any premature response resets the time relationship and the subject does not obtain reinforcement. The DRL task is quite difficult and can be mastered only with patience.

In accord with expectations, Pattern A subjects' scores were significantly lower on this test than those of Pattern B subjects (medians = 66.5 and 77.6, $p < .05$). More detailed analysis revealed that As performed more poorly because they were unable to wait long enough after prior reinforcement, not because they waited too long after their preceding response. Behavioral observations also confirm the impatience of As with delayed responding. Approximately 48% of the As, compared to only 12% of the Bs, in one of my studies showed tense and hyperactive movements during a DRL session.

Lengthy intervals between reaction time (RT) trials might also be expected to arouse impatience in As, with resultant restless behavior and distraction. Such activity should divert attention away from the task at hand, thereby causing the Type A individual to respond more slowly than his Type B counterpart when the cue for response eventually appears. Accordingly, performance on a complex RT task was assessed in a study using intertrial intervals that were either short (1.5 seconds) or relatively long (random intervals ranging from 4 to 9 seconds). Speed of response was measured as the mean latency over the 48 trials.

Analysis of the latency scores revealed that Type Bs were faster than As when intertrial intervals were long (means = 445.7 and 484.8 milliseconds), whereas As reacted slightly more quickly than Bs when intervals were short (means = 382.9 and 394.8 milliseconds). The statistical interaction in these data ($p < .06$) provides additional validation for the time urgency component of Pattern A. Type As react more slowly under conditions that place a premium on patience than they do under conditions that do not require delayed responding. By contrast, Type Bs show similar reaction times irrespective of the length of the intervals between trials.

A third facet of Pattern A is hostility and aggressiveness. Excess hostility is not always detectable in Type As, for they often keep such affect under deep cover. Although there is agreement that As are more hostile than Bs (see, for example, Friedman & Rosenman, 1974), the judgment is based largely on clinical observation and data collected in the stress interview. More systematic documentation of the hostility component of Pattern A is therefore needed.

An experiment was done in my laboratory to test the idea that relative to Bs, As would react with enhanced aggressiveness toward another person who denigrated their efforts to perform a difficult task ("instigation" condition). An opportunity was given to subjects to administer ostensible electric shocks to the harassing individual (cf. Buss, 1961). Type As and Type Bs who were randomly assigned to a "no instigation" control condition participated only in the shock phase of the study. In comparison to the control treatment, the Instigation procedure aroused substantial aggression ($p < .01$). The principal source of this main effect was the amount of shock delivered by Pattern A subjects. Individual contrasts revealed that Instigation As delivered higher levels of shock than did their counterparts in no instigation ($p < .01$). On the other hand, Type Bs in the instigation treatment did not shock at a reliably higher level than no instigation Bs ($p > .30$). While the overall interaction effect in the analysis of variance did not achieve an acceptable level of statistical significance ($p > .15$), nevertheless the contrasts indicate that As are not uniformly more aggressive than Bs:

they become so in response to a specific set of arousing circumstances (see Glass, 1977).

Interplay of Stress and Pattern A

The research I have described up to this point provides systematic documentation for the three behavioral components of Pattern A and, in so doing, evidence for the validity of the measures used to classify individuals as A or B. A more conceptual approach to the results is also possible, however, Such an analysis may provide insight into the motivational dynamics of Pattern A, as well as the relationship between the behavior pattern and uncontrollable stress. Examination of this relationship is not solely an academic exercise, for it is also likely to suggest ways in which Pattern A and stress adversely affect the cardiovascular system.

An analysis of the results of the validity experiments was undertaken in the light of the foregoing considerations, and an apparent consistency was revealed in the array of empirical facts. In contrast to Bs, Type As work hard to succeed, suppress subjective states (e.g., fatigue) that might interfere with task performance, exhibit rapid pacing of their activities, and express hostility after being harassed in their efforts at task completion—all, I would submit, in the interests of asserting control over environmental demands and requirements. I would also suggest that these demands must be at least minimally stressful, for the possibility of failure and loss of esteem was inherent in most of the experimental situations used in the validation studies. The coronary-prone behavior pattern might thus be described as a characteristic style of responding to environmental stressors that threaten an individual's sense of control (cf. Glass & Singer, 1972). Type As are engaged in a struggle for control, whereas Type Bs are relatively free of such concerns and, hence, free of characteristic Pattern A traits.

The concept of uncontrollability may be defined as follows: when an individual perceives that his responses will not determine what he gets, the outcome is considered uncontrollable. By contrast, controllability involves the subject's perception of a relationship (i.e., contingency) between responding and outcomes. An uncontrollable stressor is, then, a potentially harmful stimulus which the individual can neither escape nor avoid. A controllable stressor is a harmful stimulus which can be avoided by appropriate instrumental responses.

The initial reaction of Type As to an uncontrollable stressor may be termed *hyperresponsiveness*, since it is assumed to reflect a concerted effort to assert control over the stimulus. In comparison to Bs, Pattern A individuals experience increased motivation—at least initially—to master stressful situations that they perceive as signifying lack of control. It might thus be expected that As will try harder than Bs to master an experimental task administered after, say, a few trials of inescapable noise stimulation. Having been exposed to a brief experience with uncontrollable stress, As exert greater efforts to reestablish a sense of control by trying to master a subsequent task. Instead of developing general expectations of uncontrollability, as Seligman's (e.g., 1975) learned-helplessness hypothesis might predict, Type As actually become more motivated to assert control.

Such enhanced motivation may, of course, increase or dampen later performance, depending upon the nature of the task. Consider the reaction time (RT) study using long intertrial intervals. Pattern A subjects, it will be recalled, showed longer latencies of response than Pattern B subjects, presumably because of their inability to sustain the patience needed to remain alert during the relatively long waiting period. Assuming that uncontrollable stress enhances the motivation of As, shorter response latencies might be expected if the same RT task were administered after exposure to inescapable compared to escapable noise. Since most subjects come to recognize the importance of avoiding distraction during the waiting period of an RT task, it is not unreasonable to expect As to contain their impatience in order to perform rapidly after being threatened with loss of control. Type As should, therefore, accelerate rather than reduce their speed of RT response. Type Bs, by contrast, should show less of this effect after an experience with uncontrollability, since they are assumed to be less responsive to the incentive of environmental control.

David Krantz and I tested the foregoing line of thought in the following manner. Twenty Type As and 20 Type Bs were exposed to 12 bursts of 100-decibel noise. Twelve noise trials were arbitrarily selected as constituting brief exposure to an uncontrollable stressor. The decision was dictated by experimentation reported below which indicates that prolonged exposure (e.g., 30 noise bursts) produces learned-helplessness rather than facilitation effects (see, also, Hiroto, 1974).

Half the Type As and half the Bs in the study were randomly assigned to what may be called a "pretreatment," in which they were able to escape from each of the noise bursts by appropriate lever-pressing responses ("escape" condition). The other half of the subjects were unable to terminate the sound ("no escape" condition). A "test phase" of the study, which followed noise pretreatment, consisted of an RT task identical to the one used with long intertrial intervals. The major dependent measures were response latencies (in msec) averaged across RT trials.

The escape–no escape noise pretreatment was successful in inducing differential perceptions of lack of control. In a postexperimental questionnaire, subjects were asked, "How much control did you feel you had over the termination of the noise?" where 7 = "completely in control" and 1 = "no control at all." The mean for subjects in the escape condition was 4.8, and for the cases in no escape, 1.7. The difference was statistically significant at better than the .001 level.

The response-latency results are presented in Figure 1. The reliable interaction between behavior pattern and type of pretreatment ($p < .005$) confirms initial expectations, for As are normally slower than Bs on this particular RT task, and escapable pretreatment was not expected to alter this difference. However, the assumed threat inherent in exposure to uncontrollable noise appears to have motivated Pattern A subjects to respond

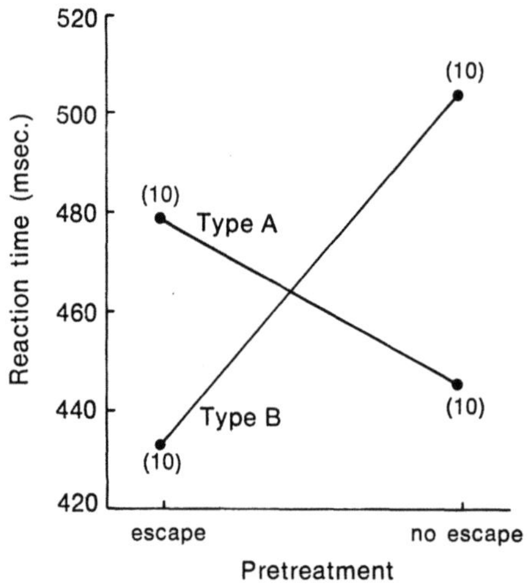

Fig. 1. Type A and Type B subjects were given a choice reaction time (RT) test after pretreatment with noise from which they could either escape or not escape. The figure shows mean reaction times for 47 trials. Compared to "escape" As, the "no escape" As seem to have been motivated by the threat of the uncontrollable noise stressor to respond rapidly in the subsequent RT task. "No escape" Bs, by contrast, show what appears to be a decrement in motivation, since they respond less rapidly to the RT signal light than their counterparts in the "escape" condition. (Group sizes are given in parentheses.)

more rapidly to the RT signal light despite the lengthy waiting period. Type Bs, in contrast, may have experienced a decrement in motivation, since their RT performance was impaired by prior uncontrollability.

The foregoing results were replicated in an experiment that induced perceived lack of control by random positive and negative reinforcements (i.e., "correct" or "incorrect" evaluations) for attempts to solve two cognitive tasks (see Hiroto & Seligman, 1975). Noncontingent reinforcement of this kind implies that the probability of being correct is independent of the subject's responses; hence the procedure is tantamount to inducing perceived uncontrollability (see Seligman, 1975). Perceived controllability was induced by giving subjects contingent reinforcement for their attempts to solve the tasks—that is, subjects were told "correct" when their answers were correct and "incorrect" when their answers were wrong. The effect of these pretreatments was measured on a DRL task in a subsequent test phase of the study. Recall that Type As do more poorly on DRL than Type Bs (see above), but to the extent that uncontrollable pretreatment enhances their motivation to succeed, we might expect better performance from As than Bs.

The results of the replication are given in Figure 2. It is readily apparent that the interaction ($p < .02$) is remarkably similar to the one depicted in Figure 1, except that a delayed response is correct here, whereas a fast response was correct in the first study. The replication shows, then, that enhanced performance among As occurred after exposure to uncontrollable stress, even though such behavior appears to require suppression of their customary impatience with a DRL task.

The two studies, taken together, suggest that Pattern A behavior emerges in the presence of a specific set of eliciting conditions—namely, perceived threats to environmental control. It would appear that Pattern A behavior is a strategy for coping with uncontrollable stress; enhanced performance reflects an attempt to assert and maintain control after its loss has been threatened. This interpretation receives further support from experimentation using other techniques for inducing lack of control, including various partial reinforcement procedures which were perceived as differentially uncontrollable (see Glass, 1977).

Extended exposure to uncontrollable stress. Enhanced responding aimed at asserting control over uncontrollable stressors must prove ineffective in the long run, for extended exposure eventually leads to the perception that no relationship exists between responses and outcomes. The Type A individual may then be expected to give up efforts at control and show what has been called learned helplessness, or *hyporesponsiveness* to uncontrollable events (see Wortman & Brehm, 1975). Type Bs might also be expected

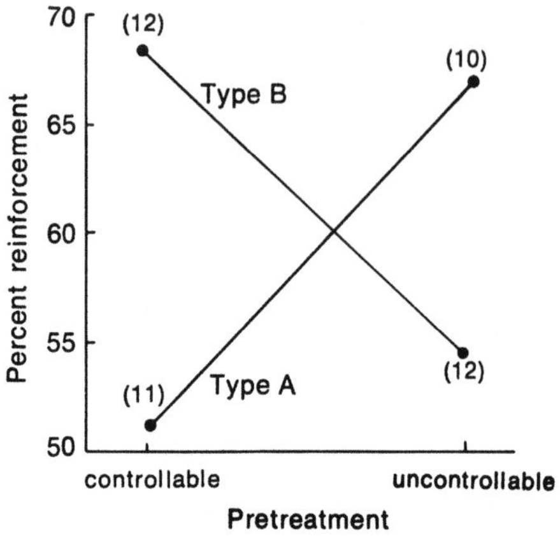

Fig. 2. After pretreatment with either controllable or uncontrollable stress, subjects were given a DRL (differential reinforcement of low rates of responding) task. The figure shows the mean percentages of reinforcement received by Type As and Type Bs during the DRL session. Type As earned a greater percentage of reinforcement after uncontrollable than controllable stressful stimulation. Type Bs, by contrast, performed the task more poorly following uncontrollable stress. (Group sizes are given in parentheses.)

to experience helplessness under these circumstances, but it is the As who are likely to show greater hyporesponsiveness, because of their tendency to experience loss of control as more threatening.

Seligman's (1975) learned-helplessness paradigm was used to test the foregoing line of thought (see Krantz, Glass & Snyder, 1974). Type As and Type Bs were exposed to a pretreatment consisting of either loud (105 decibels) or moderate (78 decibels) noise, in an effort to induce differential degrees of stress. Thirty-five noise bursts were administered to each subject. Half the cases within each stress-level condition were unable to escape from noise (no escape condition), whereas the other half could effect termination by manipulating rotary switches (escape condition). The test phase used the same intensity of noise as the first part of the experiment. However, all subjects could now escape, or even avoid, this noise by making appropriate responses with a shuttle box lever. The dependent variables were measured in the test phase and included such indices as number of trials taken to achieve a criterion of three consecutive escape and/or avoidance responses.

Table 1. Mean Number of Trials to Reach a Criterion of Three Consecutive Escapes and/or Avoidances of the Noise Bursts[a]

	Escape	No escape
High stress, Pattern A	6.3 (n = 9)	12.7 (n = 9)
High stress, Pattern B	7.2 (n = 6)	8.7 (n = 6)
Moderate stress, Pattern A	7.7 (n = 7)	8.5 (n = 6)
Moderate stress, Pattern B	9.0 (n = 8)	20.1 (n = 9)

[a] Comparisons between means for each behavior pattern and stress condition were conducted using the error-mean-square from a three-way analysis of variance. These comparisons revealed a number of significant differences ($p < .05$ or better), including those between the following means: (1) 12.7 and 6.3; (2) 20.1 and 9.0; (3) 20.1 and 8.7; (4) 20.1 and 8.5. The differences between (1) 12.7 and 8.5, (2) 9.0 and 7.2, and (3) 7.7 and 6.3 were not statistically significant ($ps > .20$).

The relevant data are presented in Table 1. Analysis of variance revealed an escape–no escape main effect ($p < .01$), a stress level by A–B interaction ($p < .02$), and a significant triple-order interaction ($p < .02$). Subsequent contrasts indicated that Type As in the no escape–high stress condition took significantly more trials to learn the escape response than did their counterparts in the escape–high stress condition ($p < .05$). Escape and no escape Bs did not differ under high stress. Just the opposite occurred in moderate stress. Thus no escape Bs took more trials to reach criterion than did escape Bs ($p < .05$), whereas there was no difference between escape and no escape As.

The results obtained in this experiment were somewhat surprising. Initial expectations called only for an interaction between behavior pattern and the escapability-inescapability manipulations. However, the data suggest a more complex relationship in which stress level somehow mediates the reactions of As and Bs to extended exposure to uncontrollable stress. A seemingly obvious interpretation would be to invoke the concept of autonomic arousal—namely, As are more aroused than Bs. However, the A–B variable failed to show reliable associations with electrodermal and self-report measures of arousal collected during and immediately after the pretreatment phase of the study. It is always possible that differences went undetected because of insufficient and/or incorrect sampling of physiological channels. On the other hand, additional studies in my laboratory have been unsuccessful in producing A–B differences in heart-rate and fingervasoconstriction responses to stressful stimulation. While I do not gainsay the possibility of an arousal interpretation—after all, As have been found to respond to stress with greater blood pressure and noradrenalin elevations than their Type B counterparts— the physiological results from the experiments under discussion do not indicate the viability of such an approach. Therefore, a cognitive interpretation was proposed and explored in subsequent research.

A cognitive interpretation. Since Pattern A individuals are presumably more concerned than their Pattern B counterparts about maintaining environmental control, we might expect As to distort cues signifying lack of control. Indeed, when uncontrollability cues do not compel attention—as, perhaps, in the case of *soft* inescapable noise (cf. Pliner, 1974)—Type As should find it relatively easy to minimize the fact that they are unable to control the situation. If, on the other hand, lack of control is a salient feature of their environment—as, for example, in the case of *loud* inescapable noise—As should experience considerable difficulty in ignoring its presence and thus exert enhanced efforts at locating control-relevant cues. These efforts will eventually result in a stronger certainty that nothing can be done to terminate the noise. Such expectations of uncontrollability may then transfer from pretreatment to the test phase of the learned-helplessness paradigm, where they appear as impaired learning of escape and avoidance responses.

A different state of affairs will occur when cues signaling lack of control are low in salience. Under these conditions, As will exert less effort at achieving control, less effectively encode the fact of uncontrollability, and, hence, fail to show subsequent learned helplessness.

While this line of thought (cf. Schachter & Rodin, 1974) appears to conform to the pattern of results obtained in the helplessness experiment, the interpretation is obviously *post hoc* and requires independent verification. Accordingly, a second study was done, which used a nonnoise manipulation of salience, and an independent variation of uncontrollability based on contingent or noncontingent reinforcements for task performance (see above). This time, however, there were four rather than two cognitive tasks, thereby extending the subjects' exposure to lack of control. Salience was manipulated by systematically varying the prominence of reinforcement—for example, by having subjects keep a detailed record of whether their responses were "correct" or "incorrect." This procedure made it relatively simple for a subject to see if there was a relationship between his answers and the reinforcements he received during the experimental session. The effects of these manipulations were assessed with an anagrams task, also used in previous learned-helplessness research (Hiroto & Seligman, 1975). A major dependent measure was the number of trials needed to achieve an arbitrary criterion of three consecutive anagram solutions in less than 15 seconds each.

Without going into further procedural and measurement details at this time (see Glass, 1977, Chapter 8), suffice it to note that the results of the second study corresponded to those reported for the helplessness experiment using noise. Indeed, comparison of the two sets of data revealed distinct similarities in the principal contrasts between experimental conditions. Type As showed greater helplessness (i.e., more trials to the anagrams criterion) after uncontrollable than controllable pretreatment, provided that the cues signifying lack of control were made salient ($p < .05$). When cues were of low salience, Type As showed minimal evidence of helplessness ($p > .20$). unlike the previous helplessness study, however, uncontrollable Bs in low salience took only marginally more trials to reach criterion than comparable Bs in the controllable condition ($p = .10$).

To sum up, the enhanced controlling behavior of As noted in earlier studies appears to change to a decrement in efforts at control after prolonged exposure to uncontrollable stress. However, this vulnerability of As to learned helplessness must be qualified to take account of the prominence or salience of the cues signifying the uncontrollable nature of the stressor. Type As exhibit helplessness only under conditions of high salience. The case for these generalizations is strengthened by the range of conditions under which predicted effects have been observed, including various subject populations, different experimenters who were blind to the subject's A–B classification, and somewhat different techniques for inducing perceived lack of control.

Control and Coronary Heart Disease

The helplessness results reported above take on added significance when viewed in the light of recent work on the relationship between disease and the magnitude of changes in an individual's life. Early research in this area suggested that life events could be positive or negative and still lead to the onset of disease; the important factor, it was believed, was the amount of change (e.g., Holmes & Rahe, 1967). More recent studies indicate, however, that events must be negative in order to potentiate illness (e.g., Dohrenwend & Dohrenwend, 1974), and there is even the suggestion that uncontrollability and helplessness induced by certain types of negative life changes are the critical variables in facilitating the onset of some diseases (cf. Paykel, 1974).

Consider the following array of events: the death of a close friend, a sudden financial setback, or a loss in occupational prestige. All are adverse aspects of our lives that may not easily be affected by our own actions. These losses often result in helplessness, depression, and a tendency to give up efforts to cope with the environment (Seligman, 1975). Engel (1968) and others (e.g., Schmale, 1972) propose that helplessness is implicated in the pathogenesis of a variety of physical diseases, ranging from the common cold to cancer. Greene, Goldstein, and Moss (1972) have shown that sudden death specifically due to coronary disease occurs in men who, according to reports by next-of-kin, were depressed for a week to several months prior to death. While these data are certainly not conclusive, they do suggest the possibility that helplessness-inducing life events are precursors to coronary heart disease. But why coronary disease and not some other disorder? In other words, what are the factors that might interact with helplessness to produce coronary disease? I would suggest that the Type A behavior pattern may be a predisposing condition that mediates the relationship between helplessness and coronary disease. The laboratory research described above indicates that extended experience with salient uncontrollable stress results in enhanced vulnerability to helplessness among Type As. It may be, therefore, that the specific interaction of Pattern A and helplessness-inducing life events is a precursor to clincal coronary disease.

An ideal test of this hypothesis would require a prospective study, since consistency of results from retrospective research might conceivably reflect a tendency for some coronary cases to rationalize their illness in terms of hurrying and hard work and/or the stress of uncontrollable life events. Practical considerations made it impossible to do longitudinal research, but it still seemed useful to conduct an exploratory retrospective project. Therefore, hospitalized coronary patients and noncoronary controls were compared in terms of their A–B scores as well as their recall of life events prior to disease onset. A one-year period was selected as the main focus of study because of previous research showing elevations in the number of significant life changes during a 12-month interval before the occurrence of clinical coronary disease (e.g., Theorell & Rahe, 1975).

In what is known as the Houston study, three basic samples were used: (1) a group of 45 patients in the coronary care unit of the Veterans Administration Hospital in Houston, Texas; (2) 77 patients in the general medical and psychiatric wards—the hospitalized control group; and (3) 50 building-maintenance employees—the "healthy" nonhospitalized controls. All participants were males aged 35 to 55. The three groups were frequency-matched in terms of social class, race, and religion.

The study instruments were the Jenkins Activity Survey and a modified version of the Schedule of Recent Experience used in research on stressful life change (e.g., Holmes & Rahe, 1967). The latter measure asked the respondent to document the number of occurrences of each of 47 life events during a one-year period prior to hospitalization or, for the healthy controls, the time the questionnaire was being completed. A loss index was computed consisting of the percentage of persons in each sample who endorsed one or more of 10 specific events in the list of 47. These 10 items were agreed upon by three members of the research staff as reflecting stressful life events over which minimal control could be exerted, for example "death of a close family member," "being fired," and "large decline in financial status." Selection of the items was made prior to the study. A so-called negative events index was also constructed, which contained 7 items designed to reflect life events that would be experienced by most individuals as stressful but not *necessarily* as uncontrollable or helplessness-inducing losses. Items in this index included "detention in jail" and "large increase in number of arguments with spouse."

Analysis of the JAS data revealed that coronary patients had significantly higher Pattern A scores than either the hospitalized or nonhospitalized controls ($ps < .01$). As for the loss index, a reliably higher percentage of each patient group (coronaries and hospitalized noncoronaries) experienced at least one loss compared to healthy controls. By contrast, percentages for the negative events index were similar in all three samples.

It would appear that helplessness-inducing life events—not just negative events—specifically discriminate individuals with illness from those without disease. Since coronary patients have higher Pattern A scores than either hospitalized or nonhospitalized control groups, coronary heart disease seems to be more likely among As than Bs, provided that an excess of life events occur that are interpretable as losses of environmental control. Future research with prospective designs is obviously needed to corroborate these findings.

A Proposed Biobehavioral Model

The studies reported in this paper were limited to an analysis of the relationship between Pattern A and uncontrollable stress. However, my long-range goal is to show how the interplay of these two variables influences the development of coronary disease. The pursuit of this goal necessarily involves systematic examination of physiological and biochemical processes. For, in the final analysis, such processes must mediate the impact of behavioral factors on cardiovascular pathology. Although the necessary research has yet to be done, preliminary specification of some of the possible mediating physiological mechanisms might still be made at this time.

Evidence cited earlier in this paper indicates that elevated levels of adrenalin and noradrenalin may potentiate the development of coronary disease. Since the two catecholamines are intimately related to autonomic nervous system discharge, it is not surprising that stress has been found to influence their rise and fall in the blood. It is also recognized that active coping with a stressor leads to an increased specific discharge of noradrenalin, whereas adrenalin levels remain relatively unchanged (e.g., Funkenstein, King, & Drolette, 1957; Elmadjian, 1963; Weiss, Stone, & Harrell, 1970). Other data indicate that while adrenalin levels may rise initially in response to stressful stimulation, they decline successively as the individual increases his felt ability to master the disturbing stimuli (Frankenhaeuser, 1971). Recent studies have also shown that severe depletion of brain noradrenalin is often associated with helplessness and giving-up responses (e.g., Weiss, Glazer, & Pohorecky, 1976).

Consider the following integration of these biochemical results with the behavioral data reported earlier in this paper. Once an individual perceives a threat to his sense of environmental control, he struggles, albeit with differential vigor, to reestablish and maintain control. During this period, we may expect active coping efforts and concomitant elevations in circulating noradrenalin. Adrenalin levels should remain unchanged or perhaps even show a decline. When the realization comes that control has been lost, the individual will become passive and give up. During this period noradrenalin levels are likely to decline.

The alternation of control efforts followed by giving up is undoubtedly repeated over and over again during the life of an individual. It is entirely possible that the more frequently this cycle occurs, the more the coronary arteries are likely to be affected by atherosclerotic disease. This extrapolation derives, in part, from results cited earlier suggesting that excessive elevations of catecholamines over time may serve as an intermediary process whereby reactions to stressful events induce biochemical and pathogenetic phenomena leading to coronary disease (see, for example, Raab *et al.*, 1964; Rosenman & Friedman, 1974). It also derives from more speculative notions implicating the rise and fall of catecholamines and rapid shifts between sympathetic and parasympathetic activity in the etiology of coronary disease and sudden death (Engel 1970; Richter, 1957; see also Seligman, 1975).

Consider next how Pattern A might fit into this general picture. We noted earlier that relative to Type B's, Type A's seem to show enhanced platelet aggregation in response to noradrenalin (Simpson, Olewine, Jenkins, Ramsey, Zyzanski, Thomas, & Rames, 1974). Moreover, at least three studies repoprt that Type A's display elevated noradrenalin reactions to stressful stimulation, whereas Type B's fail to show this type of responsiveness (Friedman *et al*, 1960; Friedman, Byers, Diamant, & Rosenman, 1975; Simpson *et al.*, 1974). Given these findings, it might be argued that the atherogenetic processes described above for individuals in general apply, *a fortiori*, to Type A individuals. In other words, Pattern A subjects experience the alternation of active coping and giving up more frequently and intensely than Pattern B subjects. This assumption is not at all unreasonable if we recall that while As vigorously engage in efforts to master their environment, nevertheless many of these struggles end in failure and helplessness. To the extent that coronary disease is influenced by a cycle of hyper-reactivity and hyporeactivity, the greater likelihood of the disease in As might be explained in terms of the cumulative effects of excessive rise and fall of catecholamines released by the repetitive interplay of Pattern A and uncontrollable stress.

I am well aware of the fact that the foregoing speculations do not tell the whole story, or even a signficant portion of it. A general explanation has been offered only as a heuristic guide to future thinking and research. In the final analysis, coronary disease must be regarded as having a multifaceted etiology. Some of the traditional risk factors (e.g., serum cholesterol and cigarette smoking) will have to be incorporated in any complete analysis of the pathogenesis of cardiac disease. However, I would emphasize that a thorough knowledge of how psychological and physiological variables interact to produce coronary disease will increase our understanding of its etiology. While many theoretical questions remain to be answered, the behavioral research described in this paper was designed to provide a partial basis for an analytic approach to the coronary disease process.

Implications for Therapy

A general aim in the treatment and prevention of coronary disease is, in addition to altering dietary and smoking habits, to correct the seemingly pathogenic life style of behavior pattern A. Since elimination of uncontrollable aversive life events or protection from them is, in all likelihood, an unattainable goal, the important consideration is how the individual attempts to deal with threats to his sense of control over environmental stressors. The Pattern A style of response may be adaptive for initial confrontations, since good adjustment is likely to require efficient mechanisms for rapidly mobilizing biopsychological resources. In the long run, however, Pattern A behavior is maladaptive and may entail considerable risk to health. A major change in coping would thus seem indicated, but whether such change is feasible is another matter. Recall that Pattern A is probably learned by individuals whose genetic constitution renders them susceptible to shaping processes that facilitate the emergence of the hard-driving and time-urgent mode of coping with the environment (see above and Glass, 1977).

There is, however, some evidence indicating that clinical and psychopharmacologic techniques might prove effective in depressing Pattern A behavior. For example, Sigg (1974) suggests that the administration of psychotropic drugs of the sedative type might reduce emotional and muscular tension characteristic of Pattern A individuals. Sigg also proposes that β-adrenergic blocking agents (e.g., propranolol) may be useful in a program designed to alter ways in which coronary prone persons cope with psychosocial stress. Since the catecholamines appear to figure in the Type A response to uncontrollable stressors, a specific blockade of beta receptors by propranolol-type drugs seems appropriate.

A number of nondrug methods of altering Pattern A have also been suggested. Benson (e.g. Benson, Marzetta, and Rosner 1974) has shown that regular practice of a secularized version of transcendental meditation (TM) reduces blood pressure and heart rate, but there is, to date, no systematic evidence to show that it alters Pattern A. On the other hand, it is not unreasonable to suggest that relaxation exercises can improve a person's ability to master environmental stressors in a less compulsively hard-driving manner. Relaxation can probably be induced not only by TM procedures but also by a variety of muscular and psychic techniques.

General relaxation therapies are but one instance of the use of psychological procedures for altering the coronary-prone behavior pattern. There are more sophisticated, though not necessarily more effective, techniques for teaching individuals to cope differently with life stresses. The use of biofeedback in reducing blood pressure and related cardiovascular symptoms is well known (e.g., Shapiro, Schwartz, & Benson, 1974). There has been, in addition, growing interest in the feasibility of applying behavior modification and group therapy to the alteration of Pattern A. Illustrative of the first approach is the work of Richard Suinn with what is called CSMP, the Cardiac Stress Management Program (e.g., Suinn, 1975). Preliminary evaluation of this approach to the treatment of Type As has been encouraging, although the relevant data are based largely on anecdotal reports of the patients involved CSMP (Suinn, Brock, & Edie, 1975). Suinn *et al.* also report decrements in serum lipids among their treated Type A patients immediately after therapy. However, such results are not very surprising, for serum cholesterol is characteristically responsive to stressful stimulation (e.g., Friedman, Rosenman, & Carroll, 1958), and the relaxation procedures included in CSMP might be expected to produce a pre- to posttest drop in lipid levels. More extended follow-up of the patients with repeated assessments of serum cholesterol is clearly indicated.

The use of group therapy for modifying behavior pattern A has been recommended in a number of quarters (e.g., Friedman & Rosenman 1974). Rahe, O'Neil, and Arthur (unpublished manuscript) report research designed to evaluate the effectiveness of brief group therapy in the management of Type A patients recovering from myocardial infarctions. The results indicated that therapy patients experienced reliably fewer rehospitalizations than similar controls. The therapy patients also demonstrated significantly greater knowledge of their disease and its rehabilitation than did controls.

These findings must be viewed with caution, however. First, the sizes of the samples were small. Second, in the course of the study, control patients learned of the educational materials being given to the therapy group, and, as Rahe correctly points out, it is difficult to argue that the therapy patients were not inadvertently given a more encouraging outlook than the controls. Third, although therapy patients seemed to modify their "previous habits of overwork, rushing against time deadlines, lack of enjoyment of life, and so forth" (Rahe *et al.*, unpublished manuscript, pp. 10–11.), these data were based, in large measure, on what subjects said in the group discussions.

To sum up, it would appear that a number of promising techniques exist for Pattern A modification, but none of them—behavioral or pharmacological—has yet received sound evaluation using controlled designs. For the present, I would only conclude that it may be feasible to alter some forms of Type A behavior, but unequivocal support for this assertion must await future research.

One theme of this paper has been the relationship between behavior and disease; hence the present section was concerned with modification of behavioral variables. However, the treatment and prevention of coronary disease is, like its etiology, a multifaceted matter. Since advances in the medical treatment of disease often occur without full understanding of the disease itself, we can expect to see a variety of pragmatic techniques developed in the next few years that effectively reduce the likelihood of clinical coronary disease. The emergence of such methods does not mean that modification of the coronary-prone behavior pattern is unnecessary in the reduction and abolition of heart disease. One can only guess at this time, but in the end, the amelioratoin of cardiovascular pathology may rely upon behavioral and pharmacological alterations in Pattern A, in conjunction with biomedical therapies aimed at reducing the effects of other risk factors for the disease.

References

Ardlie, N. G., Glew, G. & Schwartz, C. J. Influence of catecholamines on nucleotide-induced platelet aggregation. *Nature*, 1966, *212*, 415–417.

Balke, B. Optimale Koerperliche Leistungsfaehigkeisihre Messung und Veraenderung infolage Arbeitsermuedung. *Arbeitsphysiologie*, 1954, *15*, 311–323.

Balke, B., Grillo, G. P., Konecci, E. B., & Luft, U. C. Work capacity after blood donation. *Journal of Applied Physiology*, 1954, *7*, 231–238.

Benson, H., Marzetta, B. R., & Rosner, B. A. Decreased blood pressure associated with the regular elicitation of relaxation response: A study of hypertensive subjects. In R. S. Eliot (Ed.), *Stress and the heart*. New York: Futura, 1974.

Blumenthal, J. A., Williams, R. B., Kong, Y., Thompson, L. W., Jenkins, C. D., & Rosenman, R. H. Coronary-prone behavior and angiographically documented coronary disease. Paper presented at the Annual Meeting of the American Psychosomatic Society, New Orleans, March 1975.

Borhani, N. O. Magnitude of the problem of cardiovascular-renal disease. In A. M. Lilienfeld & A. J. Gifford (Eds.), *Chronic Diseases and Public Health*. Johns Hopkins University Press, 1966.

Brand, R. J., Rosenman, R. H., Sholtz, R. I., & Friedman, M. Multivariate prediction of coronary heart disease in the Western Collaborative Group Study compared to the findings of the Framingham Study. *Circulation*, 1976, *53*, 348–355.

Burnam, M. A., Pennebaker, J. W. & Glass, D. C. Time consciousness, achievement striving, and the Type A coronary-prone behavior pattern. *Journal of Abnormal Psychology*, 1973, *84*, 76–79.

Buss, A. H. *The psychology of aggression*. New York: Wiley, 1961.

Butensky, A. V., Faralli, V., Heebner, D., & Waldron, I. Elements of the coronary prone behavior pattern in children and teenagers. *Journal of Psychosomatic Research*, 1976, *20*, 439–444.

Carver, C. S., Coleman, A. E., & Glass, D. C. The coronary-prone behavior pattern and the suppression of fatigue on a treadmill test. *Journal of Personality and Social Psychology*, 1976, *33*, 460–466.

Dawber, T. R., & Kannel, W. B. Susceptibility to coronary heart disease. *Modern Concepts in Cardiovascular Disease*, 1961, *30*, 671–676.

Dohrenwend, B. S. & Dohrenwend, B. P. *Stressful life events: Their nature and effects*. New York: Wiley, 1974.

Duguid, J. B. Thrombosis as a factor in the pathogenesis of coronary atherosclerosis. *Journal of Pathology and Bacteriology*, 1946, *58*, 207–212.

Eliot, R. S., (Ed.) *Stress and the heart*. New York: Futura, 1974.

Elmadjian, F. Excretion and metabolism of epinephrine and norepinephrine in various emotional states. *Proceedings of the 5th Pan American Congress of Endocrinology*. November, 1963, 341–370.

Engel, G. L. A life setting conductive to illness: The giving-up—given-up complex. *Annals of Internal Medicine*, 1968, *69*, 293–300.

Engel, G. L. Sudden death and the "medical model" in psychiatry. *Canadian Psychiatric Association Journal*, 1970, *15*, 527–538.

Frankenhaeuser, M. Behavior and circulating catecholamines. *Brain Research*, 1971, *31*, 241–262.

Friedberg, C. K. *Diseases of the heart*. (3rd ed.) Philadelphia: W. B. Saunders, 1966.

Friedman, M. *Pathogenesis of coronary artery disease*. New York: McGraw Hill, 1969.

Friedman, M., Byers, S. O., Diamant, J., & Rosenman, R. H. Plasma catecholamine response of coronary-prone subjects (Type A) to a specific challenge. *Metabolism*, 1975, *24*, 205–210.

Friedman, M., & Rosenman, R. H. 1959. Association of specific overt behavior pattern with blood and cardiovascular findings. *J of the A.M.A.* 169:1286–96.

Friedman, M., & Rosenman, R. H. *Type A behavior and your heart*. New York: Knopf, 1974.

Friedman, M., Rosenman, R. H., & Carroll, V. Changes in the serum cholesterol and blood-clotting time in men subjected to cyclic variation of occupational stress. *Circulation*, 1958, *17*, 852–861.

Friedman, M., St. George, S., Byers, S. O., & Rosenman, R. H. Excretion of catecholamines, 17-ketosteroids, 17-hydroxycorticoids, and 5-hydroxyindole in men exhibiting a particular behavior pattern associated with high incidence of clinical coronary artery disease. *Journal of Clincal Investigation*, 1960, *39*, 758–764.

Funkenstein, D. H., King, S. H., & Drolette, M. E. *Mastery of stress*. New Haven: Harvard University Press, 1957.

Glass, D. C. *Behavior patterns, stress, and coronary disease*. Hillsdale, N.J.: Erlbaum, 1977.

Glass, D. C., & Singer, J. E. *Urban stress: Experiments on noise and social stressors*. Academic, 1972.

Glass, D. C., Synder, M. L., & Hollis, J. F. Time urgency and the Type A coronary-prone behavior pattern. *Journal of Applied Social Psychology*, 1974, *4*, 125–140.

Greene, W. A., Goldstein, S., & Moss, A. J. Psychosocial aspects of sudden death: A preliminary report. *Archives of Internal Medicine*, 1972, *129*, 725–731.

Hiroto, D. S. 1974. Locus of control and learned helplessness. *Journal of Experimental Psychology*, 1974, *102*, 187–193.

Hiroto, D. S., & Seligman, M. E. P. Generality of learned helplessness in man. *Journal of Personality and Social Psychology*, 1975, *31*, 311–327.

Holmes, T. H., & Rahe, R. H. The social readjustment rating scale. *Journal of Psychosomatic Research*, 1967, *11*, 213–218.

House, J. S. Occupational stress as a precursor to coronary disease. 1975. In W. D. Gentry & R. B. Williams, Jr. (Eds.), *Psychological Aspects of Myocardial Infarction and Coronary Care*. St. Louis: C. V. Mosby, 1975.

Jenkins, C. D. Psychologic and social precursors of coronary disease. *New England Journal of Medicine*, 1971, *284*, 244–255, 307–317.

Jenkins, C. D. Recent evidence supporting psychologic and social risk factors for coronary disease. *New England Journal of Medicine*, 1976, *294*, 987–994, 1033–1038.

Jenkins, C. D., Rosenman, R. H., & Friedman, M. Replicability of rating the coronary-prone behavior pattern. *British Journal of Preventive and Social Medicine*, 1968, *22*, 16–22.

Jenkins, C. D., Rosenman, R. H., & Zyzanski, S. J. The Jenkins Activity Survey for Health Prediction, Form B. Boston: Authors, 1972.

Jenkins, C. D., Zyzanski, S. J., & Rosenman, R. H. Risk of new myocardial infarction of middle-age men with manifest coronary disease. *Circulation*, 1976, *53*, 342–347.

Krantz, D. S., Glass, D. C., & Snyder, M. L. Helplessness, stress level, and the coronary-prone behavior pattern. *Journal of Experimental Social Psychology*, 1974, *10*, 284–300.

Lazarus, R. S. *Psychological stress and the coping process*. New York: McGraw-Hill, 1966.

Mason, J. W. Organization of psychoendocrine mechanisms: A review and reconsideration of research. In N. S. Greenfield & R. A. Sternback (Eds.), *Handbook of psychophysiology*. New York: Holt, Rinehart & Winston, 1972.

Matthews, K. A., & Krantz, D. S. Resemblance of twins and their parents in Pattern A behavior. *Psychosomatic Medicine*, 1976, *38*, 140–144.

McGinn, N. F., Harburg, E., Julius, S., & McLeod, J. M. Psychological correlates of blood pressure. *Psychological Bulletin*, 1964, *61*, 209–219.

Parkes, C. M., Benjamin, B., & Fitzgerald, R. G. Broken heart: A statistical study of increased mortality among widowers. *British Medical Journal*, 1969, *1*, 740–743.

Paykel, E. S. Life Stress and Psychiatric disorder: Applications of the clinical approach. In B. S. Dohrenwend & B. P. Dohrenwend (Eds.), *Stressful life events: Their nature and effects*. New York: Wiley, 1974.

Pliner, P. The effects of auditory cues on time-estimation judgments. In S. Schachter and J. Rodin (Eds.) *Obese humans and rats*. Hillsdale, N.J.: Erlbaum, 1974.

Raab, W., Stark, E., MacMillan, W. H., & Gigee, W. R. Sympathetic origin and antiadrenergic prevention of stress-induced myocardial lesions. *American Journal of Cardiology*, 1961, *8*, 203–211.

Raab, W., Chaplin, J. P., & Bajusz, E. Myocardial neuroses produced in domesticated rats and in wild rats by sensory and emotional stresses. Proceedings of the Society of Experimental Biology and Medicine, 1964, *116*, 665–669.

Rahe, R. H., O'Neil, T., Arthur, R. J. Brief group therapy following myocardial infarction: Eighteen-month follow-up of a controlled trial. Unpublished manuscript, National Health Research Center, San Diego, 1975.

Richter, C. P. On the phenomenon of sudden death in animals and man. *Psychosomatic Medicine*, 1957, *19*, 191–198.

Rosenman, R. H., & Friedman, M. Neurogenic factors in pathogenesis of coronary heart disease. *Medical Clinics of North America*, 1974, *58*, 269–279.

Rosenman, R. H., Brand, R. J., Jenkins, C. D., Friedman, M., Strauss, R., & Wurm, M. Coronary heart disease in the Western Collaborative Group Study: Final follow-up experience of 8½ years. *Journal of the American Medical Association*, 1975, *233*, 872–877.

Rosenman, R. H., Friedman, M., Strauss, R., Wurm, M., Jenkins, C. D., & Messinger, H. B. Coronary heart disease of the Western Collaborative Group Study: A follow-up experience of two years. *Journal of the American Medical Association*, 1966, *195*, 130–136.

Rosenman, R. H., Rahe, R. H., Borhani, N. O., & Feinlieb, M. Heritability of personality and behavior pattern. Proceedings of the First International Congress on Twins, Rome, 1975.

Schachter, S., & Rodin, J. *Obese humans and rats*. Hillsdale, N.J.: Erlbaum, 1974.

Scherwitz, L., Berton, K., & Leventhal, H. *Type A assessment in the behavior pattern interview*. Unpublished manuscript, University of Wisconsin.

Schmale, A. H. Giving up as a final common pathway to changes in health. *Advances in Psychosomatic Medicine*, 1972, *8*, 18–38.

Seligman, M. E. P. *Helplessness: On depression, development, and death*. San Francisco: Freeman, 1975.

Shapiro, D., Schwartz, G. E., & Benson, H. Biofeedback: A behavioral approach to cardiovascular control. In R. S. Eliot (Ed.), *Stress and the heart*. Mt. Kisco, N.Y.: Futura, 1974.

Shekelle, R. B., Schoenberger, J. A., Stamler, J. Correlates of the JAS Type A behavior pattern score. *Journal of Chronic Diseases*, 1976, *29*, 381–394.

Sigg, E. B. The pharmacological approaches to cardiac stress. In R. S. Eliot (Eds.), *Stress and the heart*. Mt. Kisco, N.Y.: Futura, 1974.

Simpson, M. T., Olewine, D. A., Jenkins, C. D., Ramsey, F. H., Zyzanski, S. J., Thomas, G., & Hames, C. G. Exercise-induced catecholamines and platelet aggregation in coronary-prone behavior pattern. *Psychosomatic Medicine*, 1974, *36*, 476–487.

Suinn, R. M. The cardiac stress management program for Type A patients. *Cardiac Rehabilitation*, 1975, *5*, 13–15.

Suinn, R. M., Brock, L. & Edie, C. Behavior therapy for Type A patients. *American Journal of Cardiology*, 1975, *36*, 269–270.

Theorell, T. Life events before and after the onset of a premature myocardial infarction. In B. S. Dohrenwend & B. P. Dohrenwend (Eds.), *Stressful life events: Their nature and effects*. New York: Wiley, 1974.

Theorell, T. & Rahe, R. H. Life change events, ballistocardiography, and coronary death. *Journal of Human Stress*, 1975, *1*, 18–24.

Weiss, J. M., Glazer, H. I., & Pohorecky, L. A. Coping behavior and neurochemical changes: An alternative explanation for the original "learned helplessness" experiments. In G. Serban (Ed.), *Psychopathology of human adaptation*. New York: Plenum, 1976.

Weiss, J. M., Stone, E. A., & Harrell, N. Coping behavior and brain norepinephrine level in rats. *Journal of Comparative and Physiological Psychology*, 1970, *72*, 153–160.

Wortman, C. B., & Brehm, J. W. Responses to uncontrollable outcomes: An integration of reactance theory and the learned helplessness model. In L. Berkowitz (Ed.), *Advances in experimental social psychology*, vol. 8. New York: Academic, 1975.

Zyzanski, S. J., Jenkins, C. D., Ryan, T. J., Flessas, A., & Everist, M. Psychological correlates of coronary angiographic findings. *Archives of Internal Medicine*, 1976, *136*, 1234–1237.

Index

MIX
Papier aus verantwortungsvollen Quellen
Paper from responsible sources
FSC® C105338

If you have any concerns about our products,
you can contact us on
ProductSafety@springernature.com

In case Publisher is established outside the EU,
the EU authorized representative is:
Springer Nature Customer Service Center GmbH
Europaplatz 3, 69115 Heidelberg, Germany

Printed by Libri Plureos GmbH
in Hamburg, Germany